KU-422-044

ultimate knit
stitch bible

First published in the United Kingdom in 2015 by
Collins & Brown
1 Gower Street
London
WC1E 6HD

An imprint of Pavilion Books Company Ltd

Copyright © Pavilion Books Company Ltd 2015

All rights reserved. No part of this publication may
be copied, displayed, extracted, reproduced,
utilized, stored in a retrieval system or transmitted
in any form or by any means, electronic,
mechanical or otherwise including but not limited
to photocopying, recording, or scanning without
the prior written permission of the publishers.

ISBN 9781909397989

A CIP catalogue record for this book is available
from the British Library.

10 9 8 7 6 5 4 3 2 1

Reproduction by Rival Colour Ltd, UK
Printed and bound by Craft Print Ltd, Singapore

This book can be ordered direct from the
publisher at

www.pavilionbooks.com

ultimate knit stitch bible

750 knit, purl, cable, lace and colour stitches

COLLINS & BROWN

contents

Introduction   6

Tools and equipment   8
Starting off   10
Key to stitch diagrams   24
Abbreviations   26
Knit and purl stitches   28
Cable and aran stitches   80
Lace and eyelet stitches   132
Colourwork stitches   182
Edgings and trims   234

Index   284
Acknowledgements   288

Introduction

Whether you're a knitting novice who is picking up a pair of needles for the first time, or a seasoned professional with years of experience, you will find inspiration and technical know-how within these pages; there is always something to learn and to pass on.

This book is divided into five sections. The first one introduces basic combinations of knit and purl. These two stitches can be configured into patterns and constructed into all kinds of fabrics. Texture is the main inspiration for this section.

The second section features cable and aran stiches. These patterns are traditionally romantic, rugged and instantly recognizable; they create wonderful surface interest and give scale to any knitted fabric. You can apply these patterns to an Aran sweater; these are characterized by a large central panel bordered by varying numbers of side panels on a textural background. Usually symmetrical, these side panels are knitted in simpler stitch patterns – a useful device for scaling up larger sizes. Even the welts, cuffs and neckbands can be worked with complex stitches to create highly decorative and unique textiles.

Lace and eyelets are the focus of the third section. These intricate stitches are intriguing and absorbing and offer endless possibilities for experimentation. For the beginner knitter, lace knitting may seem daunting as it requires a little more technique – wrapping the yarn around the needle a few times, dropping a stitch or two, or (intentionally) slipping unknitted stitches over a knitted one, for example. However, the sense of accomplishing a simple eyelet will encourage you to attempt and experiment with the more complex and challenging effects.

The fourth section focuses on colourwork, with most of the designs drawing inspiration from traditional Scottish and Scandinavian patterns knitted using the Fair Isle technqiue. Fair Isle knitting uses design repeats and motifs in horizontal and vertical bands, and in small and large panels. Typically, these patterns feature diagonal lines, which means that the colour-change positions are offset, creating an elastic fabric. No more than two colours are used in any row, one colour being 'stranded' across the back of the other. There is also a symmetry to the patterns, which means they can be easily memorized. Intarsia knitting is a similar technique, though yarn is usually not stranded across the back of the work and patterns often involve larger blocks of colour and picture motifs.

The final section concentrates on edgings and trims. From simple yet decorative ribs to intricate lace borders, there is an almost endless variety of edgings. They offer a quick way of turning a plain knit garment into something supremely stylish. Often you will be able to simply add the edging to an existing pattern, but if you need to make some calculations to make a new trim fit an old pattern, you will find advice on page 23. It is usually possible to combine an existing pattern with a fresh edging. As most edgings are worked over just a few stitches, it is easy to knit up a few centimetres to see how a pattern might suit your project.

Tools and equipment

To master any skill, it is imperative to have a solid foundation in the techniques. This section provides useful information for knitting.

Knitting needles

Knitting needles are used in pairs to produce a flat knitted fabric. They are pointed at one end to form the stitches and have a knob at the other to retain the stitches. They may be made in plastic, wood, steel or alloy and range in size from 2mm to 20mm in diameter. Needles are also made in different lengths that will comfortably hold the number of stitches required for each project. It is useful to have a range of sizes so that tension swatches can be knitted up and compared. Discard any needles that become bent. Points should be fairly sharp, as blunt needles reduce the speed and ease of working.

Circular and double-pointed needles are used to produce a tubular fabric or flat rounds. Many traditional fishermen's sweaters are knitted in the round. Double-pointed needles are sold in sets of four or five. Circular needles consist of two needle points joined by a flexible length of plastic. The plastic varies in length. You can use the shorter lengths for knitting sleeves and neckbands and the longer lengths for larger pieces such as the bodies of sweaters.

Cable needles are short double-pointed needles with a kink in them that are used to hold the stitches of a cable to the back or front of the main body of knitting.

Other useful equipment

Needle gauges are punched with holes corresponding to the needle sizes. They are usually marked with both US and metric sizing, so you can easily check the size of any needle.

Stitch holders resemble large safety pins and are used to hold stitches while they are not being worked – for example, around a neckline when the neckband stitches will be picked up and worked after the back and front have been joined. As an alternative, thread a blunt-pointed sewing needle with a generous length of contrast-coloured yarn, thread it through the stitches to be held while they are still on the needle, then slip the stitches off the needle and knot both ends of the contrast yarn to secure the stitches.

Wool sewing needles or tapestry needles are used to sew completed pieces of knitting together. They are large, with a broad eye for easy threading and a blunt point that will slip between the knitted stitches without splitting and fraying the yarn. Do not use sharp-pointed sewing needles to sew up knitting.

A row counter is a cylinder with a numbered dial that is used to count the number of rows that have been knitted. Push it onto the needle and turn the dial at the end of each row.

A tape measure is essential for checking tension swatches and for measuring the length and width of completed knitting. For an accurate result, always smooth the knitting (without stretching) on a firm flat surface before measuring it.

A crochet hook is useful for picking up dropped stitches.

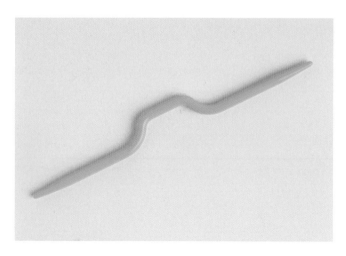

Cable needle

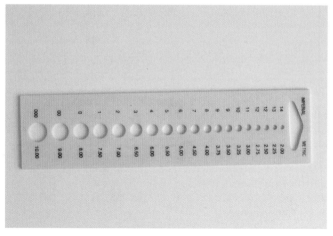

Needle gauge

Knitting yarn

Yarn is the term used for strands of spun fibre that are twisted together into a continuous length of the required thickness. Yarn can be of animal origin (wool, angora, mohair, silk, alpaca), of vegetable origin (cotton, linen), or man-made (nylon, acrylic, rayon). Knitting yarn may be made up from a combination of different fibres.

Each single strand of yarn is known as a ply. A number of plies are twisted together to form the yarn. The texture and characteristics of the yarn may be varied by the combination of fibres and by the way in which the yarn is spun. Wool and other natural fibres are often combined with man-made fibres to make a yarn that is more economical and hard-wearing. Wool can also be treated to make it machine-washable. The twist of the yarn is firm and smooth and knits up into a hard-wearing fabric. Loosely twisted yarn has a softer finish when knitted.

Buying yarn

Yarn is most commonly sold wound into balls of specific weight measured in grams or ounces. Some yarn, particularly very thick yarn, is sold in a coiled hank or skein that must be wound into a ball before you can begin knitting.

Yarn manufacturers wrap each ball with a paper band on which is printed information such as the weight of the yarn and its composition. It will give instructions for washing and ironing and will state the ideal range of needle sizes to be used with the yarn. The ball band also carries the shade number and dye lot number. It is important that you use yarn of the same dye lot for an entire project. Different dye lots vary subtly in shading; this may not be apparent when you are holding the two balls, but it will show as a variation in shade on the finished piece of knitting.

Always keep the ball band as a reference. The best way is to pin it to the tension swatch and keep them together with any leftover yarn and spare buttons or other trimmings. That way, you can always check the washing instructions and also have materials for repairs.

Starting off

Once you have mastered the basics of knitting, you can go on to develop your skills and start making more challenging projects.

Casting on

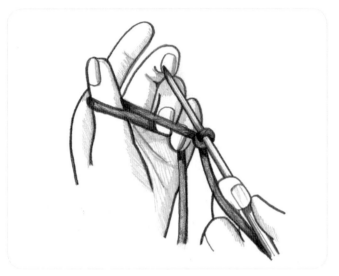

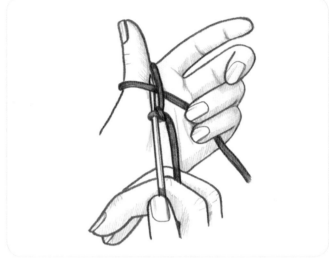

1. Make a slip knot 1m (39in) from the end of the yarn. Hold the needle in your right hand, with the ball end of the yarn over your index finger. Wind the loose end of the yarn around your left thumb from front to back.

2. Insert the point of the needle under the first strand of yarn on your thumb.

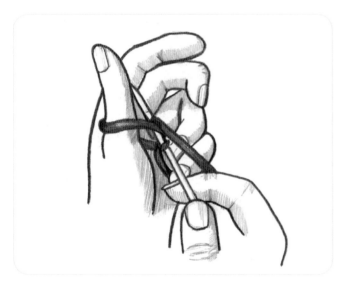

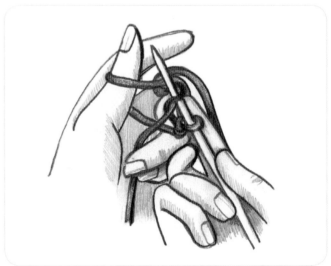

3. With your right index finger, take the ball end of the yarn over the point of the needle.

4. Pull a loop through to form the first stitch. Remove your left thumb from the yarn. Pull the loose end to secure the stitch. Repeat until all stitches have been cast on.

Knit stitch

Hold the needle with the cast-on stitches in your left hand, with the loose yarn at the back of the work. Insert the right-hand needle from left to right through the front of the first stitch on the left-hand needle.

Wind the yarn from left to right over the point of the right-hand needle.

Draw the yarn through the stitch, thus forming a new stitch on the right-hand needle.

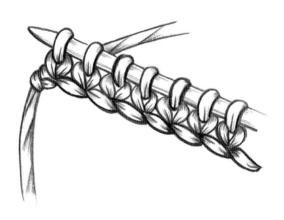

Slip the original stitch off the left-hand needle, keeping the new stitch on the right-hand needle.

To knit a row, repeat steps 1 to 4 until all the stitches have been transferred from the left-hand needle to the right-hand needle. Turn the work, transferring the needle that holds the stitches to your left hand to work the next row.

Purl stitch

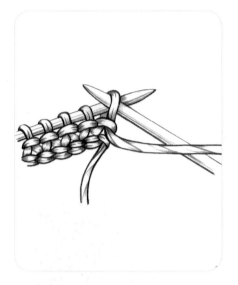

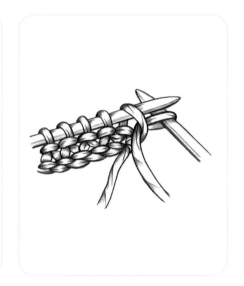

1. Hold the needle with the stitches in your left hand with the loose yarn at the front of the work. Insert the right-hand needle from right to left into the front of the first stitch on the left-hand needle.

2. Wind the yarn from right to left over the point of the right-hand needle.

3. Draw the yarn through the stitch, thus forming a new stitch on the right-hand needle.

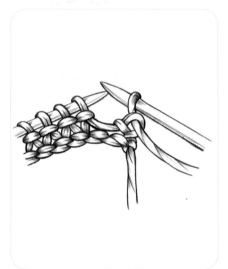

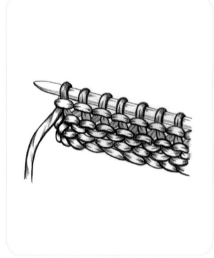

4. Slip the original stitch off the left-hand needle, keeping the new stitch on the right-hand needle.

5. To purl a row, repeat steps 1 to 4 until all the stitches have been transferred from the left-hand needle to the right-hand needle. Turn the work, transferring the needle that holds the stitches into your left hand to work the next row.

Casting off

There is one simple, most commonly used method of securing stitches once you have finished a piece of knitting – casting off. The cast-off edge should always have the same 'give' or elasticity as the fabric and you should always cast off in the stitch pattern used for the main fabric unless the pattern directs otherwise.

Knitwise

Knit two stitches. *Using the point of the left-hand needle, lift the first stitch on the right-hand needle over the second, then drop it off the needle. Knit the next stitch and repeat from * until all stitches have been worked off the left-hand needle and only one stitch remains on the right-hand needle. Cut the yarn (leaving enough to sew in the end), thread the end through the stitch, and then slip it off the needle. Draw the yarn up firmly to fasten off.

Purlwise

Purl two stitches. *Using the point of the left-hand needle, lift the first stitch on the right-hand needle over the second and drop it off the needle. Purl the next stitch and repeat from * until all the stitches have been worked off the left-hand needle and only one stitch remains on the right-hand needle. Secure the last stitch as described for casting off knitwise.

Increasing

The simplest method of increasing one stitch is to work into the front and back of the same stitch.

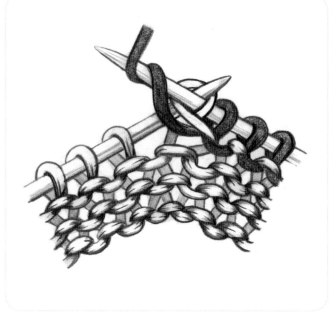

On a knit row

Knit into the front of the stitch to be increased into; then, before slipping it off the needle, place the right-hand needle behind the left-hand needle and knit again into the back of the same stitch. Slip the original stitch off the left-hand needle.

On a purl row

Purl into the front of the stitch to be increased into; then, before slipping it off the needle, purl again into the back of the same stitch. Slip the original stitch off the left-hand needle.

Tip

In this book, you will most often find that increases and decreases are used to create the lace and eyelet patterns. With lace stitches, it is commonplace for sets of increases and decreases to be paired together. This creates the open, 'holey' nature of the pattern while keeping the overall stitch count consistent.

Decreasing

The simplest method of decreasing one stitch is to work two stitches together.

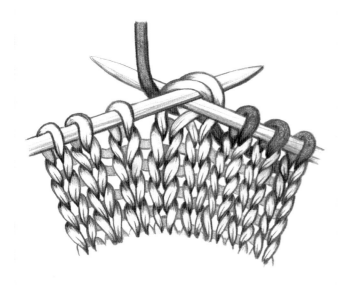

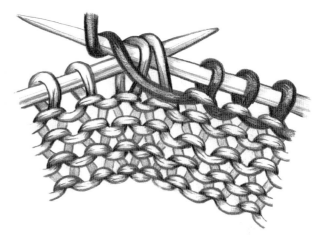

On a knit row

Insert the right-hand needle from left to right through two stitches instead of one, then knit them together as one stitch. This is called knit two together (k2tog).

On a purl row

Insert the right-hand needle from right to left through two stitches instead of one, then purl them together as one stitch. This is called purl two together (p2tog).

Joining in a new colour on a knit row

When working Fair Isle, it is better to join in a new colour at the beginning of a row, but in some cases, you may have to join in the middle of a row. This is how you join in a new colour mid-row on a knit row.

 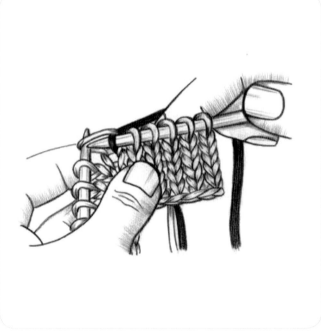

1 Lay the new colour (B) over the original colour (A). Twist the yarns over themselves and hold them in place.

2 Knit with the new colour (B). You can always go back and tighten the join after a couple of stitches.

The Ploughed furrows design (see page 193) requires you to join yarn in the middle of a row

Joining in a new colour on a purl row

This is how you join in a new colour mid-row on a purl row.

1   Lay the new colour (B) over the original colour (A). Twist the yarns over themselves and hold them in place.

2   Purl with the new colour (B).

Joining in a new colour in the middle of a row

When working in intarsia you will find yourself needing to join in a new colour in the middle of a row.

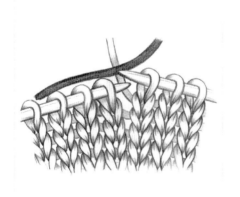

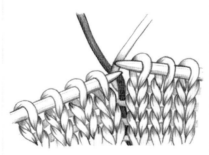

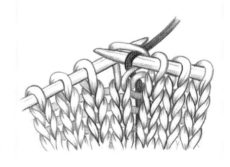

1   On a knit row, knit to the change in colour. Lay the new colour over the existing colour and between the two needles, with the tail to the left.

2   Bring the new colour under and then over the existing colour.

3   Knit the stitch with the new colour. Go back and pull gently on the tail to tighten up the first stitch in the new colour after you have knitted a couple more stitches.

Changing colours in a straight vertical line

Once you have joined in a new colour you may need to work for a number of rows, changing these colours on both the knit rows and purl rows. This is often confusingly referred to as 'twisting' the yarns but it is a link rather than a twist. It is a common mistake to over-twist the yarns at this point, with the result that the fabric will not lie flat.

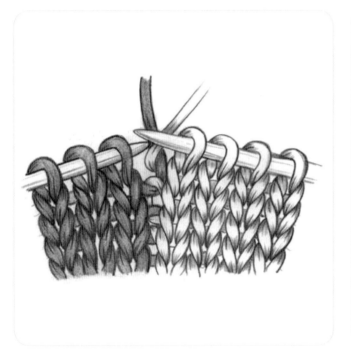 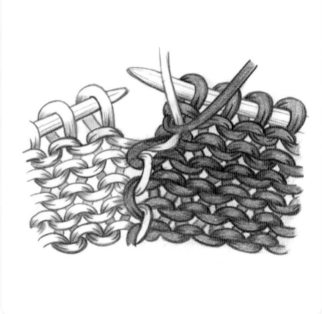

1 On a knit row, knit to the change in colour. Bring the new colour up from under the old colour and drop the old colour so that the new colour is ready to work with.

2 On a purl row, knit to the change in colour. Bring the new colour from the left under the old colour and up to the top. Drop the old colour and continue with the new colour.

Tip

When working blocks of colour in an intarsia pattern you may find it easiest to wind a small skein of yarn, called a bobbin, for each colour section, rather than working off a full ball of yarn. This makes the process less fiddly and is less likely to get your various yarns tangled.

Eliminating ends

If you are working a complex design it is always best to look for ways of eliminating ends so that you can cut down the amount of time that will be needed to sew them all in. Look for shapes that perhaps have an outline, as with a diamond motif.

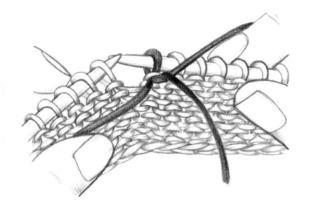

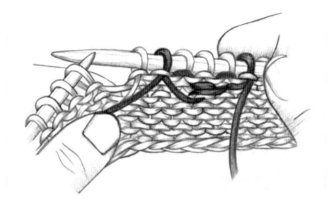

Take a length of the yarn required to work the whole motif and fold it in half. On the centre stitch of the motif, loop the fold over the right-hand needle.

On the next row, take one end of the yarn to the right and the other to the left, linking the outline and background colours on each row. If the motif is very small and the background colour remains the same, it is best to carry the background colour across the back of the motif, weaving it in if necessary.

How to read charts

Charts are featured in many of the instructions for the cable and aran stitches (pages 80–131) and for the colourwork designs (pages 182–233).

Charts are read exactly as the knitting is worked – from the bottom to the top. After the last row at the top has been worked, repeat the sequence from row 1 if required.

Each symbol represents an instruction. Symbols have been designed to resemble the actual appearance of the knitting. This is more difficult to do with multicolour slip-stitch patterns, which have to be knitted before the mosaic effects become obvious.

Before starting to knit, look up all the symbols on your chosen chart (see page 24 for a key to the stitch diagrams) so that you are familiar with the techniques involved. These may be shown with the pattern as a special abbreviation. The most common abbreviations that are not shown as special abbreviations are listed on page 26. Make sure that you understand the difference between working similar symbols on a right-side and on a wrong-side row.

Each square represents a stitch and each horizontal line represents a row. Place a ruler above the line you are working and work the symbols one by one. If you are new to reading charts, try comparing the charted instructions with the written ones.

For knitters who wish to follow the written directions, it is still a good idea to look at the chart (where one is available) before starting, to see what the repeat looks like and how the pattern has been balanced.

Right-side and wrong-side rows

'Right-side rows' are where the right side of the fabric is facing you when you work; 'wrong-side rows' are where the wrong side is facing you when you work. Row numbers are shown at the side of the charts at the beginning of the row. Right-side rows are always read from right to left. Wrong-side rows are always read from left to right.

Symbols on charts are shown as they appear from the right side of the work. Therefore, a horizontal dash stands for a purl 'bump' on the right side, regardless of whether it was achieved by purling on a right-side row or by knitting on a wrong-side row. To make things clearer, symbols on right-side rows are slightly darker than those on wrong-side rows.

Pattern repeats and multiples

The 'multiple' or repeat of the pattern is given with each set of instructions – for example, 'multiple of 7 + 4'. This means you can cast on any number of stitches that is a multiple of 7, plus 4 balancing stitches – for instance, 14 + 4, 21 + 4, 28 + 4, and so on.

In written instructions, the 7 stitches are shown in parentheses or follow an asterisk *. These stitches are repeated across the row the required number of times. In charted instructions, the pattern repeat is contained between heavier vertical lines. The extra stitches not included in the pattern repeat are there to 'balance' the row or make it symmetrical and are only worked once.

Some patterns require a foundation row that is worked once before commencing the pattern but does not form part of the repeat. On charts, this row is marked by a letter 'F' and is separated from the pattern repeat by a heavier horizontal line.

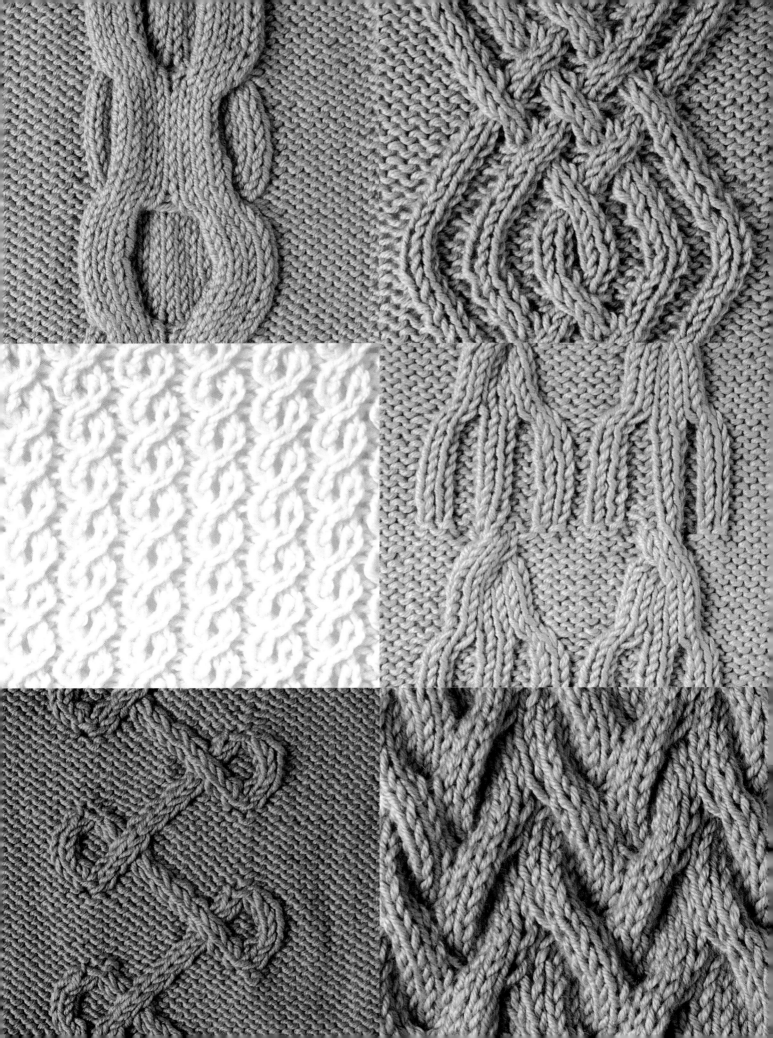

Advice on knitting lace

Lace knitting can be used in many different ways – as an allover pattern, a horizontal or vertical panel, or as single or random motifs. Lace stitch patterns are most effective when worked in plain yarns, as fluffy or textured yarns do not show the detail of the pattern. Finer yarns are also more suitable than bulky yarns, as they give the stitch a more delicate appearance. Lace knitting is especially popular for baby garments such as heirloom shawls and christening blankets.

Lace patterns are produced by using the eyelet method of increasing. These increases are usually worked in conjunction with decreases, so that the number of stitches remains constant at the end of each row. However, some of the most beautiful lace effects are achieved by increasing stitches on one or more rows and decreasing the extra stitches on subsequent rows. Circular shawls are produced by continually increasing stitches on every round (or every alternate round), while working the increases into the lace pattern.

The eyelet method of increasing is used in lace patterns to form a hole. The exact way that the yarn is taken over the needle depends on the stitches at either side of the eyelet – whether they are knitted, purled or a combination of both. They are then accompanied by one of the decrease methods, depending on whether the slant is to be towards the left or the right.

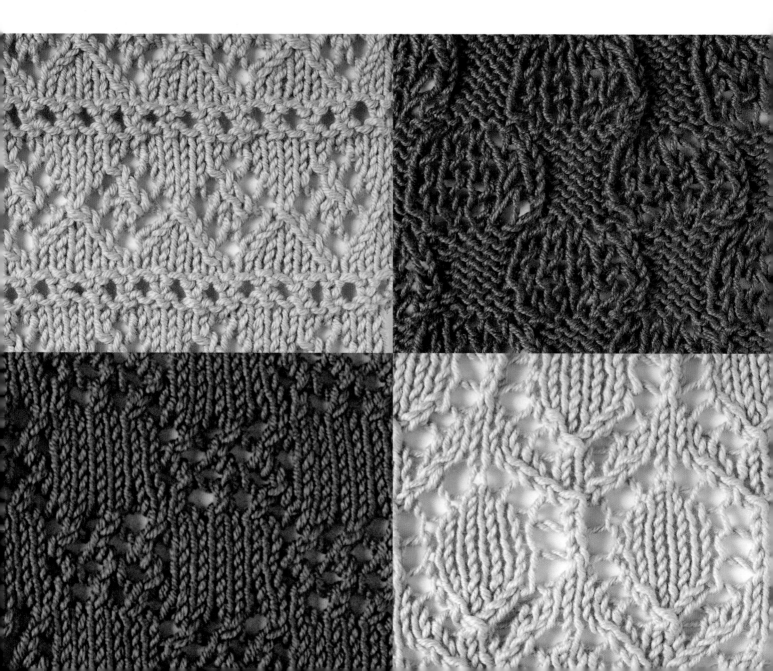

Advice on knitting edgings

If an edging is worked lengthways then the instruction at the start of the pattern will say, for example, 'Worked lengthways over 10 sts'. This means that you cast on 10 stitches to work the first row. Once you have worked all the pattern rows, you simply repeat them until the edging is the required length.

The instructions may tell you to finish the final repeat on a particular row. This is usually so that if the ends of the knitted edging are joined to form a circle, the pattern will run as evenly as possible across the join. If a particular row is not given, end the last repeat with the last pattern row.

Depending on the pattern, the number of stitches on the needle may vary on rows. When the number changes, a stitch count is given in brackets at the end of the row. This count includes all loops on the needle, whether they are full stitches or yarnovers. If no stitch count is given then the number of stitches has not changed since the last count. So, a lengthways pattern with no stitch counts at all has the same number of stitches on every row as originally cast on.

Some patterns need a foundation row that does not form part of the repeat. These are marked as such in the patterns.

Edgings that are worked from the top down or bottom up have different instructions. The 'multiple' or repeat of the pattern is given at the start – for example, 'Starts with multiple of 7 sts + 4 sts'. This means you can cast on any number of stitches that is a multiple of 7, plus 4 balancing stitches – for instance, 14 + 4, 21 + 4, 28 + 4, and so on. These patterns do not have stitch counts at the ends of the rows, so you will need to follow the increases and decreases carefully to keep the pattern correct.

The number of times the pattern rows need to be repeated to make the edging shown in the swatch will be specified, though

on many of the patterns you could work the repeat more often to create a deeper edging if required.

If you are going to work a bottom-up edging and then continue knitting the project, you need to make sure that the number of stitches the edging finishes with – for example, 'Ends with multiple of 6 sts + 2 sts' – can be multiplied to make the correct number of stitches for the first row of the project. So, in this example, the first row of the project needs to be any multiple of 6 stitches, plus 2 balancing stitches.

For a top-down edging worked on the lower edge of a project, check the multiple the edging starts with. Edging patterns won't work without the correct multiple, so you will usually need to adjust the number of project stitches.

However, if the number of project stitches is just one or two more than is needed for the edging, then you can add one or two selvedge stitches to the end of the edging pattern, but remember they are there and don't try to work them into the pattern. Make careful notes of any changes and consider how they might affect other areas of the project. Of course, both bottom-up and top-down edgings can be worked as strips and sewn on afterwards if preferred.

Attaching edgings

Lengthways edgings need to be sewn to the finished project. Usually it is best to use a tapestry needle and matching yarn and whip stitch the top edge of the edging to the knitted fabric. To attach an edging to cloth fabric, use a sewing needle and matching sewing thread.

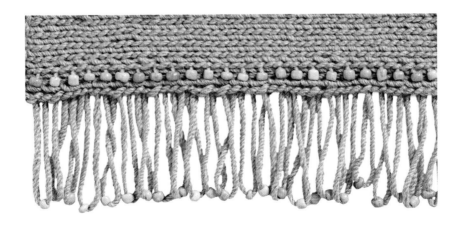

Key to stitch diagrams

C2B (CROSS 2 BACK)

Slip next st onto cable needle and hold at back of work, knit next st from left-hand needle, then knit st from cable needle.

C2BW (CROSS 2 BACK ON WRONG SIDE)

Slip next st onto cable needle and hold at back (right side) of work, purl next st from left-hand needle, then purl st from cable needle.

C2F (CROSS 2 FRONT)

Slip next st onto cable needle and hold at front of work, knit next st from left-hand needle, then knit st from cable needle.

C2FW (CROSS 2 FRONT ON WRONG SIDE)

Slip next st onto cable needle and hold at front (wrong side) of work, purl next st from left-hand needle, then purl st from cable needle.

C3B (CABLE 3 BACK)

Slip next st onto cable needle and hold at back of work, knit next 2 sts from left-hand needle, then knit st from cable needle.

C3F (CABLE 3 FRONT)

Slip next 2 sts onto cable needle and hold at front of work, knit next st from left-hand needle, then knit 2 sts from cable needle.

C3L (CABLE 3 LEFT)

Slip next st onto cable needle and hold at front of work, knit next 2 sts from left-hand needle, then knit st from cable needle.

C3R (CABLE 3 RIGHT)

Slip next 2 sts onto cable needle and hold at back of work, knit next st from left-hand needle, then knit 2 sts from cable needle.

C4B (CABLE 4 BACK)

Slip next 2 sts onto cable needle and hold at back of work, knit next 2 sts from left-hand needle, then knit 2 sts from cable needle.

C4F (CABLE 4 FRONT)

Slip next 2 sts onto cable needle and hold at front of work, knit next 2 sts from left-hand needle, then knit 2 sts from cable needle.

C5B (CABLE 5 BACK)

Slip next 3 sts onto cable needle and hold at back of work, knit next 2 sts from left-hand needle, then knit 3 sts from cable needle.

C5F (CABLE 5 FRONT)

Slip next 2 sts onto cable needle and hold at front of work, knit next 3 sts from left-hand needle, then knit 2 sts from cable needle.

C6B (CABLE 6 BACK)

Slip next 3 sts onto cable needle and hold at back of work, knit next 3 sts from left-hand needle, then knit 3 sts from cable needle.

C6F (CABLE 6 FRONT)

Slip next 3 sts onto cable needle and hold at front of work, knit next 3 sts from left-hand needle, then knit 3 sts from cable needle.

C7B (CABLE 7 BACK)

Slip next 4 sts onto cable needle and hold at back of work, knit next 3 sts from left-hand needle, then knit 4 sts from cable needle.

C8B (CABLE 8 BACK)

Slip next 4 sts onto cable needle and hold at back of work, knit next 4 sts from left-hand needle, then knit 4 sts from cable needle.

C8F (CABLE 8 FRONT)

Slip next 4 sts onto cable needle and hold at front of work, knit next 4 sts from left-hand needle, then knit 4 sts from cable needle.

C10B (CABLE 10 BACK)

Slip next 5 sts onto cable needle and hold at back of work, knit next 5 sts from left-hand needle, then knit 5 sts from cable needle.

C10F (CABLE 10 FRONT)

Slip next 5 sts onto cable needle and hold at front of work, knit next 5 sts from left-hand needle, then knit 5 sts from cable needle.

C12B (CABLE 12 BACK)

Slip next 6 sts onto cable needle and hold at back of work, knit next 6 sts from left-hand needle, then knit 6 sts from cable needle.

T2B (TWIST 2 BACK)

Slip next st onto cable needle and hold at back of work, knit next st from left-hand needle, then purl st from cable needle.

T2F (TWIST 2 FRONT)

Slip next st onto cable needle and hold at front of work, purl next st from left-hand needle, then knit st from cable needle.

T3B (TWIST 3 BACK)

Slip next st onto cable needle and hold at back of work, knit next 2 sts from left-hand needle, then purl st from cable needle.

T3F (TWIST 3 FRONT)

Slip next 2 sts onto cable needle and hold at front of work, purl next st from left-hand needle, then knit 2 sts from cable needle.

T4B (TWIST 4 BACK)

Slip next 2 sts onto cable needle and hold at back of work, knit next 2 sts from left-hand needle, then purl 2 sts from cable needle.

T4BP (TWIST 4 BACK PURL)

Slip next 2 sts onto cable needle and hold at back of work, knit next 2 sts from left-hand needle, then p1, k1 from cable needle.

T4F (TWIST 4 FRONT)

Slip next 2 sts onto cable needle and hold at front of work, purl next 2 sts from left-hand needle, then knit 2 sts from cable needle.

T4FP (TWIST 4 FRONT PURL)

Slip next 2 sts onto cable needle and hold at front of work, k1, p1 from left-hand needle, then knit 2 sts from cable needle.

T5B (TWIST 5 BACK)

Slip next 3 sts onto cable needle and hold at back of work, knit next 2 sts from left-hand needle, then purl 3 sts from cable needle.

T5BP (TWIST 5 BACK PURL)

Slip next 3 sts onto cable needle and hold at back of work, knit next 2 sts from left-hand needle, then p1, k2 from cable needle.

T5L (TWIST 5 LEFT)

Slip next 3 sts onto cable needle and hold at front of work, purl next 2 sts from left-hand needle, then knit 3 sts from cable needle.

T5R (TWIST 5 RIGHT)

Slip next 2 sts onto cable needle and hold at back of work, knit next 3 sts from left-hand needle, then purl 2 sts from cable needle.

T6B (TWIST 6 BACK)

Slip next 3 sts onto cable needle and hold at back of work, knit next 3 sts from left-hand needle, then purl 3 sts from cable needle.

I

K

Knit on right-side rows.

‒

K

Knit on wrong-side rows.

K2tog

Knit two sts together.

<

KB1

Knit into back of st on wrong-side rows.

V

KB1

Knit into back of st on right-side rows.

V

M3 (Make 3 sts)

[k1, p1, k1] all into next st.

‒

P

Purl on right-side rows.

I

P

Purl on wrong-side rows.

P2tog

Purl two sts together.

V

PB1

Purl into back of st on wrong-side rows.

S

Sl 1

Slip one st with yarn at back (wrong side) of work.

Sl 1, k1, psso

Slip one st, knit one, pass the slipped st over.

Sl 1, k2tog, psso

Slip one st, knit two sts together, pass the slipped st over.

Sl 2tog knitwise, k1, p2sso

Slip two sts knitwise, knit one st, pass the two slipped sts over.

Abbreviations

Knitting patterns are usually written with abbreviated instructions in order to save space. Below is an explanation of all the abbreviations that are used in this book.

[ ] work instructions within brackets as many times as directed

( ) work instructions within parentheses in the place directed

* repeat instructions following the single asterisk as directed

* * repeat instructions following the asterisks as directed

alt alternate

beg begin(s)(ning)

C2B cross 2 back – slip next st onto cable needle and hold at back, knit next st from LH needle, knit st from cable needle

C2BW cross 2 back on wrong side – slip next st onto cable needle and hold at back (RS), purl next st from LH needle, purl next st from cable needle

C2F cross 2 front – slip next st onto cable needle and hold at front, knit next st from LH needle, knit st from cable needle

C2FW cross 2 front on wrong side – slip next st onto cable needle and hold at front (WS), purl next st from LH needle, purl st from cable needle

C2L cross 2 left – slip next st onto cable needle and hold at front, knit next st from LH needle, knit st from cable needle

C2R cross 2 right – slip next st onto cable needle and hold at back, knit next st from LH needle, knit st from cable needle

C3B cable 3 back – slip next st onto cable needle and hold at back, knit next 2 sts from LH needle, knit st from cable needle

C3F cable 3 front – slip next 2 sts onto cable needle and hold at front, knit next st from LH needle, knit 2 sts from cable needle

C3L cable/cross 3 left – slip next st onto cable needle and hold at front, knit next 2 sts from LH needle, knit st from cable needle

C3R cable/cross 3 right – slip next 2 sts onto cable needle and hold at back, knit next st from LH needle, knit 2 sts from cable needle

C4B cable 4 back – slip next 2 sts onto cable needle and hold at back, knit next 2 sts from LH needle, knit 2 sts from cable needle

C4F cable 4 front – slip next 2 sts onto cable needle and hold at front, knit next 2 sts from LH needle, knit 2 sts from cable needle

C5B cable 5 back – slip next 3 sts onto cable needle and hold at back, knit next 2 sts from LH needle, knit 3 sts from cable needle

C5F cable 5 front – slip next 2 sts onto cable needle and hold at front, knit next 3 sts from LH needle, knit 2 sts from cable needle

C6 cross 6 – slip next 4 sts onto cable needle and hold at front, knit next 2 sts from LH needle, slip 2 purl sts from cable needle back to LH needle. Pass cable needle back with 2 rem knit sts to back of work, purl 2 sts from LH needle, knit 2 sts from cable needle

C6B cable 6 back – slip next 3 sts onto cable needle and hold at back, knit next 3 sts from LH needle, knit 3 sts from cable needle

C6F cable 6 front – slip next 3 sts onto cable needle and hold at front, knit next 3 sts from LH needle, knit 3 sts from cable needle

C7B cable 7 back – slip next 4 sts onto cable needle and hold at back, knit next 3 sts from LH needle, knit 4 sts from cable needle

C7F cable 7 front – slip next 3 sts onto cable needle and hold at front, knit next 4 sts from LH needle, knit 3 sts from cable needle

C8B cable 8 back – slip next 4 sts onto cable needle and hold at back, knit next 4 sts from LH needle, knit 4 sts from cable needle

C8F cable 8 front – slip next 4 sts onto cable needle and hold at front, knit next 4 sts from LH needle, knit 4 sts from cable needle

C9 cross 9 – slip next 4 sts onto cable needle and hold at front, knit next 5 sts from LH needle, knit 4 sts from cable needle

C10B cable 10 back – slip next 5 sts onto cable needle and hold at back, knit next 5 sts from LH needle, knit 5 sts from cable needle

C10F cable 10 front – slip next 5 sts onto cable needle and hold at front, knit next 5 sts from LH needle, knit 5 sts from cable needle

cm centimetre(s)

cont continue

foll(s) follow(s)(ing)

in   inch(es)

inc   increase

inc2   increase 2 – work into front, back and front of next st

k   knit

K1B   knit 1 below

K1B   back from the top, insert point of RH needle into back of st below next st on LH needle and knit it

k2tog   knit 2 sts together

k5tog   knit 5 sts together

K5W   knit next 5 sts wrapping yarn twice around needle for each st

KB1   knit into back of next st

LH   left hand

M1   make 1

M1K   make 1 knit

M1P   make 1 purl

M5K   make 5 knit

MB   make bobble – knit into front, back and front of next st, [turn and knit these 3 sts] 3 times, then turn and sl 1, k2tog, psso to complete bobble

ML   make loop – k1 but do not slip st off LH needle, bring yarn between needles to the front, take it under and over your left thumb, take yarn back between needles to the wrong side, k st on LH needle again, then slip second st on RH needle over first st

p   purl

p2sso   pass 2 slipped sts over

p2tog   purl 2 sts together

p3tog   purl 3 sts together

PB1   purl into back of next st

psso   pass slipped st over

p3sso   pass 3 slipped sts over

rem   remain(ing)

rep   repeat(s)

rev st st   reverse stocking stitch

RH   right hand

RS   right side

sk2po   slip one st, knit two sts together, pass slipped st over

skpo   slip one st, knit one st, pass slipped st over

sl   slip

ssk   slip one st knitwise, slip next st knitwise, insert LH needle through fronts of slipped sts and knit the two sts together

st(s)   stitch(es)

st st   stocking stitch

T2B   twist 2 back – slip next st onto cable needle and hold at back, knit next st from LH needle, purl st from cable needle

T2F   twist 2 front – slip next st onto cable needle and hold at front, purl next st from LH needle, knit st from cable needle

T3B   twist 3 back – slip next st onto cable needle and hold at back, knit next 2 sts from LH needle, purl st from cable needle

T3F   twist 3 front – slip next 2 sts onto cable needle and hold at front of work, purl next st from LH needle,

knit 2 sts from cable needle

T4B   twist 4 back – slip next 2 sts onto cable needle and hold at back of work, knit 2 sts, purl 2 sts from cable needle

T4BR   twist 4 back right – slip next st onto cable needle, hold at back, knit next 3 sts from LH needle, purl st from cable needle

T4F   twist 4 front – slip next 2 sts onto cable needle and hold at front, purl 2 sts, knit 2 sts from cable needle

T4FL   twist 4 front left – slip next 3 sts onto cable needle and hold at front, purl next st from LH needle, knit 3 sts from cable needle

T4FP   twist 4 front purl – slip next 2 sts onto cable needle and hold at front, k1, p1 from LH needle, knit 2 sts from cable needle

T5BP   twist 5 back purl – slip next 3 sts onto cable needle and hold at back, knit next 2 sts from LH needle, p1, k2 from cable needle

T5L   twist 5 left – slip next 3 sts onto cable needle and hold at front, purl next 2 sts from LH needle, knit 3 sts from cable needle

T5R   twist 5 right – slip next 2 sts onto cable needle and hold at back, knit next 3 sts

from LH needle, purl 2 sts from cable needle

T6B   twist 6 back – slip next 3 sts onto cable needle and hold at back, knit next 3 sts from LH needle, purl 3 sts from cable needle

T6F   twist 6 front – slip next 3 sts onto cable needle and hold at front, knit next 3 sts from LH needle, purl 3 sts from cable needle

tbl   through back of loop

tog   together

WS   wrong side

wyib   with yarn in back

wyif   with yarn in front

yb   yarn to the back

yf   yarn to the front

yfon   yarn forward and over needle

yfrn   with yarn in front

yo/yon   yarnover/needle

yo2   yarn forward, round or over needle twice to make 2 sts

yrn   yarn round needle

Garter stitch

Knit every row.

Stocking stitch

Any number of stitches.
Row 1 (RS): Knit.
Row 2: Purl.
Rep these 2 rows.

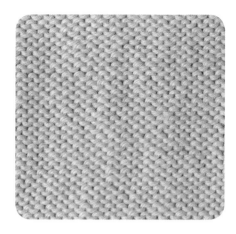

Reverse stocking stitch

Any number of stitches.
Row 1 (RS): Purl.
Row 2: Knit.
Rep these 2 rows.

Linen stitch

Multiple of 2.
Row 1: *K1, yfwd, sl 1, yb*; rep from * to end.
Row 2: *P1, yb, sl 1, yfwd*; rep from * to end.
Rep these 2 rows.

K1, p1 rib

On an even number of sts:
*K1, p1; rep from * to end.
Rep this row.

On an odd number of sts:
Row 1: K1, *p1, k1; rep from * to end.
Row 2: P1, *k1, p1; rep from * to end.
Rep these 2 rows.

K2, p2 rib

Multiple of 4.
Row 1: *K2, p2; rep from * to end.
Rep this row.

Multiple of 4 plus 2.
Row 1: K2, *p2, k2; rep from * to end.
Row 2: P2, *k2, p2; rep from * to end.
Rep these 2 rows.

Cartridge stitch

Any number of stitches.
Rows 1 (RS), 3, 4 and 6: Knit.
Rows 2 and 5: Purl.
Rep these 6 rows.

Alternated smooth stitch and tier

Any number of stitches.
Rows 1 (RS), 3 and 4: Knit.
Row 2: Purl.
Rep these 4 rows.

Texture stitch

Multiple of 2 + 1.
Row 1 (RS): Purl.
Row 2: K1, *yf, sl 1 purlwise, yb, k1; rep from * to end.
Rep these 2 rows.

Herringbone I

Multiple of 2.
Row 1: K2tog tbl dropping only first loop off left needle, *k2tog tbl (rem st and next st), again dropping only the first loop off the needle*, k1tbl.
Row 2: P2tog dropping only the first loop off left needle, *p2tog (rem st and next stitch), again dropping only first loop off needle*, p1.
Rep these 2 rows.

Gathered stitch

Any number of stitches.
Rows 1–6: Knit.
Row 7: Knit into front and back of each st.
Rows 8, 10 and 12: Purl.
Rows 9 and 11: Knit.
Row 13: K2tog to end.
Rep from row 2.

Loop pattern

Multiple of 2 + 2.
Row 1 (RS): Knit.
Row 2: *K1, sl 1; rep from * to last 2 sts, k2.
Row 3: Knit.
Row 4: K2, *sl 1, k1; rep from * to end.
Rep these 4 rows.

Bobble stitch

Multiple of 12 + 11.
Row 1: Knit.
Row 2: Purl.
Row 3: K5, *make 5 sts out of 1 st by knitting into front and back of next st twice, then into front again, turn, work 4 rows in st st (starting purl) on these 5 sts, with left-hand needle lift 2nd, 3rd, 4th and 5th sts over the first st (one bobble made), k11; rep from * to last 6 sts, work a bobble in next st, k5.
Rows 4–14: Starting with a purl row work 11 rows in st st.
Row 15 (RS): K11, *work a bobble in next st, k11; rep from * to end.
Rows 16–26: Work 11 rows in st st.
Rep from row 3.

Fur stitch

Multiple of 2 + 2.
Row 1 (WS): Knit.
Row 2: *K1, k1 keeping st on left-hand needle, bring yf, pass yarn over left thumb to make a loop (approx 4cm/1½in), yb and knit this st again, slipping st off the needle, yo and pass the 2 sts just worked over this loop (1 loop made = ML); rep from * to last 2 sts, k2.
Row 3: Knit.
Row 4: K2, *ML, k1; rep from * to end.
Rep these 4 rows.

Whelk pattern

Multiple of 4 + 3.
Row 1 (RS): K3, *sl 1 purlwise, k3; rep from * to end.
Row 2: K3, *yo, sl 1 purlwise, yb, k3; rep from * to end.
Row 3: K1, *sl 1 purlwise, k3; rep from * to last 2 sts, sl 1 purlwise, k1.
Row 4: P1, sl 1 purlwise, *p3, sl 1 purlwise; rep from * to last st, p1.
Rep these 4 rows.

Diagonal ridge I

Multiple of 4 + 2.

Row 1: Edge st, * p1, k3; rep from * to last st, edge st.

Row 2 (back): Edge st, p2 * k1, p3; rep from * to last 3 sts, k1, p1, edge st.

Row 3: Edge st, k2 * p1, k3; rep from * to last 3 sts, p1, k1, edge st.

Row 4: Edge st, * k1, p3; rep from * to last st, edge st.

Rep these 4 rows.

This pattern can be used on either side.

Bowknot

Multiple of 10 + 7.

Rows 1 (WS) and 3: Purl.

Rows 2, 4, 6 and 8: Knit.

Rows 5, 7 and 9: P6, *yb, sl 5 sts, yf, p5; rep from* to last st, p1.

Row 10: K8, *make bowknot [slip right needle under 3 strands, knit next st pulling the loop through under the strands], k8; rep from * to end.

Rows 11 and 13: Purl.

Rows 12, 14, 16 and 18: Knit.

Rows 15, 17 and 19: P1, *yb, sl 5 sts, yf, p5; rep from * to last 6 sts, yb, sl 5 sts, p1.

Row 20: K3, *bowknot, k9*; rep from * to last 4 sts, bowknot, k3.

Rep these 20 rows.

Ornamental stitches

Multiple of 10 + 8.

Rows 1, 3 and 5: Knit.

Rows 2, 4 and 6: Purl.

Row 7: K2, make daisy [insert needle in loop 3 rows below the 2nd st on left-hand needle, draw up a loop, k2, draw 2nd loop through same st, k2, draw 3rd loop through same st], *k6, make daisy; rep from * to last 2 sts, k2.

Row 8: P2, *[p2tog, p1] twice, p2tog, p5; rep from * to last 9 sts, [p2tog, p1] twice, p2tog, p1.

Rows 9, 11 and 13: Knit.

Rows 10, 12 and 14: Purl.

Row 15: K7, *make daisy, k6; rep from * to last st, k1.

Row 16: P2, *p5, [p2tog, p1] twice, p2tog; rep from * to last 6 sts, p6.

Rep these 16 rows.

Pleats

Multiple of 2 +1 + 2 sts each edge.

Row 1 (RS): 1 edge st, *k1, p1*; rep from * to * k1, 1 edge st.

Row 2: 1 edge st, p1, *k1, p1*; rep from * to *, 1 edge st.

Rows 3, 5, 7 and 9: 1 edge st, *k1, yf, sl 1 purlwise, yb*; rep from * to *, k1, 1 edge st.

Rows 4, 6, 8 and 10: 1 edge st, *yf, sl 1 purlwise, yb, k1*; rep from * to * to last 2 sts, yf, sl 1 purlwise, yb, 1 edge st.

Rep these 10 rows.

Ribbed extended stitches

Multiple of 8 + 4 + 2 edge sts.

Row 1 (RS): 1 edge st, *p4, k4 (winding yarn around needle 3 times for each st)*; rep from * to last st, 1 edge st.

Rows 2 and 4: 1 edge st, k4, *yf, slip 4 sts purlwise dropping extra loops off needle, yb, k4; rep from * to last st, 1 edge st.

Row 3: 1 edge st, *p4, yb, slip 4 sts knitwise, yf; rep from * to last st, 1 edge st.

Rep these 4 rows.

Diagonal ridge II

Multiple of 18, plus 2 edge sts.

Row 1: Edge st, *p4, k4, p1, k4, p1, k4*; rep from * to last st, edge st.

Row 2: Edge st, *k1, p4, k4, p4, k1, p4*; rep from * to last st, edge st.

Row 3: Edge st, k5, *p1, k10, p1, k6*; rep from * to last 14 sts, p1, k10, p1, k1, edge st.

Row 4: Edge st, p2, *k1, p8, k1, p8*, rep from * to last 17 sts, k1, p8, k1, p6, edge st.

Row 5: Edge st, k7, *p1, k6, p1, k10*; rep from * to last 12 sts, p1, k6, p1, k3, edge st.

Row 6: Edge st, *p4, k1, p4, k1, p4, k4*; rep from * to last st, edge st.

Row 7: Edge st, *k4, p1, k4, p4, k4, p1*; rep from * to last st, edge st.

Row 8: Edge st, p1, *k1, p10, k1, p6*; rep from * to last 18 sts, k1, p10, k1, p5, edge st.

Row 9: Edge st, k6, *p1, k8, p1, k8*, rep from * to last 13 sts, p1, k8, p1, k2, edge st.

Row 10: Edge st, p3, *k1, p6, k1, p10*; rep from * to last 16 sts, k1, p6, k1, p7, edge st.

Rep these 10 rows.

Labyrinth

Panel of 40 sts.

Rows 1 (RS) and 3: K2, p2, k2, p2, k2, p8, k2, p2, k2, p16.

Row 2 and even rows: Knit all knit sts and purl all purl sts.

Rows 5 and 7: K2, p2 (3 times), k8, p2, k2, p2, k14.

Rows 9 and 11: K2, p2 (4 times), p6, k2, p2, k2, p12.

Rows 13 and 15: K2, p2 (4 times), k8, p2, k2, p2, k10.

Rows 17 and 19: K2, p2 (4 times), p10, k2, p2, k2, p8.

Rows 21 and 23: K2, p2 (4 times), k12, p2, k2, p2, k6.

Rows 25 and 27: K6, p2, k2, p2, k2, p12, k2, p2, k2, p2, k2, p4.

Rows 29 and 31: P8, k2, p2, k2, p2, k12, p2, k2 (3 times).

Rows 33 and 35: K10, p2, k2, p2, k2, p12, k2, p2, k2, p2, k2.

Rows 37 and 39: P12, k2, p2, k16, p2, k12, p2, k2.

Rows 41 and 43: K14, p2, k2, p16, k2, p2, k2.

Rows 45 and 47: P12, k2, p2, k20, p2, k2.

Row 48: As row 2.

Rep these 48 rows.

Plain diamonds

Multiple of 9.

Row 1 (RS): K4, *p1, k8; rep from * to last 5 sts, p1, k4.

Row 2: P3, *k3, p6; rep from * to last 6 sts, k3, p3.

Row 3: K2, *p5, k4; rep from * to last 7 sts, p5, k2.

Row 4: P1, *k7, p2; rep from * to last 8 sts, k7, p1.

Row 5: Purl.

Row 6: As row 4.

Row 7: As row 3.

Row 8: As row 2.

Rep these 8 rows.

Embossed diamonds

Multiple of 10 + 3.

Row 1 (RS): P1, k1, p1, *[k3, p1] twice, k1, p1; rep from * to end.

Row 2: P1, k1, *p3, k1, p1, k1, p3, k1; rep from * to last st, p1.

Row 3: K4, *[p1, k1] twice, p1, k5; rep from * to last 9 sts, [p1, k1] twice, p1, k4.

Row 4: P3, *[k1, p1] 3 times, k1, p3; rep from * to end.

Row 5: As row 3.

Row 6: As row 2.

Row 7: As row 1.

Row 8: P1, k1, p1, *k1, p5, [k1, p1] twice; rep from * to end.

Row 9: [P1, k1] twice, *p1, k3, [p1, k1] 3 times; rep from * to last 9 sts, p1, k3, [p1, k1] twice, p1.

Row 10: As row 8.

Rep these 10 rows.

Pleat pattern

Multiple of 5 + 1.
Row 1 (RS): K1B, *p1, k2, p1, k1B; rep from *.
Row 2: P1, *k1, p2, k1, p1; rep from *.
Row 3: K1B, *p4, k1B; rep from *.
Row 4: P1, *k4, p1; rep from *.
Rep these 4 rows.

Vertical bar lines

Multiple of 4 + 2.
Row 1 (RS): P2, *k2, p2; rep from * to end.
Row 2: K2, *keeping yarn to the back sl next 2 sts purlwise, k2; rep from * to end.
Rep these 2 rows.

Openwork mullions

Multiple of 5 + 1.
Row 1 (RS): P1, *k4, p1; rep from * to end.
Row 2: K1, *k twice into st below st on needle, k2tog, k into st below st on needle, p1; rep from * to end.
Rep these 2 rows.

Supple rib

Multiple of 3 + 1.
Row 1 (RS): K1, *knit the next st but do not slip it off the left-hand needle, then purl the same st and the next st tog, k1; rep from * to end.
Row 2: Purl.
Rep these 2 rows.

Dot stitch

Multiple of 4 + 3.
Row 1 (RS): K1, *p1, k3; rep from * to last 2 sts, p1, k1.
Row 2: Purl.
Row 3: *K3, p1; rep from * to last 3 sts, k3.
Row 4: Purl.
Rep these 4 rows.

Farrow rib

Multiple of 3 + 1.
Row 1 (RS): *K2, p1; rep from * to last st, k1.
Row 2: P1, *k2, p1; rep from * to end.
Rep these 2 rows.

Box stitch

Multiple of 4 + 2.
Row 1: K2, *p2, k2; rep from * to end.
Row 2: P2, *k2, p2; rep from * to end.
Row 3: As row 2.
Row 4: As row 1.
Rep these 4 rows.

Moss stitch

Multiple of 2 + 1.
Row 1: K1, *p1, k1; rep from * to end.
Rep this row.

Double moss stitch

Multiple of 2 + 1.
Row 1: K1, *p1, k1; rep from * to end.
Row 2: P1, *k1, p1; rep from * to end.
Row 3: As row 2.
Row 4: As row 1.
Rep these 4 rows.

Oblique rib

Multiple of 4.
Row 1 (RS): *K2, p2; rep from * to end.
Row 2: K1, *p2, k2; rep from * to last 3 sts, p2, k1.
Row 3: *P2, k2; rep from * to end.
Row 4: P1, *k2, p2; rep from * to last 3 sts, k2, p1.
Rep these 4 rows.

Lizard lattice

Multiple of 6 + 3.
Work 4 rows in st st, starting knit (row 1 is RS).
Row 5: P3, *k3, p3; rep from * to end.
Row 6: Purl.
Rep the last 2 rows once more, then row 5 again.
Work 4 rows in st st, starting with purl.
Row 14: P3, *k3, p3; rep from * to end.
Rep these 14 rows.

Stocking stitch triangles

Multiple of 5.
Row 1 (RS): Knit.
Row 2: *K1, p4; rep from * to end.
Row 3: *K3, p2; rep from * to end.
Row 4: *K3, p2; rep from * to end.
Row 5: *K1, p4; rep from * to end.
Row 6: Knit.
Rep these 6 rows.

Cross motif pattern

Multiple of 12.

Row 1 (RS): P1, k10, *p2, k10; rep from * to last st, p1.

Row 2: K1, p10, *k2, p10; rep from * to last st, k1.

Rep the last 2 rows once more.

Row 5: P3, k6, *p6, k6; rep from * to last 3 sts, p3.

Row 6: K3, p6, *k6, p6; rep from * to last 3 sts, k3.

Row 7: As row 1.

Row 8: As row 2.

Rep the last 2 rows once more.

Row 11: Knit.

Row 12: Purl.

Row 13: K5, p2, *k10, p2; rep from * to last 5 sts, k5.

Row 14: P5, k2, *p10, k2; rep from * to last 5 sts, p5.

Rep the last 2 rows once more.

Row 17: K3, p6, *k6, p6; rep from * to last 3 sts, k3.

Row 18: P3, k6, *p6, k6; rep from * to last 3 sts, p3.

Row 19: K5, p2, *k10, p2; rep from * to last 5 sts, k5.

Row 20: P5, k2, *p10, k2; rep from * to last 5 sts, p5.

Rep the last 2 rows once more.

Row 23: Knit.

Row 24: Purl.

Rep these 24 rows.

Pyramids I

Multiple of 15 + 7.

Row 1 (RS): *P1, [KB1] 5 times, p1, k8; rep from * to last 7 sts, p1, [KB1] 5 times, p1.

Row 2: *K1, [PB1] 5 times, k1, p8; rep from * to last 7 sts, k1, [PB1] 5 times, k1.

Row 3: P1, *[KB1] 5 times, p10; rep from * to last 6 sts, [KB1] 5 times, p1.

Row 4: K1, *[PB1] 5 times, k10; rep from * to last 6 sts, [PB1] 5 times, k1.

Row 5: P2, *[KB1] 3 times, p3, k6, p3; rep from * to last 5 sts, [KB1] 3 times, p2.

Row 6: K2, *[PB1] 3 times, k3, p6, k3; rep from * to last 5 sts, [PB1] 3 times, k2.

Row 7: P2, *[KB1] 3 times, p12; rep from * to last 5 sts, [KB1] 3 times, p2.

Row 8: K2, *[PB1] 3 times, k12; rep from * to last 5 sts, [PB1] 3 times, k2.

Row 9: P3, *KB1, p5, k4, p5; rep from * to last 4 sts, KB1, p3.

Row 10: K3, *PB1, k5, p4, k5; rep from * to last 4 sts, PB1, k3.

Row 11: P3, *KB1, p14; rep from * to last 4 sts, KB1, p3.

Row 12: K3, *PB1, k14; rep from * to last 4 sts, PB1, k3.

Rep these 12 rows.

Moss stitch parallelograms

Multiple of 10.

Row 1 (RS): *K5, [p1, k1] twice, p1; rep from * to end.

Row 2: [P1, k1] 3 times, *p5, [k1, p1] twice, k1; rep from * to last 4 sts, p4.

Row 3: K3, *[p1, k1] twice, p1, k5; rep from * to last 7 sts, [p1, k1] twice, p1, k2.

Row 4: P3, *[k1, p1] twice, k1, p5; rep from * to last 7 sts, [k1, p1] twice, k1, p2.

Row 5: [K1, p1] 3 times, *k5, [p1, k1] twice, p1; rep from * to last 4 sts, k4.

Row 6: Purl.

Rep these 6 rows.

Woven horizontal herringbone

Multiple of 4.

Row 1 (RS): K3, *yf, sl 2, yb, k2; rep from * to last st, k1.

Row 2: P2, *yb, sl 2, yf, p2; rep from * to last 2 sts, p2.

Row 3: K1, yf, sl 2, yb, *k2, yf, sl 2, yb; rep from * to last st, k1.

Row 4: P4, *yb, sl 2, yf, p2; rep from * to end.

Rep the last 4 rows twice more.

Row 13: As row 3.

Row 14: As row 2.

Rep these 14 rows.

Moss stitch triangles

Multiple of 8.

Row 1 (RS): *P1, k7; rep from * to end.

Row 2: P6, *k1, p7; rep from * to last 2 sts, k1, p1.

Row 3: *P1, k1, p1, k5; rep from * to end.

Row 4: P4, *k1, p1, k1, p5; rep from * to last 4 sts, [k1, p1] twice.

Row 5: *[P1, k1] twice, p1, k3; rep from * to end.

Row 6: P2, *[k1, p1] twice, k1, p3; rep from * to last 6 sts, [k1, p1] 3 times.

Row 7: *P1, k1; rep from * to end.

Row 8: As row 6.

Row 9: As row 5.

Row 10: As row 4.

Row 11: As row 3.

Row 12: As row 2.

Rep these 12 rows.

Moss stitch squares

Multiple of 12 + 3.

Row 1 (RS): Knit.

Row 2: Purl.

Row 3: K4, *[p1, k1] 3 times, p1, k5, rep from * to last 11 sts, [p1, k1] 3 times, p1, k4.

Row 4: P3, *[k1, p1] 4 times, k1, p3; rep from * to end.

Row 5: K4, *p1, k5; rep from * to last 5 sts, p1, k4.

Row 6: P3, *k1, p7, k1, p3; rep from * to end.

Rep the last 2 rows twice more, then row 5 again.

Row 12: As row 4.

Row 13: As row 3.

Row 14: Purl.

Rep these 14 rows.

Little birds

Multiple of 14 + 8.

Row 1 (RS): Knit.

Row 2: Purl.

Row 3: K10, *sl 2 purlwise, k12; rep from * to last 12 sts, sl 2 purlwise, k10.

Row 4: P10, *sl 2 purlwise, p12; rep from * to last 12 sts, sl 2 purlwise, p10.

Row 5: K8, *C3R, C3L, k8; rep from * to end.

Row 6: Purl.

Rep rows 1–2 once.

Row 9: K3, *sl 2, k12; rep from * to last 5 sts, sl 2, k3.

Row 10: P3, *sl 2, p12; rep from * to last 5 sts, sl 2, p3.

Row 11: K1, *C3R, C3L, k8; rep from * to last 7 sts, C3R, C3L, k1.

Row 12: Purl.

Rep these 12 rows.

Chevron stripes

Multiple of 18 + 9.

Row 1 (RS): P4, k1, p4, *k4, p1, k4, p4, k1, p4; rep from * to end.

Row 2: K3, *p3, k3; rep from * to end.

Row 3: P2, k5, p2, *k2, p5, k2, p2, k5, p2; rep from * to end.

Row 4: K1, p7, k1, *p1, k7, p1, k1, p7, k1; rep from * to end.

Row 5: K4, p1, k4, *p4, k1, p4, k4, p1, k4; rep from * to end.

Row 6: P3, *k3, p3; rep from * to end.

Row 7: K2, p5, k2, *p2, k5, p2, k2, p5, k2; rep from * to end.

Row 8: P1, k7, p1, *k1, p7, k1, p1, k7, p1; rep from * to end.

Rep these 8 rows.

Hexagon stitch

Multiple of 10 + 1.

Row 1 (RS): Knit.

Row 2: Purl.

Row 3: K4, *p1, k1, p1, k7; rep from * to last 7 sts, p1, k1, p1, k4.

Row 4: P3, *[k1, p1] twice, k1, p5; rep from * to last 8 sts, [k1, p1] twice, k1, p3.

Row 5: K2, *[p1, k1] 3 times, p1, k3, rep from * to last 9 sts, [p1, k1] 3 times, p1, k2.

Rep the last 2 rows once more.

Row 8: As row 4.

Row 9: As row 3.

Row 10: Purl.

Row 11: Knit.

Row 12: Purl.

Row 13: K1, p1, *k7, p1, k1, p1; rep from * to last 9 sts, k7, p1, k1.

Row 14: K1, p1, k1, *p5, [k1, p1] twice, k1; rep from * to last 8 sts, p5, k1, p1, k1.

Row 15: [K1, p1] twice, *k3, [p1, k1] 3 times, p1; rep from * to last 7 sts, k3, [p1, k1] twice.

Rep the last 2 rows once more.

Row 18: As row 14.

Row 19: As row 13.

Row 20: Purl.

Rep these 20 rows.

Open chain ribbing

Multiple of 6 + 2.

Row 1 (WS): K2, *p4, k2; rep from * to end.

Row 2: P2, *k2tog, yf twice, sl 1, k1, psso, p2; rep from * to end.

Row 3: K2, *p1, purl into front of first yf, purl into back of 2nd yf, p1, k2; rep from * to end.

Row 4: P2, *yo, sl 1, k1, psso, k2tog, yf, p2; rep from * to end.

Rep these 4 rows.

Moss stitch diagonal

Multiple of 8 + 3.

Row 1 (RS): K4, *p1, k1, p1, k5; rep from * to last 7 sts, p1, k1, p1, k4.

Row 2: P3, *[k1, p1] twice, k1, p3; rep from * to end.

Row 3: K2, *p1, k1, p1, k5; rep from * to last st, p1.

Row 4: P1, k1, *p3, [k1, p1] twice, k1; rep from * to last st, p1.

Row 5: *P1, k1, p1, k5; rep from * to last 3 sts, p1, k1, p1.

Row 6: *[P1, k1] twice, p3, k1; rep from * to last 3 sts, p1, k1, p1.

Row 7: P1, *k5, p1, k1, p1; rep from * to last 2 sts, k2.

Row 8: [P1, k1] 3 times, *p3, [k1, p1] twice, k1; rep from * to last 5 sts, p3, k1, p1.

Rep these 8 rows.

Seed stitch checks

Multiple of 10 + 5.

Row 1 (RS): K5, *[p1, k1] twice, p1, k5; rep from * to end.

Row 2: P6, *k1, p1, k1, p7; rep from * to last 9 sts, k1, p1, k1, p6.

Rep the last 2 rows once more, then row 1 again.

Row 6: *[K1, p1] twice, k1, p5; rep from * to last 5 sts, [k1, p1] twice, k1.

Row 7: [K1, p1] twice, *k7, p1, k1, p1; rep from * to last st, k1.

Rep the last 2 rows once more, then row 6 again.

Rep these 10 rows.

Alternate bobble stripe

Multiple of 10 + 5.

Row 1 (RS): P2, k1, *p4, k1; rep from * to last 2 sts, p2.

Row 2: K2, p1, *k4, p1; rep from * to last 2 sts, k2.

Row 3: P2, *MB (Make bobble) as follows: work [k1, p1, k1, p1, k1] into the next st, turn and k5, turn and k5tog (bobble completed), p4, k1, p4; rep from * to last 3 sts, MB, p2.

Row 4: As row 2.

Rep the last 4 rows 4 times more.

Row 21: As row 1.

Row 22: As row 2.

Row 23: P2, *k1, p4, MB, p4; rep from * to last 3 sts, k1, p2.

Row 24: As row 2.

Rep the last 4 rows 4 times more.

Rep these 40 rows.

Moss stitch panes

Multiple of 10 + 3.

Row 1 (RS): P1, *k1, p1; rep from * to end.

Row 2: P1, *k1, p1; rep from * to end.

Row 3: P1, k1, p1, *k7, p1, k1, p1; rep from * to end.

Row 4: P1, k1, p9, *k1, p9; rep from * to last 2 sts, k1, p1.

Rep the last 2 rows 3 times more.

Rep these 10 rows.

Vertical zigzag moss stitch

Multiple of 7.

Row 1 (RS): *P1, k1, p1, k4; rep from * to end.

Row 2: *P4, k1, p1, k1; rep from * to end.

Row 3: *[K1, p1] twice, k3; rep from * to end.

Row 4: *P3, [k1, p1] twice; rep from * to end.

Row 5: K2, p1, k1, p1, *k4, p1, k1, p1; rep from * to last 2 sts, k2.

Row 6: P2, k1, p1, k1, *p4, k1, p1, k1; rep from * to last 2 sts, p2.

Row 7: K3, p1, k1, p1, *k4, p1, k1, p1; rep from * to last st, k1.

Row 8: [P1, k1] twice, *p4, k1, p1, k1; rep from * to last 3 sts, p3.

Row 9: *K4, p1, k1, p1; rep from * to end.

Row 10: *K1, p1, k1, p4; rep from * to end.

Rows 11–12: As rows 7–8.

Rows 13–14: As rows 5–6.

Rows 15–16: As rows 3–4.

Rep these 16 rows.

Top hat pattern

Multiple of 6 + 4.

Row 1 (RS): K4, *p2, k4; rep from * to end.

Row 2: P4, *k2, p4; rep from * to end. Rep the last 2 rows once more.

Row 5: P1, k2, *p4, k2; rep from * to last st, p1.

Row 6: K1, p2, *k4, p2; rep from * to last st, k1. Rep the last 2 rows once more.

Row 9: Purl.

Row 10: Knit.

Rep these 10 rows.

Diagonal garter ribs

Multiple of 5 + 2.

Row 1 (RS) and every alt row: Knit.

Row 2: *P2, k3; rep from * to last 2 sts, p2.

Row 4: K1, *p2, k3; rep from * to last st, p1.

Row 6: K2, *p2, k3; rep from * to end.

Row 8: *K3, p2; rep from * to last 2 sts, k2.

Row 10: P1, *k3, p2; rep from * to last st, k1.

Rep these 10 rows.

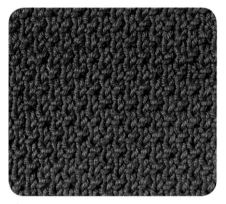

Double rice stitch

Multiple of 2 + 1.
Row 1 (WS): P1, *KB1, p1; rep from *
to end.
Row 2: Knit.
Row 3: *KB1, p1; rep from * to last
st, KB1.
Row 4: Knit.
Rep these 4 rows.

Checkerboard

Multiple of 8 + 4.
Row 1: K4, *p4, k4; rep from * to end.
Row 2: P4, *k4, p4; rep from * to end.
Rep the last 2 rows once more.
Row 5: As row 3.
Row 6: As row 1.
Rep the last 2 rows once more.
Rep these 8 rows.

Woven stitch I

Multiple of 2 + 1.
Row 1 (RS): K1, *yf, sl 1, yb, k1; rep from
* to end.
Row 2: Purl.
Row 3: K2, *yf, sl 1, yb, k1; rep from * to
last st, k1.
Row 4: Purl.
Rep these 4 rows.

Beaded rib

Multiple of 5 + 2.
Row 1 (RS): P2, *k1, p1, k1, p2; rep from
* to end.
Row 2: K2, *p3, k2; rep from * to end.
Rep these 2 rows.

Double woven stitch

Multiple of 4.
Row 1 (RS): K3, *yf, sl 2, yb, k2; rep from
* to last st, k1.
Row 2: Purl.
Row 3: K1, *yf, sl 2, yb, k2; rep from * to
last 3 sts, yf, sl 2, yb, k1.
Row 4: Purl.
Rep these 4 rows.

Two-stitch ribs

Multiple of 4 + 2.
Row 1: K2, *p2, k2; rep from * to end.
Rep this row.

Four-stitch ribs

Multiple of 8 + 4.
Row 1: K4, *p4, k4; rep from * to end.
Rep this row.

Eyelet mock cable ribbing

Multiple of 5 + 2.
Row 1 (RS): P2, *sl 1, k2, psso, p2; rep from * to end.
Row 2: K2, *p1, yrn, p1, k2; rep from * to end.
Row 3: P2, *k3, p2; rep from * to end.
Row 4: K2, *p3, k2; rep from * to end.
Rep these 4 rows.

Fleck stitch

Multiple of 2 + 1.
Row 1 (RS): Knit.
Row 2: Purl.
Row 3: K1, *p1, k1; rep from * to end.
Row 4: Purl.
Rep these 4 rows.

Large eyelet rib

Multiple of 6 + 2.
Row 1 (RS): *P2, k2tog, [yf] twice, sl 1, k1, psso; rep from * to last 2 sts, p2.
Row 2: K2, *p1, knit into first yf, purl into 2nd yf, p1, k2; rep from * to end.
Row 3: *P2, k4; rep from * to last 2 sts, p2.
Row 4: K2, *p4, k2; rep from * to end.
Rep these 4 rows.

Double basket weave

Multiple of 4 + 3.
Row 1 (RS) and every alt row: Knit.
Row 2: *K3, p1; rep from * to last 3 sts, k3.
Row 4: As row 3.
Row 6: K1, *p1, k3; rep from * to last 2 sts, p1, k1.
Row 8: As row 6.
Rep these 8 rows.

Open check stitch

Multiple of 2.
Row 1 (RS): Purl.
Row 2: Knit.
Row 3: K2, *sl 1, k1; rep from * to end.
Row 4: *K1, yf, sl 1, yb; rep from * to last 2 sts, k2.
Row 5: K1, *yf, k2tog; rep from * to last st, k1.
Row 6: Purl.
Rep these 6 rows.

Maze pattern

Multiple of 13.

Row 1 (RS): Knit.

Row 2: Purl.

Row 3: Knit.

Row 4: P1, k11, *p2, k11; rep from * to last st, p1.

Row 5: K1, p11, *k2, p11; rep from * to last st, k1.

Row 6: As row 4.

Row 7: K1, p2, k7, p2, *k2, p2, k7, p2; rep from * to last st, k1.

Row 8: P1, k2, p7, k2, *p2, k2, p7, k2; rep from * to last st, p1.

Row 9: As row 7.

Row 10: P1, k2, p2, k3, *[p2, k2] twice, p2, k3; rep from * to last 5 sts, p2, k2, p1.

Row 11: K1, p2, k2, p3, *[k2, p2] twice, k2, p3; rep from * to last 5 sts, k2, p2, k1.

Rep the last 2 rows once more.

Row 14: As row 8.

Row 15: As row 7.

Row 16: As row 8.

Row 17: As row 5.

Row 18: As row 4.

Row 19: As row 5.

Row 20: As row 3.

Rep these 20 rows.

Double parallelogram stitch

Multiple of 10.

Row 1 (RS): *P5, k5; rep from * to end.

Row 2: K1, *p5, k5; rep from * to last 9 sts, p5, k4.

Row 3: P3, *k5, p5; rep from * to last 7, k5, p2.

Row 4: K3, *p5, k5; rep from * to last 7 sts, p5, k2.

Row 5: P1, *k5, p5; rep from * to last 9 sts, k5, p4.

Row 6: P4, *k5, p5; rep from * to last 6 sts, k5, p1.

Row 7: K2, *p5, k5; rep from * to last 8 sts, p5, k3.

Row 8: P2, *k5, p5; rep from * to last 8 sts, k5, p3.

Row 9: K4, *p5, k5; rep from * to last 6 sts, p5, k1.

Row 10: *K5, p5; rep from * to end.

Rep these 10 rows.

Double signal check

Multiple of 18 + 9.

Row 1 (RS): K1, p7, k1, *p1, k7, p1, k1, p7, k1; rep from * to end.

Row 2: P2, k5, p2, *k2, p5, k2, p2, k5, p2; rep from * to end.

Row 3: K3, *p3, k3; rep from * to end.

Row 4: P4, k1, p4, *k4, p1, k4, p4, k1, p4; rep from * to end.

Row 5: P1, k7, p1, *k1, p7, k1, p1, k7, p1; rep from * to end.

Row 6: K2, p5, k2, *p2, k5, p2, k2, p5, k2; rep from * to end.

Row 7: P3, *k3, p3; rep from * to end.

Row 8: K4, p1, k4, *p4, k1, p4, k4, p1, k4; rep from * to end.

Rep these 8 rows.

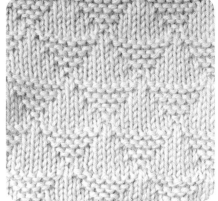

King Charles brocade

Multiple of 12 + 1.

Row 1 (RS): K1, *p1, k9, p1, k1; rep from * to end.

Row 2: K1, p1, k1, *p7, [k1, p1] twice, k1; rep from * to last 10 sts, p7, k1, p1, k1.

Row 3: [K1, p1] twice, *k5, [p1, k1] 3 times, p1; rep from * to last 9 sts, k5, [p1, k1] twice.

Row 4: P2, *k1, p1, k1, p3; rep from * to last 5 sts, k1, p1, k1, p2.

Row 5: K3, *[p1, k1] 3 times, p1, k5, rep from * to last 10 sts, [p1, k1] 3 times, p1, k3.

Row 6: P4, *[k1, p1] twice, k1, p7; rep from * to last 9 sts, [k1, p1] twice, k1, p4.

Row 7: K5, *p1, k1, p1, k9; rep from * to last 8 sts, p1, k1, p1, k5.

Row 8: As row 6.

Row 9: As row 5.

Row 10: As row 4.

Row 11: As row 3.

Row 12: As row 2.

Rep these 12 rows.

Garter stitch triangles

Multiple of 8 +1.

Row 1 (RS): P1, *k7, p1; rep from * to end.

Row 2 and every alt row: Purl.

Row 3: P2, *k5, p3; rep from * to last 7 sts, k5, p2.

Row 5: P3, *k3, p5; rep from * to last 6 sts, k3, p3.

Row 7: P4, *k1, p7; rep from * to last 5 sts, k1, p4.

Row 9: K4, *p1, k7; rep from * to last 5 sts, p1, k4.

Row 11: K3, *p3, k5; rep from * to last 6 sts, p3, k3.

Row 13: K2, *p5, k3; rep from * to last 7 sts; p5, k2.

Row 15: K1, *p7, k1; rep from * to end.

Row 16: Purl.

Rep these 16 rows.

Diagonals

Multiple of 8 + 6.

Row 1 (RS): P3, *k5, p3; rep from * to last 3 sts, k3.

Row 2: P4, *k3, p5; rep from * to last 2 sts, k2.

Row 3: P1, k5, *p3, k5; rep from * to end.

Row 4: K1, p5, *k3, p5; rep from * to end.

Row 5: K4, *p3, k5; rep from * to last 2 sts, p2.

Row 6: K3, *p5, k3; rep from * to last 3 sts, p3.

Row 7: K2, p3, *k5, p3; rep from * to last st, k1.

Row 8: P2, k3, *p5, k3; rep from * to last st, p1.

Rep these 8 rows.

Diamond and block

Multiple of 14 + 5.

Row 1 (RS): P5, *k4, p1, k4, p5; rep from * to end.

Row 2: K5, *p3, k3, p3, k5; rep from * to end.

Row 3: K7, p5, *k9, p5; rep from * to last 7 sts, k7.

Row 4: P6, k7, *p7, k7; rep from * to last 6 sts, p6.

Row 5: K5, *p9, k5; rep from * to end.

Row 6: As row 4.

Row 7: As row 3.

Row 8: As row 2.

Rep these 8 rows.

Divided triangles

Multiple of 14 + 1.

Row 1 (WS): Knit.

Row 2: Knit.

Row 3: K1, *p13, k1; rep from * to end.

Row 4: K1, *p1, k11, p1, k1; rep from * to end.

Row 5: P1, *k2, p9, k2, p1; rep from * to end.

Row 6: K1, *p3, k7, p3, k1; rep from * to end.

Row 7: P1, *k4, p5, k4, p1; rep from * to end.

Row 8: K1, *p5, k3, p5, k1; rep from * to end.

Row 9: P1, *[k6, p1] twice; rep from * to end.

Rows 10–11: Purl.

Row 12: K7, p1, *k13, p1; rep from * to last 7 sts, k7.

Row 13: P6, k1, p1, k1, *p11, k1, p1, k1; rep from * to last 6 sts, p6.

Row 14: K5, p2, k1, p2, *k9, p2, k1, p2; rep from * to last 5 sts, k5.

Row 15: P4, k3, p1, k3, *p7, k3, p1, k3; rep from * to last 4 sts, p4.

Row 16: K3, p4, k1, p4, *k5, p4, k1, p4; rep from * to last 3 sts, k3.

Row 17: P2, k5, p1, k5, *p3, k5, p1, k5; rep from * to last 2 sts, p2.

Row 18: K1, *p6, k1; rep from * to end.

Rep these 18 rows.

Rib checks

Multiple of 10 + 5.

Row 1 (RS): P5, *[KB1, p1] twice, KB1, p5; rep from * to end.

Row 2: K5, *[PB1, k1] twice, PB1, k5; rep from * to end.

Rep the last 2 rows once more, then row 1 again.

Row 6: [PB1, k1] twice, PB1, *k5, [PB1, k1] twice, PB1; rep from * to end.

Row 7: [KB1, p1] twice, KB1, *p5, [KB1, p1] twice, KB1; rep from * to end.

Rep the last 2 rows once more, then row 6 again.

Rep these 10 rows.

Purl triangles

Multiple of 8 + 1.

Row 1 (RS): K1, *p7, k1; rep from * to end.

Row 2: P1, *k7, p1; rep from * to end.

Row 3: K2, *p5, k3; rep from * to last 7 sts, p5, k2.

Row 4: P2, *k5, p3; rep from * to last 7 sts, k5, p2.

Row 5: K3, *p3, k5; rep from * to last 6 sts, p3, k3.

Row 6: P3, *k3, p5; rep from * to last 6 sts, k3, p3.

Row 7: K4, *p1, k7; rep from * to last 5 sts, p1, k4.

Row 8: P4, *k1, p7; rep from * to last 5 sts, k1, p4.

Row 9: As row 8.

Row 10: As row 7.

Row 11: As row 6.

Row 12: As row 5.

Row 13: As row 4.

Row 14: As row 3.

Row 15: As row 2.

Row 16: K1, *p7, k1; rep from * to end.

Rep these 16 rows.

Textured triangle stack

Multiple of 10 + 1.

Row 1 (RS): P5, *k1, p9; rep from * to last 6 sts, k1, p5.

Row 2: K5, *p1, k9; rep from * to last 6 sts, p1, k5.

Row 3: P4, *k3, p7; rep from * to last 7 sts, p3, k4.

Row 4: K4, *p3, k7; rep from * to last 7 sts, k3, p4.

Row 5: P3, *k5, p5; rep from * to last 8 sts, k5, p3.

Row 6: K3, *p5, k5; rep from * to last 8 sts, p5, k3.

Row 7: P2, *k7, p3; rep from * to last 9 sts, k7, p2.

Row 8: K2, *p7, k3; rep from * to last 9 sts, p7, k2.

Row 9: P1, *k9, p1; rep from * to end.

Row 10: K1, *p9, k1; rep from * to end.

Rep these 10 rows.

Moss stitch diamonds

Multiple of 10 + 9.

Row 1 (RS): K4, *p1, k9; rep from * to last 5 sts, p1, k4.

Row 2: P3, *k1, p1, k1, p7; rep from * to last 6 sts, k1, p1, k1, p3.

Row 3: K2, *[p1, k1] twice, p1, k5; rep from * to last 7 sts, [p1, k1] twice, p1, k2.

Row 4: [P1, k1] 4 times, *p3, [k1, p1] 3 times, k1; rep from * to last st, p1.

Row 5: P1, *k1, p1; rep from * to end.

Row 6: As row 4.

Row 7: As row 3.

Row 8: As row 2.

Row 9: As row 1.

Row 10: Purl.

Rep these 10 rows.

Check stitch

Multiple of 4 + 2.
Row 1: K2, *p2, k2; rep from * to end.
Row 2: P2, *k2, p2; rep from * to end.
Rep these last 2 rows once more.
Row 5: As row 2.
Row 6: As row 1.
Rep these last 2 rows once more.
Rep these 8 rows.

Horizontal herringbone

Multiple of 2.
Row 1 (RS): K1, *sl 1, k1, psso but instead of dropping slipped st from left-hand needle knit into the back of it; rep from * to last st, k1.
Row 2: *P2tog, then purl 1st st again slipping both sts off needle tog; rep from * to end.
Rep these 2 rows.

Double fleck stitch

Multiple of 6 + 4.
Rows 1 (RS) and 3: Knit.
Row 2: P4, *k2, p4; rep from * to end.
Row 4: P1, *k2, p4; rep from * to last 3 sts, k2, p1.
Rep these 4 rows.

Woven rib

Multiple of 6 + 3.
Row 1 (RS): P3, *sl 1 purlwise, yb, k1, yf, sl 1 purlwise, p3; rep from * to end.
Row 2: K3, *p3, k3; rep from * to end.
Row 3: *P3, k1, yf, sl 1 purlwise, yb, k1; rep from * to last 3 sts, p3.
Row 4: As row 2.
Rep these 4 rows.

Garter stitch checks

Multiple of 10 + 5.
Row 1 (RS): K5, *p5, k5; rep from * to end.
Row 2: Purl.
Rep the last 2 rows once more, then row 1 again.
Row 6: K5, *p5, k5; rep from * to end.
Row 7: Knit.
Rep the last 2 rows once more, then row 6 again.
Rep these 10 rows.

Medallion rib

Multiple of 8 + 4.
Row 1 (RS): P4, *yb, sl 2 purlwise, C2B, p4; rep from * to end.
Row 2: K4, *yf, sl 2 purlwise, purl the 2nd st on left-hand needle, then the 1st st, slipping both sts from needle tog, k4; rep from * to end.
Row 3: Knit.
Row 4: Purl.
Rep these 4 rows.

Cactus ladder

Multiple of 10 + 7.

Row 1 (RS): P3, KB1, *p4, KB1; rep from * to last 3 sts, p3.

Row 2: K3, PB1, *k4, PB1; rep from * to last 3 sts, k3.

Row 3: P2, [KB1] 3 times, *p3, KB1, p3, [KB1] 3 times; rep from * to last 2 sts, p2.

Row 4: K2, [PB1] 3 times, *k3, PB1, k3, [PB1] 3 times; rep from * to last 2 sts, k2.

Rep the last 2 rows once more.

Rows 7–8: As rows 1–2.

Rep the last 2 rows once more.

Row 11: P3, KB1, p3, *[KB1] 3 times, p3, KB1, p3; rep from * to end.

Row 12: K3, PB1, k3, *[PB1] 3 times, k3, PB1, k3; rep from * to end.

Rep the last 2 rows once more.

Rows 15–16: As rows 1–2.

Rep these 16 rows.

Moss stitch double parallelograms

Multiple of 10.

Row 1 (RS): *K5, [p1, k1] twice, p1; rep from * to end.

Row 2: P1, *[k1, p1] twice, k1, p5; rep from * to last 9 sts, [k1, p1] twice, k1, p4.

Row 3: K3, *[p1, k1] twice, p1, k5; rep from * to last 7 sts, [p1, k1] twice, p1, k2.

Row 4: P3, *[k1, p1] twice, k1, p5; rep from * to last 7 sts, [k1, p1] twice, k1, p2.

Row 5: K1, *[p1, k1] twice, p1, k5; rep from * to last 9 sts, [p1, k1] twice, p1, k4.

Row 6: *[P1, k1] twice, p5, k1; rep from * to end.

Row 7: K1, p1, *k5, [p1, k1] twice, p1; rep from * to last 8 sts, k5, p1, k1, p1.

Row 8: P1, k1, *p5, [k1, p1] twice, k1; rep from * to last 8 sts, p5, k1, p1, k1.

Row 9: *[K1, p1] twice, k5, p1; rep from * to end.

Row 10: *P5, [k1, p1] twice, k1; rep from * to end.

Rep these 10 rows.

Flag pattern

Multiple of 11.

Row 1 (RS): *P1, k10; rep from * to end.

Row 2: *P9, k2; rep from * to end.

Row 3: *P3, k8; rep from * to end.

Row 4: *P7, k4; rep from * to end.

Row 5: *P5, k6; rep from * to end.

Row 6: As row 5.

Row 7: As row 5.

Row 8: As row 4.

Row 9: As row 3.

Row 10: As row 2.

Row 11: As row 1.

Row 12: *K1, p10; rep from * to end.

Row 13: *K9, p2; rep from * to end.

Row 14: *K3, p8; rep from * to end.

Row 15: *K7, p4; rep from * to end.

Row 16: *K5, p6; rep from * to end.

Row 17: As row 16.

Row 18: As row 16.

Row 19: As row 15.

Row 20: As row 14.

Row 21: As row 13.

Row 22: As row 12.

Rep these 22 rows.

Crosses

Multiple of 12 + 1.

Row 1 (RS): Purl.

Row 2: Knit.

Row 3: P5, *[KB1] 3 times, p9; rep from * to last 8 sts, [KB1] 3 times, p5.

Row 4: K5, *p3, k9; rep from * to last 8 sts, p3, k5.

Rep the last 2 rows once more.

Row 7: P2, *[KB1] 9 times, p3; rep from * to last 11 sts, [KB1] 9 times, p2.

Row 8: K2, *p9, k3; rep from * to last 11 sts, p9, k2.

Rep the last 2 rows once more.

Row 11: As row 3.

Row 12: As row 4.

Rep the last 2 rows once more.

Row 15: Purl.

Row 16: Knit.

Rep these 16 rows.

Reverse stocking stitch chevrons

Multiple of 6 + 5.

Row 1 (RS): K5, *p1, k5; rep from * to end.

Row 2: K1, *p3, k3; rep from * to last 4 sts, p3, k1.

Row 3: P2, *k1, p2; rep from * to end.

Row 4: P1, *k3, p3; rep from * to last 4 sts, k3, p1.

Row 5: K2, *p1, k5; rep from * to last 3 sts, p1, k2.

Row 6: Purl.

Rep these 6 rows.

Twisted cable rib

Multiple of 4 + 2.

Row 1 (RS): P2, *k2, p2; rep from * to end.

Row 2: K2, *p2, k2; rep from * to end.

Row 3: P2, *k2tog but do not slip off needle, then insert right-hand needle between these 2 sts and knit the 1st st again, slipping both sts off needle tog, p2; rep from * to end.

Row 4: As row 2.

Rep these 4 rows.

Ladder stitch

Multiple of 8 + 5.
Row 1 (RS): K5, *p3, k5; rep from *
to end.
Row 2: P5, *k3, p5; rep from * to end.
Rep the last 2 rows once more.
Row 5: K1, *p3, k5; rep from * to last
4 sts, p3, k1.
Row 6: P1, *k3, p5; rep from * to last
4 sts, k3, p1.
Rep the last 2 rows once more.
Rep these 8 rows.

Small basket stitch

Multiple of 10 + 5.
Row 1 (RS): [K1, p1] twice, *k7, p1, k1,
p1; rep from * to last st, k1.
Row 2: P1, [k1, p1] twice, *k5, [p1, k1]
twice, p1; rep from * to end.
Rep the last 2 rows once more.
Row 5: K6, *p1, k1, p1, k7; rep from * to
last 9 sts, p1, k1, p1, k6.
Row 6: *K5, [p1, k1] twice, p1; rep from *
to last 5 sts, k5.
Rep the last 2 rows once more.
Rep these 8 rows.

Herringbone II

Multiple of 7 + 1.
Special abbreviation:
K1B Back = From the top, insert point of
right-hand needle into back of st below
next st on left-hand needle and knit it.
Row 1 (WS): Purl.
Row 2: *K2tog, k2, K1B Back then knit st
above, k2; rep from * to last st, k1.
Row 3: Purl.
Row 4: K3, K1B Back then knit st above,
k2, k2tog, *k2, K1B Back then knit st
above, k2, k2tog; rep from * to end.
Rep these 4 rows.

Double moss stitch triangles

Multiple of 8 + 1.

Row 1 (RS): *K1, p7; rep from * to last st, k1.

Row 2: *P1, k7; rep from * to last st, p1.

Row 3: *P1, k1, p5, k1; rep from * to last st, p1.

Row 4: *K1, p1, k5, p1; rep from * to last st, k1.

Row 5: K1, p1, *k1, p3, [k1, p1] twice; rep from * to last 7 sts, k1, p3, k1, p1, k1.

Row 6: P1, k1, *p1, k3, [p1, k1] twice; rep from * to last 7 sts, p1, k3, p1, k1, p1.

Row 7: *P1, k1; rep from * to last st, p1.

Row 8: *K1, p1; rep from * to last st, k1.

Row 9: P4, *k1, p7; rep from * to last 5 sts, k1, p4.

Row 10: K4, *p1, k7; rep from * to last 5 sts, p1, k4.

Row 11: P3, *k1, p1, k1, p5; rep from * to last 6 sts, k1, p1, k1, p3.

Row 12: K3, *p1, k1, p1, k5; rep from * to last 6 sts, p1, k1, p1, k3.

Row 13: P2, *[k1, p1] twice, k1, p3; rep from * to last 7 sts, [k1, p1] twice, k1, p2.

Row 14: K2, *[p1, k1] twice, p1, k3; rep from * to last 7 sts, [p1, k1] twice, p1, k2.

Row 15: As row 7.

Row 16: As row 8.

Rep these 16 rows.

Spaced knots

Multiple of 6 + 5.

Note: Stitches should not be counted after row 5 or 11.

Work 4 rows in st st, starting with knit.

Row 5: K5, *[k1, p1] twice into next st, k5; rep from * to end.

Row 6: P5, *sl 3, k1, pass 3 sl sts separately over last st (knot completed), p5; rep from * to end.

Work 4 rows in st st.

Row 11: K2, *[k1, p1] twice into next st, k5; rep from * to last 3 sts, [k1, p1] twice into next st, k2.

Row 12: P2, *sl 3, k1, pass sl sts over as before, p5; rep from * to last 6 sts, sl 3, k1, pass sl sts over as before, p2.

Rep these 12 rows.

Twisted check

Multiple of 4 + 2.

Row 1 (RS): Knit all sts through back loops.

Row 2: Purl.

Row 3: [KB1] twice, *p2, [KB1] twice; rep from * to end.

Row 4: P2, *k2, p2; rep from * to end.

Rep rows 1–2 once more.

Row 7: P2, *[KB1] twice, p2; rep from * to end.

Row 8: K2, *p2, k2; rep from * to end.

Rep these 8 rows.

Dotted ladder stitch

Multiple of 8 + 5.

Row 1 (RS): K2, p1, k2, *p3, k2, p1, k2; rep from * to end.

Row 2: [P1, k1] twice, p1, *k3, [p1, k1] twice, p1; rep from * to end.

Rep the last 2 rows once more.

Row 5: K1, *p3, k2, p1, k2; rep from * to last 4 sts, p3, k1.

Row 6: P1, k3, p1, *[k1, p1] twice, k3, p1; rep from * to end.

Rep the last 2 rows once more.

Rep these 8 rows.

Knot pattern

Multiple of 6 + 5.

Special abbreviation:

Make knot = p3tog leaving sts on left-hand needle, now knit them tog, then purl them tog again, slipping sts off needle at end.

Work 2 rows in st st, starting with knit.

Row 3 (RS): K1, *make knot, k3; rep from * to last 4 sts, make knot, k1.

Work 3 rows in st st, starting with purl.

Row 7: K4, *make knot, k3; rep from * to last st, k1.

Row 8: Purl.

Rep these 8 rows.

Trellis stitch

Multiple of 6 + 5.

Row 1 (RS): K1, p3, *keeping yarn at front of work sl 3 purlwise, p3; rep from * to last st, k1.

Row 2: P1, k3, *keeping yarn at back of work sl 3 purlwise, k3; rep from * to last st, p1.

Row 3: K1, p3, *k3, p3; rep from * to last st, k1.

Row 4: P1, k3, *p3, k3; rep from * to last st, p1.

Row 5: K5, *insert point of right-hand needle upwards under the 2 strands in front of the sl sts and knit the next st, then lift the 2 strands off over the point of the right-hand needle (called pull up loop), k5; rep from * to end.

Row 6: As row 3.

Row 7: P1, *keeping yarn at front sl 3 purlwise, p3; rep from * to last 4 sts, sl 3 purlwise, p1.

Row 8: K1, *keeping yarn at back sl 3 purlwise, k3; rep from * to last 4 sts, sl 3 purlwise, k1.

Row 9: As row 4.

Row 10: As row 3.

Row 11: K2, *pull up loop, k5; rep from * to last 3 sts, pull up loop, k2.

Row 12: As row 4.

Rep these 12 rows.

Tip

If you have made a number of swatches to see which stitch patterns you like or work best with your yarn, you can try turning a collection of your swatches into a project. You could make the front of a patchwork cushion, a baby blanket, or some scented sachets.

Bud stitch

Multiple of 6 + 5.

Note: Stitches should only be counted after rows 6 or 12.

Row 1 (RS): P5, *k1, yf, p5; rep from * to end.

Row 2: K5, *p2, k5; rep from * to end.

Row 3: P5, *k2, p5; rep from * to end.

Rep the last 2 rows once more.

Row 6: K5, *p2tog, k5; rep from * to end.

Row 7: P2, *k1, yf, p5; rep from * to last 3 sts, k1, yf, p2.

Row 8: K2, *p2, k5; rep from * to last 4 sts, p2, k2.

Row 9: P2, *k2, p5; rep from * to last 4 sts, k2, p2.

Rep the last 2 rows once more.

Row 12: K2, *p2tog, k5; rep from * to last 4 sts, p2tog, k2.

Rep these 12 rows.

Compass check pattern

Multiple of 14 + 7.

Row 1 (WS): [P1, KB1] twice, *k10, [p1, KB1] twice; rep from * to last 3 sts, k3.

Row 2: K3, [PB1, k1] twice, *p7, k3, [PB1, k1] twice; rep from * to end.

Rep the last 2 rows once more.

Row 5: Knit.

Row 6: [K1, PB1] twice, *p10, [k1, PB1] twice; rep from * to last 3 sts, p3.

Row 7: P3, [KB1, p1] twice, *k7, p3, [KB1, p1] twice; rep from * to end.

Rep the last 2 rows once more.

Row 10: P7, *[k1, PB1] twice, p10; rep from * to end.

Row 11: K7, *p3, [KB1, p1] twice, k7; rep from * to end.

Rep the last 2 rows once more.

Row 14: Purl.

Row 15: K7, *[p1, KB1] twice, k10; rep from * to end.

Row 16: P7, *k3, [PB1, k1] twice, p7; rep from * to end.

Rep the last 2 rows once more.

Rep these 18 rows.

Mock cable on moss stitch

Multiple of 9 + 5.

Row 1 (RS): [K1, p1] twice, k1, *KB1, p2, KB1, [k1, p1] twice, k1; rep from * to end.

Row 2: *[K1, p1] 3 times, k2, p1; rep from * to last 5 sts, [k1, p1] twice, k1.

Rep these 2 rows once more.

Row 5: [K1, p1] twice, k1, *yf, k1, p2, k1, lift yf over last 4 sts and off needle, [k1, p1] twice, k1; rep from * to end.

Row 6: As row 2.

Rep these 6 rows.

Puffed rib

Multiple of 3 + 2.
Note: Stitches should only be counted after row 4.
Row 1 (RS): P2, *yo, k1, yf, p2; rep from * to end.
Row 2: K2, *p3, k2; rep from * to end.
Row 3: P2, *k3, p2; rep from * to end.
Row 4: K2, *p3tog, k2; rep from * to end.
Rep these 4 rows.

Interrupted rib

Multiple of 2 + 1.
Row 1 (RS): P1, *k1, p1; rep from * to end.
Row 2: K1, *p1, k1; rep from * to end.
Row 3: Purl.
Row 4: Knit.
Rep these 4 rows.

Uneven rib

Multiple of 4 + 3.
Row 1: *K2, p2; rep from * to last 3 sts, k2, p1.
Rep this row.

Stocking stitch checks

Multiple of 10 + 5.
Row 1 (RS): K5, *p5, k5; rep from * to end.
Row 2: P5, *k5, p5; rep from * to end.
Rep the last 2 rows once more, then row 1 again.
Row 6: K5, *p5, k5; rep from * to end.
Row 7: As row 2.
Rep the last 2 rows once more, then row 6 again.
Rep these 10 rows.

Ridged rib

Multiple of 2 + 1.
Rows 1–2: Knit.
Row 3 (RS): P1, *k1, p1k rep from * to end.
Row 4: K1, *p1, k1; rep from * to end.
Rep these 4 rows.

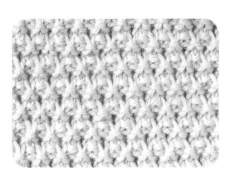

Garter slip stitch

Multiple of 2 + 1.
Row 1 (RS): Knit.
Row 2: Knit.
Row 3: K1, *sl 1 purlwise, k1; rep from * to end.
Row 4: K1, *yf, sl 1 purlwise, yb, k1; rep from * to end.
Knit 2 rows.
Row 7: K2, *sl 1 purlwise, k1; rep from * to last st, k1.
Row 8: K2, *yf, sl 1 purlwise, yb, k1; rep from * to last st, k1.
Rep these 8 rows.

Lattice stitch

Multiple of 6 + 1.

Row 1 (RS): K3, *p1, k5; rep from * to last 4 sts, p1, k3.

Row 2: P2, *k1, p1, k1, p3; rep from * to last 5 sts, k1, p1, k1, p2.

Row 3: K1, *p1, k3, p1, k1; rep from * to end.

Row 4: K1, *p5, k1; rep from * to end.

Row 5: As row 3.

Row 6: As row 2.

Rep these 6 rows.

Slanting diamonds

Multiple of 10.

Row 1 (RS): *K9, p1; rep from * to end.

Row 2: *K2, p8; rep from * to end.

Row 3: *K7, p3; rep from * to end.

Row 4: *K4, p6; rep from * to end.

Rows 5–6: *K5, p5; rep from * to end.

Row 7: K5, p4, *k6, p4; rep from * to last st, k1.

Row 8: P2, k3, *p7, k3; rep from * to last 5 sts, p5.

Row 9: K5, p2, *k8, p2; rep from * to last 3 sts, k3.

Row 10: P4, k1, *p9, k1; rep from * to last 5 sts, p5.

Row 11: K4, p1, *k9, p1; rep from * to last 5 sts, k5.

Row 12: P5, k2, *p8, k2; rep from * to last 3 sts, p3.

Row 13: K2, p3, *k7, p3; rep from * to last 5 sts, k5.

Row 14: P5, k4, *p6, k4; rep from * to last st, p1.

Rows 15–16: *P5, k5; rep from * to end.

Row 17: *P4, k6; rep from * to end.

Row 18: *P7, k3; rep from * to end.

Row 19: *P2, k8; rep from * to end.

Row 20: *P9, k1; rep from * to end.

Rep these 20 rows.

Steps

Multiple of 8 + 2.

Row 1 (RS): *K4, p4; rep from * to last 2 sts, k2.

Row 2: P2, *k4, p4; rep from * to end.

Rep the last 2 rows once more.

Row 5: K2, *p4, k4; rep from * to end.

Row 6: *P4, k4; rep from * to last 2 sts, p2.

Row 7: As row 5.

Row 8: As row 6.

Row 9: *P4, k4; rep from * to last 2 sts, p2.

Row 10: K2, *p4, k4; rep from * to end.

Rep the last 2 rows once more.

Row 13: As row 2.

Row 14: *K4, p4; rep from * to last 2 sts, k2.

Rep the last 2 rows once more.

Rep these 16 rows.

Harbour flag

Multiple of 10.
Row 1 (RS): P7, k2, *p8, k2; rep from * to last st, p1.
Row 2: *P1, k1, p2, k6; rep from * to end.
Row 3: *P5, k2, p1, k2; rep from * to end.
Row 4: *P3, k1, p2, k4; rep from * to end.
Row 5: *P3, k2, p1, k4; rep from * to end.
Row 6: *P5, k1, p2, k2; rep from * to end.
Row 7: *P1, k2, p1, k6; rep from * to end.
Row 8: As row 6.
Row 9: As row 5.
Row 10: As row 4.
Row 11: As row 3.
Row 12: As row 2.
Row 13: As row 1.
Row 14: *P2, k8; rep from * to end.
Rep these 14 rows.

Diagonal bobble stitch

Multiple of 6.
Row 1 (RS): *K2, Make Bobble (MB) as follows: [knit into front and back] 3 times into next st, take 1st, 2nd, 3rd, 4th and 5th sts over 6th made st (bobble completed), p3; rep from * to end.
Row 2: *K3, p3; rep from * to end.
Row 3: P1, *k2, MB, p3; rep from * to last 5 sts, k2, MB, p2.
Row 4: K2, *p3, k3; rep from * to last 4 sts, p3, k1.
Row 5: P2, *k2, MB, p3; rep from * to last 4 sts, k2, MB, p1.
Row 6: K1, *p3, k3; rep from * to last 5 sts, p3, k2.
Row 7: *P3, k2, MB; rep from * to end.
Row 8: *P3, k3; rep from * to end.
Row 9: *MB, p3, k2; rep from * to end.
Row 10: P2, *k3, p3; rep from * to last 4 sts, k3, p1.
Row 11: K1, *MB, p3, k2; rep from * to last 5 sts, MB, p3, k1.
Row 12: P1, *k3, p3; rep from * to last 5 sts, k3, p2.
Rep these 12 rows.

Shingle stitch

Multiple of 10 + 5.
Row 1 (RS): K5, *KB1, [p1, KB1] twice, k5; rep from * to end.
Row 2: K5, *PB1, [k1, PB1] twice, k5; rep from * to end.
Rep the last 2 rows twice more.
Row 7: KB1, [p1, KB1] twice, *k5, KB1, [p1, KB1] twice; rep from * to end.
Row 8: PB1, [k1, PB1] twice, *k5, PB1, [k1, PB1] twice; rep from * to end.
Rep the last 2 rows twice more.
Rep these 12 rows.

Basket rib

Multiple of 2 + 1.
Row 1 (RS): Knit.
Row 2: Purl.
Row 3: K1, *sl 1 purlwise, k1; rep from * to end.
Row 4: K1, *yf, sl 1 purlwise, yb, k1; rep from * to end.
Rep these 4 rows.

Basket weave

Multiple of 4 + 3.
Rows 1 (RS) and 3: Knit.
Row 2: *K3, p1; rep from * to last 3 sts, k3.
Row 4: K1, *p1, k3; rep from * to last 2 sts, p1, k1.
Rep these 4 rows.

Mini bobble stitch

Multiple of 2 + 1.
Special abbreviation:
MB (Make Bobble) = work (p1, k1, p1, k1) all into next st, pass 2nd, 3rd and 4th sts over first st.
Row 1 (RS): Knit.
Row 2: K1, *MB, k1; rep from * to end.
Row 3: Knit.
Row 4: K2, *MB, k1; rep from * to last st, k1.
Rep these 4 rows.

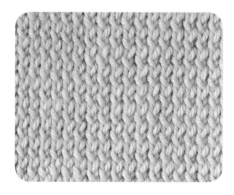

Twisted stocking stitch

Any number of stitches.
Row 1 (RS): Knit into the back of every st.
Row 2: Purl.
Rep these 2 rows.

Alternating triangles

Multiple of 5.
Row 1 (RS): *P1, k4; rep from * to end.
Rows 2–3: *P3, k2; rep from * to end.
Row 4: *P1, k4; rep from * to end.
Row 5: *K4, p1; rep from * to end.
Rows 6–7: *K2, p3; rep from * to end.
Row 8: As row 5.
Rep these 8 rows.

Bramble stitch

Multiple of 4 + 2.
Row 1 (RS): Purl.
Row 2: K1, *(k1, p1, k1) into next st, p3tog; rep from * to last st, k1.
Row 3: Purl.
Row 4: K1, *p3tog, (k1, p1, k1) into next st; rep from * to last st, k1.
Rep these 4 rows.

Slipped rib

Multiple of 4 + 3.
Row 1 (RS): K1, sl 1 purlwise, *k3, sl 1 purlwise; rep from * to last st, k1.
Row 2: P1, sl 1 purlwise, *p3, sl 1 purlwise; rep from * to last st, p1.
Row 3: *K3, sl 1 purlwise; rep from * to last 3 sts, k3.
Row 4: *P3, sl 1 purlwise; rep from * to last 3 sts, p3.
Rep these 4 rows.

Half brioche stitch (purl version)

Multiple of 2 + 1.
Row 1 (WS): Purl.
Row 2: K1, *K1B, k1; rep from * to end.
Row 3: Purl.
Row 4: K1B, *k1, K1B; rep from * to end.
Rep these 4 rows.

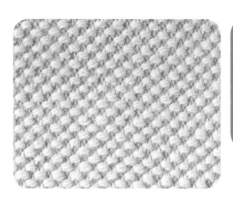

Moss slip stitch

Multiple of 2 + 1.
Row 1 (RS): K1, *sl 1 purlwise, k1; rep from * to end.
Row 2: K1, *yf, sl 1 purlwise, yb, k1; rep from * to end.
Row 3: K2, *sl 1 purlwise, k1; rep from * to last st, k1.
Row 4: K2, *yf, sl 1 purlwise, yb, k1; rep from * to last st, k1.
Rep these 4 rows.

Garter stitch twisted rib

Multiple of 4.
Row 1 (RS): K1, *C2B, k2; rep from * to last 3 sts, C2B, k1.
Row 2: K1, *yf, C2P, yb, k2; rep from * to last 3 sts, yf, C2P, yb, k1.
Rep these 2 rows.

Knotted rib

Multiple of 5.
Note: Stitches should only be counted after row 2.
Row 1 (RS): P2, *knit into front and back of next st, p4; rep from * to last 3 sts, knit into front and back of next st, p2.
Row 2: K2, *p2tog, k4; rep from * to last 4 sts, p2tog, k2.
Rep these 2 rows.

Three-stitch twisted rib

Multiple of 5 + 2.
Row 1 (WS): K2, *p3, k2; rep from * to end.
Row 2: P2, *C3, p2; rep from * to end.
Rep these 2 rows.

Triple wave

Worked over 14 sts on a background of st st.

Row 1 (RS): P3, k8, p3.

Row 2: [K1, p1] twice, k2, p2, k2, [p1, k1] twice.

Row 3: P3, k3, p2, k3, p3.

Row 4: K1, p1, k1, p8, k1, p1, k1.

Row 5: P3, k1, p2, k2, p2, k1, p3.

Row 6: K1, p1, k1, p3, k2, p3, k1, p1, k1.

Rep these 6 rows.

Linked ribs

Multiple of 8 + 4.

Row 1 (RS): P4, *k1, p2, k1, p4; rep from * to end.

Row 2: K4, *p1, k2, p1, k4; rep from * to end.

Rep the last 2 rows once more.

Row 5: P4, *C2L, C2R, p4; rep from * to end.

Row 6: K4, *p4, k4; rep from * to end.

Rep these 6 rows.

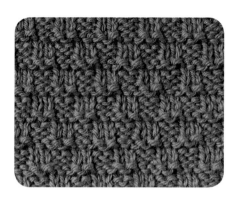

Purled ladder stitch

Multiple of 4 + 2.

Rows 1–2: Knit.

Row 3 (RS): P2, *k2, p2; rep from * to end.

Row 4: K2, *p2, k2; rep from * to end.

Rows 5–6: Knit.

Row 7: As row 4.

Row 8: P2, *k2, p2; rep from * to end.

Rep these 8 rows.

Broken rib

Multiple of 2 + 1.

Row 1 (RS): Knit.

Row 2: P1, *k1, p1; rep from * to end.

Rep these 2 rows.

Rose stitch

Multiple of 2 + 1.

Row 1 (WS): K2, *p1, k1; rep from * to last st, k1.

Row 2: K1, *K1B, k1; rep from * to end.

Row 3: K1, *p1, k1; rep from * to end.

Row 4: K2, *K1B, k1; rep from * to last st, k1.

Rep these 4 rows.

Moss rib

Multiple of 4 + 1.

Row 1: K2, *p1, k3; rep from * to last 3 sts, p1, k2.

Row 2: P1, *k3, p1; rep from * to end.

Rep these 2 rows.

Embossed rib

Multiple of 6 + 2.
Row 1 (RS): P2, *KB1, k1, p1, KB1, p2;
rep from * to end.
Row 2: K2, *PB1, k1, p1, PB1, k2; rep
from * to end.
Row 3: P2, *KB1, p1, k1, KB1, p2; rep
from * to end.
Row 4: K2, *PB1, p1, k1, PB1, k2; rep
from * to end.
Rep these 4 rows.

Garter stitch steps

Multiple of 8.
Row 1 and every alt row (RS): Knit.
Rows 2 and 4: *K4, p4; rep from * to end.
Rows 6 and 8: K2, *p4, k4; rep from * to
last 6 sts, p4, k2.
Rows 10 and 12: *P4, k4; rep from *
to end.
Rows 14 and 16: P2, *k4, p4; rep from *
to last 6 sts, k4, p2.
Rep these 16 rows.

Ridge and furrow

Worked over 23 sts on a background of
st st.
Row 1 (RS): P4, k7, p1, k7, p4.
Row 2: K1, p2, k1, p5, [k1, p1] twice, k1,
p5, k1, p2, k1.
Row 3: P4, k4, [p1, k2] twice, p1, k4, p4.
Row 4: K1, p2, [k1, p3] 4 times, k1, p2, k1.
Row 5: P4, k2, [p1, k4] twice, p1, k2, p4.
Row 6: K1, p2, k1, p1, [k1, p5] twice, k1,
p1, k1, p2, k1.
Rep these 6 rows.

Divided boxes

Multiple of 5.
Row 1 (RS): Knit.
Row 2: *K1, p4; rep from * to end.
Row 3: *K3, p2; rep from * to end.
Row 4: As row 3.
Row 5: As row 2.
Row 6: Knit.
Rep these 6 rows.

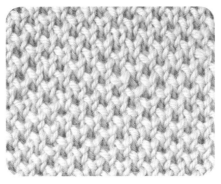

Twisted moss

Multiple of 2 + 1.
Row 1 (WS): Knit.
Row 2: K1, *K1B, k1; rep from * to end.
Row 3: Knit.
Row 4: K1B, *k1, K1B; rep from * to end.
Rep these 4 rows.

Tile stitch

Multiple of 6 + 4.
Row 1 (RS): K4, *p2, k4; rep from *
to end.
Row 2: P4, *k2, p4; rep from * to end.
Rep the last 2 rows twice more.
Row 7: As row 2.
Row 8: K4, *p2, k4; rep from * to end.
Rep these 8 rows.

Biba trellis

Multiple of 14 + 5.

Note: Slip sts purlwise with yarn at WS of work.

Row 1 (RS): Purl.

Row 2: Knit.

Row 3: Purl.

Row 4: P8, sl 3, *p11, sl 3; rep from * to last 8 sts, p8.

Row 5: K8, sl 3, *k11, sl 3; rep from * to last 8 sts, k8.

Rep the last 2 rows once more, then row 4 again.

Rows 9–11: As rows 1–3.

Row 12: P1, sl 3, *p11, sl 3; rep from * to last st, p1.

Row 13: K1, sl 3, *k11, sl 3; rep from * to last st, k1.

Rep the last 2 rows once more, then row 12 again.

Rep these 16 rows.

Diagonal checks

Multiple of 5 sts.

Row 1 (RS): *P1, k4; rep from * to end.

Row 2: *P3, k2; rep from * to end.

Row 3: As row 2.

Row 4: *P1, k4; rep from * to end.

Row 5: *K1, p4; rep from * to end.

Row 6: *K3, p2; rep from * to end.

Row 7: As row 6.

Row 8: As row 5.

Rep these 8 rows.

Diagonal rib I

Multiple of 4.

Row 1 (RS): *K2, p2; rep from * to end.

Row 2: As row 1.

Row 3: K1, *p2, k2; rep from * to last 3 sts, p2, k1.

Row 4: P1, *k2, p2; rep from * to last 3 sts, k2, p1.

Row 5: *P2, k2; rep from * to end.

Row 6: As row 5.

Row 7: As row 4.

Row 8: As row 3

Rep these 8 rows.

Tip

If you are designing a garment, take your swatches and pin them onto an old jumper or a shape you like to get a sense of scale and what the finished item might look like. Alternatively, pin the swatch onto a stand or a tailor's dummy (a patient family member or friend will also do!) and work out the number of stitches and rows required.

Diamond net mask

Worked over 19 sts on a background of st st.

Row 1 (RS): P3, k6, p1, k6, p3.
Row 2: K1, p1, k1, [p6, k1] twice, p1, k1.
Row 3: P3, k5, p1, k1, p1, k5, p3.
Row 4: K1, p1, k1, [p5, k1, p1, k1] twice.
Row 5: P3, k4, [p1, k1] twice, p1, k4, p3.
Row 6: K1, p1, k1, p4, [k1, p1] twice, k1, p4, k1, p1, k1.
Row 7: P3, k3, [p1, k1] 3 times, p1, k3, p3.
Row 8: K1, p1, k1, p3, [k1, p1] 3 times, k1, p3, k1, p1, k1.
Row 9: P3, k2, p1, k1, p1, k3, p1, k1, p1, k2, p3.
Row 10: K1, p1, k1, p2, k1, p1, k1, p3, k1, p1, k1, p2, k1, p1, k1.
Row 11: P3, [k1, p1] twice, k5, [p1, k1] twice, p3.
Row 12: [K1, p1] 3 times, k1, p5, [k1, p1] 3 times, k1.
Row 13: As row 9.
Row 14: As row 10.
Row 15: As row 7.
Row 16: As row 8.
Row 17: As row 5.
Row 18: As row 6.
Row 19: As row 3.
Row 20: As row 4.
Rep these 20 rows.

Moss panels

Multiple of 8 + 7.
Row 1 (WS): K3, *p1, k3; rep from * to end.
Row 2: P3, *k1, p3; rep from * to end.
Row 3: K2, p1, k1, *[p1, k2] twice, p1, k1; rep from * to last 3 sts, p1, k2.
Row 4: P2, k1, p1, *[k1, p2] twice, k1, p1; rep from * to last 3 sts, k1, p2.
Row 5: K1, *p1, k1; rep from * to end.
Row 6: P1, *k1, p1; rep from * to end.
Row 7: As row 3.
Row 8: As row 4.
Row 9: As row 1.
Row 10: As row 2.
Rep these 10 rows.

Anchor

Worked over 17 sts on a background of st st.

Row 1 (RS): P3, k11, p3.
Row 2: K1, p1, [k1, p5] twice, k1, p1, k1.
Row 3: P3, k4, p1, k1, p1, k4, p3.
Row 4: K1, p1, k1, p3, [k1, p1] twice, k1, p3, k1, p1, k1.
Row 5: P3, k2, p1, k5, p1, k2, p3.
Row 6: [K1, p1] twice, [k1, p3] twice, [k1, p1] twice, k1.
Row 7: P3, k1, p1, k7, p1, k1, p3.
Row 8: K1, p1, [k1, p5] twice, k1, p1, k1.
Row 9: As row 1.
Rep the last 2 rows once more.
Row 12: K1, p1, k1, p3, k5, p3, k1, p1, k1.
Row 13: P3, k3, p5, k3, p3.
Row 14: As row 12.
Row 15: As row 1.
Row 16: As row 8.
Rep the last 2 rows once more.
Row 19: As row 3.
Row 20: K1, p1, [k1, p3] 3 times, k1, p1, k1.
Row 21: As row 3.
Row 22: As row 2.
Row 23: As row 1.
Row 24: K1, p1, k1, p11, k1, p1, k1.
Rep these 24 rows.

Topiary stitch

Multiple of 24 + 3.

Row 1 (RS): P1, KB1, *p5, KB1, [p1, KB1] 6 times, p5, KB1; rep from * to last st, p1.

Row 2: K1, p1, *k5, p1, [k1, p1] 6 times, k5, p1; rep from * to last st, k1.

Row 3: As row 1.

Row 4: K1, p1, *k7, p1, [k1, p1] 4 times, k7, p1; rep from * to last st, k1.

Row 5: P1, KB1, *p7, KB1, [p1, KB1] 4 times, p7, KB1; rep from * to last st, p1.

Row 6: K1, p1, k9, p1, [k1, p1] twice, *[k9, p1] twice, [k1, p1] twice; rep from * to last 11 sts, k9, p1, k1.

Row 7: P1, KB1, p9, KB1, [p1, KB1] twice, *[p9, KB1] twice, [p1, KB1] twice; rep from * to last 11 sts, p9, KB1, p1.

Row 8: K1, p1, *k11, p1; rep from * to last st, k1.

Row 9: P1, KB1, *p11, KB1; rep from * to last st, p1.

Row 10: *[K1, p1] twice, [k9, p1] twice; rep from * to last 3 sts, k1, p1, k1.

Row 11: *[P1, KB1] twice, [p9, KB1] twice; rep from * to last 3 sts, p1, KB1, p1.

Row 12: [K1, p1] 3 times, [k7, p1] twice, *[k1, p1] 4 times, [k7, p1] twice; rep from * to last 5 sts, k1, [p1, k1] twice.

Row 13: [P1, KB1] 3 times, [p7, KB1] twice, *[p1, KB1] 4 times, [p7, KB1] twice; rep from * to last 5 sts, p1, [KB1, p1] twice.

Row 14: [K1, p1] 4 times, [k5, p1] twice, *[k1, p1] 6 times, [k5, p1] twice; rep from * to last 7 sts, k1, [p1, k1] 3 times.

Row 15: [P1, KB1] 4 times, [p5, KB1] twice, *[p1, KB1] 6 times, [p5, KB1] twice; rep from * to last 7 sts, p1, [KB1, p1] 3 times.

Rep the last 2 rows twice more.

Rows 20–21: As rows 12–13.

Rows 22–23: As rows 10–11.

Rows 24–25: As rows 8–9.

Rows 26–27: As rows 6–7.

Rows 28–29: As rows 4–5.

Row 30: As row 2.

Rows 31–32: As rows 1–2.

Rep these 32 rows.

Moss diamonds

Multiple of 10 + 7.

Row 1 (RS): *[K3, p1] twice, k1, p1; rep from * to last 7 sts, k3, p1, k3.

Row 2: *[P3, k1] twice, p1, k1; rep from * to last 7 sts, p3, k1, p3.

Row 3: K2, p1, k1, p1, *[k3, p1] twice, k1, p1; rep from * to last 2 sts, k2.

Row 4: P2, k1, p1, k1, *[p3, k1] twice, p1, k1; rep from * to last 2 sts, p2.

Row 5: [K1, p1] 3 times, *[k2, p1] twice, [k1, p1] twice; rep from * to last st, k1.

Row 6: [P1, k1] 3 times, *[p2, k1] twice, [p1, k1] twice; rep from * to last st, p1.

Row 7: As row 3.

Row 8: As row 4.

Row 9: As row 1.

Row 10: As row 2.

Row 11: K3, p1, *k2, [p1, k1] twice, p1, k2, p1; rep from * to last 3 sts, k3.

Row 12: P3, k1, *p2, [k1, p1] twice, k1, p2, k1; rep from * to last 3 sts, p3.

Rep these 12 rows.

Pyramid triangles

Multiple of 14 + 1.

Row 1 (RS): K7, p1, *k13, p1; rep from * to last 7 sts, k7.

Row 2 and every alt row: Purl.

Row 3: K6, p3, *k11, p3; rep from * to last 6 sts, k6.

Row 5: K5, p5, *k9, p5; rep from * to last 5 sts, k5.

Row 7: K4, p7, *k7, p7; rep from * to last 4 sts, k4.

Row 9: K3, p9, *k5, p9; rep from * to last 3 sts, k3.

Row 11: K2, p11, *k3, p11; rep from * to last 2 sts, k2.

Row 13: K1, *p13, k1; rep from * to end.

Row 15: P1, *k13, p1; rep from * to end.

Row 17: P2, k11, *p3, k11; rep from * to last 2 sts, p2.

Row 19: P3, k9, *p5, k9; rep from * to last 3 sts, p3.

Row 21: P4, k7, *p7, k7; rep from * to last 4 sts, p4.

Row 23: P5, k5, *p9, k5; rep from * to last 5 sts, p5.

Row 25: P6, k3, *p11, k3; rep from * to last 6 sts, p6.

Row 27: P7, k1, *p13, k1; rep from * to last 7 sts, p7.

Row 28: Purl.

Rep these 28 rows.

Unusual pattern check

Multiple of 8.

Row 1 (RS): Knit.

Row 2: *K4, p4; rep from * to end.

Row 3: P1, *k4, p4; rep from * to last 7 sts, k4, p3.

Row 4: K2, *p4, k4; rep from * to last 6 sts, p4, k2.

Row 5: P3, *k4, p4; rep from * to last 5 sts, k4, p1.

Row 6: *P4, k4; rep from * to end.

Row 7: Knit.

Row 8: *K4, p4; rep from * to end.

Rep the last row 3 times more.

Row 12: Purl.

Row 13: As row 6.

Row 14: K1, *p4, k4; rep from * to last 7 sts, p4, k3.

Row 15: P2, *k4, p4; rep from * to last 6 sts, k4, p2.

Row 16: K3, *p4, k4; rep from * to last 5 sts, p4, k1.

Row 17: As row 2.

Row 18: Purl.

Row 19: *P4, k4; rep from * to end.

Rep the last row 3 times more.

Rep these 22 rows.

Chevron rib

Multiple of 18 + 1.
Row 1 (RS): P1, *k1, p2, k2, p2, k1, p1; rep from * to end.
Row 2: *K3, p2, k2, p2, k1, [p2, k2] twice; rep from * to last st, k1.
Row 3: *[P2, k2] twice, p3, k2, p2, k2, p1, rep from * to last st, p1.
Row 4: *K1, p2, k2, p2, k5, p2, k2, p2; rep from * to last st, k1.
Rep these 4 rows.

Woven stitch II

Multiple of 4 + 2.
Row 1 (RS): Knit.
Row 2: Purl.
Row 3: K2, *p2, k2; rep from * to end.
Row 4: P2, *k2, p2; rep from * to end.
Row 5: Knit.
Row 6: Purl.
Row 7: As row 4.
Row 8: As row 3.
Rep these 8 rows.

Stocking stitch ridge

Multiple of 2.
Note: Stitches should not be counted after row 2.
Row 1 (RS): Knit.
Row 2: P1, *k2tog; rep from * to last st, p1.
Row 3: K1, *knit into front and back of next st; rep from * to last st, k1.
Row 4: Purl.
Rep these 4 rows.

Centipede stitch

Multiple of 6 + 4.
Row 1 (RS): Knit.
Row 2: P1, k2, *p4, k2; rep from * to last st, p1.
Rep the last 2 rows 5 times more.
Row 13: Knit.
Row 14: P4, *k2, p4; rep from * to end.
Rep the last 2 rows 5 times more.
Rep these 24 rows.

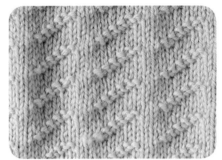

Caterpillar stitch

Multiple of 8 + 6.
Row 1 (RS): K4, p2, *k6, p2; rep from * to end.
Row 2: P1, k2, *p6, k2; rep from * to last 3 sts, p3.
Row 3: K2, p2, *k6, p2; rep from * to last 2 sts, k2.
Row 4: P3, k2, *p6, k2; rep from * to last st, p1.
Row 5: P2, *k6, p2; rep from * to last 4 sts, k4.
Row 6: Purl.
Rep these 6 rows.

Little chevron rib

Multiple of 10 + 1.
Row 1 (RS): P1, *k1, p1, [k2, p1] twice, k1, p1; rep from * to end.
Row 2: K1, *p2, [k1, p1] twice, k1, p2, k1; rep from * to end.
Row 3: P1, *k3, p3, k3, p1; rep from * to end.
Row 4: K2, *p3, k1, p3, k3; rep from * to last 9 sts, p3, k1, p3, k2.
Rep these 4 rows.

Pillar stitch

Multiple of 2.
Row 1 (WS): Purl.
Row 2: K1, *yf, k2, pass yf over k2; rep from * to last st, k1.
Rep these 2 rows.

Waffle stitch

Multiple of 3 + 1.
Row 1 (RS): P1, *k2, p1; rep from * to end.
Row 2: K1, *p2, k1; rep from * to end.
Row 3: As row 1.
Row 4: Knit.
Rep these 4 rows.

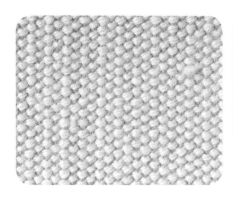

Tweed stitch

Multiple of 2 + 1.
Row 1 (RS): K1, *yf, sl 1 purlwise, yb, k1; rep from * to end.
Row 2: P2, *yb, sl 1 purlwise, yf, p1; rep from * to last st, p1.
Rep these 2 rows.

Horizontal dash stitch

Multiple of 10 + 6.
Row 1 (RS): P6, *k4, p6; rep from * to end.
Row 2 and every alt row: Purl.
Row 3: Knit.
Row 5: P1, *k4, p6; rep from * to last 5 sts, k4, p1.
Row 7: Knit.
Row 8: Purl.
Rep these 8 rows.

Open twisted rib

Multiple of 5 + 3.
Note: Stitches should not be counted after rows 2 and 3 of this pattern.
Row 1 (WS): K1, PB1, k1, *p2, k1, PB1, k1; rep from * to end.
Row 2: P1, KB1, p1, *k1, yf, k1, p1, KB1, p1; rep from * to end.
Row 3: K1, PB1, k1, *p3, k1, PB1, k1; rep from * to end.
Row 4: P1, KB1, p1, *k3, pass 3rd st on right-hand needle over first 2 sts, p1, KB1, p1; rep from * to end.
Rep these 4 rows.

Diagonal rib II

Multiple of 4.
Rows 1–2: *K2, p2; rep from * to end.
Row 3 (RS): K1, *p2, k2; rep from * to last 3 sts, p2, k1.
Row 4: P1, *k2, p2; rep from * to last 3 sts, k2, p1.
Rows 5–6: *P2, k2; rep from * to end.
Row 7: As row 4.
Row 8: As row 3.
Rep these 8 rows.

knit and purl stitches

Large basket weave

Multiple of 6 + 2.

Row 1 (RS): Knit.

Row 2: Purl.

Row 3: K2, *p4, k2; rep from * to end.

Row 4: P2, *k4, p2; rep from * to end.

Rep the last 2 rows once more.

Row 7: Knit.

Row 8: Purl.

Row 9: P3, *k2, p4; rep from * to last 5 sts, k2, p3.

Row 10: K3, *p2, k4; rep from * to last 5 sts, p2, k3.

Rep the last 2 rows once more.

Rep these 12 rows.

Broken rib diagonal

Multiple of 6.

Row 1 (RS): *K4, p2; rep from * to end.

Row 2: *K2, p4; rep from * to end.

Row 3: As row 1.

Row 4: As row 2.

Row 5: K2, *p2, k4; rep from * to last 4 sts, p2, k2.

Row 6: P2, *k2, p4; rep from * to last 4 sts, k2, p2.

Row 7: As row 5.

Row 8: As row 6.

Row 9: *P2, k4; rep from * to end.

Row 10: *P4, k2; rep from * to end.

Row 11: As row 9.

Row 12: As row 10.

Rep these 12 rows.

Stripe pillars

Multiple of 6 + 3.

Work 4 rows in st st, starting with knit (RS).

Row 5: K1, *p1, k1; rep from * to end.

Row 6: P1, *k1, p1; rep from * to end.

Rep the last 2 rows once more.

Row 9: K1, p1, k1, *p3, k1, p1, k1; rep from * to end.

Row 10: P1, k1, p1, *k3, p1, k1, p1; rep from * to end.

Rep the last 2 rows once more.

Rep these 12 rows.

Tip

When creating a garment design, think about assembling the swatches on a mood board. Consider adding the trims, buttons, ribbons and edging you may wish to use. You could also add buttons to the swatch for further reference to make sure they work with the design and don't get lost.

Diamond panels

Multiple of 8 + 1.

Row 1 (RS): Knit.

Row 2: K1, *p7, k1; rep from * to end.

Row 3: K4, *p1, k7; rep from * to last 5 sts, p1, k4.

Row 4: K1, *p2, k1, p1, k1, p2, k1; rep from * to end.

Row 5: K2, *[p1, k1] twice, p1, k3; rep from * to last 7 sts, [p1, k1] twice, p1, k2.

Row 6: As row 4.

Row 7: As row 3.

Row 8: As row 2.

Rep these 8 rows.

Textured tiles

Multiple of 10 + 6.

Row 1 (RS): P1, *k4, p1; rep from * to end.

Row 2: K1, *p4, k1; rep from * to end.

Rep the last 2 rows once more, then row 1 again.

Row 6: K6, *p4, k6; rep from * to end.

Row 7: As row 1.

Rep the last 2 rows twice more.

Row 12: As row 2.

Row 13: As row 1.

Rep the last 2 rows once more.

Row 16: K1, p4, *k6, p4; rep from * to last st, k1.

Row 17: As row 1.

Rep the last 2 rows once more, then row 16 again.

Rep these 20 rows.

Enlarged basket stitch

Multiple of 18 + 10.

Row 1 (RS): K11, *p2, k2, p2, k12; rep from * to last 17 sts, p2, k2, p2, k11.

Row 2: P1, *k8, [p2, k2] twice, p2; rep from * to last 9 sts, k8, p1.

Row 3: K1, *p8, [k2, p2] twice, k2; rep from * to last 9 sts, p8, k1.

Row 4: P11, *k2, p2, k2, p12; rep from * to last 17 sts, k2, p2, k2, p11.

Rep the last 4 rows once more.

Row 9: Knit.

Row 10: [P2, k2] twice, p12, *k2, p2, k2, p12; rep from * to last 8 sts, [k2, p2] twice.

Row 11: [K2, p2] twice, k2, *p8, [k2, p2] twice, k2; rep from * to end.

Row 12: [P2, k2] twice, p2, *k8, [p2, k2] twice, p2; rep from * to end.

Row 13: [K2, p2] twice, k12, *p2, k2, p2, k12; rep from * to last 8 sts, [p2, k2] twice.

Rep the last 4 rows once more.

Row 18: Purl.

Rep these 18 rows.

Garter and slip stitch

Multiple of 6 + 4.

Row 1 (RS): Knit.

Row 2: K1, *yf, sl 2 purlwise, yb, k4; rep from * to last 3 sts, yf, sl2 purlwise, yb, k1.

Row 3: K1, *keeping yarn at back sl 2 purlwise, k4; rep from * to last 3 sts, sl 2 purlwise, k1.

Rep the last 2 rows once more.

Row 6: As row 2.

Row 7: Knit.

Row 8: K4, *yf, sl 2 purlwise, yb, k4; rep from * to end.

Row 9: K4, *keeping yarn at back sl 2 purlwise, k4; rep from * to end.

Rep the last 2 rows once more.

Row 12: As row 8.

Rep these 12 rows.

Chevron

Multiple of 8 + 1.

Row 1 (RS): K1, *p7, k1; rep from * to end.

Row 2: P1, *k7, p1; rep from * to end.

Row 3: K2, *p5, k3; rep from * to last 7 sts, p5, k2.

Row 4: P2, *k5, p3; rep from * to last 7 sts, k5, p2.

Row 5: K3, *p3, k5; rep from * to last 6 sts, p3, k3.

Row 6: P3, *k3, p5; rep from * to last 6 sts, k3, p3.

Row 7: K4, *p1, k7; rep from * to last 5 sts, p1, k4.

Row 8: P4, *k1, p7; rep from * to last 5 sts, k1, p4.

Row 9: As row 2.

Row 10: As row 1.

Row 11: As row 4.

Row 12: As row 3.

Row 13: As row 6.

Row 14: As row 5.

Row 15: As row 8.

Row 16: As row 7.

Rep these 16 rows.

Intertwined texture stitch

Multiple of 15 + 2.

Row 1 (RS): *P13, k2; rep from * to last 2 sts, p2.

Row 2: K2, *p2, k13; rep from * to end.

Row 3: As row 1.

Row 4: Purl.

Row 5: P2, *k2, p1, [k1, p1] 4 times, k2, p2; rep from * to end.

Row 6: K2, *p3, k1, [p1, k1] 3 times, p3, k2; rep from * to end.

Rep the last 2 rows 4 times more.

Row 15: P2, *k2, p13; rep from * to end.

Row 16: *K13, p2; rep from * to last 2 sts, k2.

Row 17: As row 15.

Row 18: Purl.

Rep these 18 rows.

Bobble rib

Multiple of 8 + 3.

Row 1 (RS): K3, *p2, [p1, k1] twice into next st, pass the first 3 of these sts, one at a time, over the 4th st (bobble made), p2, k3; rep from * to end.

Row 2: P3, *k2, p1, k2, p3; rep from * to end.

Row 3: K3, *p2, k1, p2, k3; rep from * to end.

Row 4: As row 2.

Rep these 4 rows.

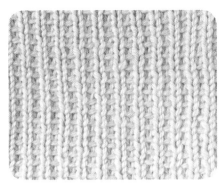

Slip stitch rib

Multiple of 2 + 1.

Row 1 (WS): Purl.

Row 2: K1, *yf, sl 1 purlwise, yb, k1; rep from * to end.

Rep these 2 rows.

Granite rib

Multiple of 8 + 2.

Row 1 (RS): K2, *C2F 3 times, k2; rep from * to end.

Row 2: Purl.

Row 3: K2, *[knit 3rd st from left-hand needle, then 2nd st, then 1st stitch, slipping all 3 sts off needle together] twice, k2; rep from * to end.

Row 4: Purl.

Rep these 4 rows.

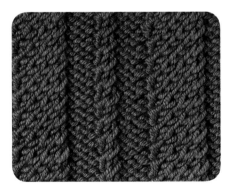

Basket weave rib

Multiple of 15 + 8.

Row 1 (RS): *P3, k2, p3, k1, [C2F] 3 times; rep from * to last 8 sts, p3, k2, p3.

Row 2: *K3, purl into 2nd st on needle, then purl 1st st slipping both sts off needle together (called C2P), k3, p1, [C2P] 3 times; rep from * to last 8 sts, k3, C2P, k3.

Rep these 2 rows.

Garter stitch ridges

Any number of stitches.

Row 1 (RS): Knit.

Row 2: Purl.

Rep the last 2 rows once more.

Purl 6 rows.

Rep these 10 rows.

Piqué rib

Multiple of 10 + 3.

Row 1 (RS): K3, *p3, k1, p3, k3; rep from * to end.

Row 2: P3, *k3, p1, k3, p3; rep from * to end.

Row 3: As row 1.

Row 4: Knit.

Rep these 4 rows.

Ladder tile

Multiple of 12.

Row 1 (RS): K4, p1, *k11, p1; rep from * to last 7 sts, k7.

Row 2 and every alt row: Purl.

Rows 3 and 5: K4, p2, *k10, p2; rep from * to last 6 sts, k6.

Row 7: K4, p7, *k5, p7; rep from * to last st, k1.

Row 9: *K4, p8; rep from * to end.

Row 11: K1, p7, *k5, p7; rep from * to last 4 sts, k4.

Row 13: *P8, k4; rep from * to end.

Rows 15 and 17: K6, p2, *k10, p2; rep from * to last 4 sts, k4.

Row 19: K7, p1, *k11, p1; rep from * to last 4 sts, k4.

Row 20: Purl.

Rep these 20 rows.

Spiral rib

Multiple of 6 + 3.

Row 1 (RS): K3, *p3, k3; rep from * to end.

Row 2: P3, *k3, p3; rep from * to end.

Row 3: As row 1.

Row 4: K1, *p3, k3; rep from * to last 2 sts, p2.

Row 5: K2, *p3, k3; rep from * to last st, p1.

Row 6: As row 4.

Row 7: As row 4.

Row 8: As row 5.

Row 9: As row 4.

Row 10: K3, *p3, k3; rep from * to end.

Row 11: As row 2.

Row 12: As row 10.

Row 13: P2, *k3, p3; rep from * to last st, k1.

Row 14: P1, *k3, p3; rep from * to last 2 sts, k2.

Row 15: As row 13.

Row 16: As row 13.

Row 17: As row 14.

Row 18: As row 13.

Rep these 18 rows.

Dotted chevron

Multiple of 18.

Row 1 (RS): K8, *p2, k16; rep from * to last 10 sts, p2, k8.

Row 2: P7, *k4, p14; rep from * to last 11 sts, k4, p7.

Row 3: P1, *k5, p2, k2, p2, k5, p2, rep from * to last 17 sts, k5, p2, k2, p2, k5, p1.

Row 4: K2, *p3, k2, p4, k2, p3, k4, rep from * to last 16 sts, p3, k2, p4, k2, p3, k2.

Row 5: P1, *k3, p2, k6, p2, k3, p2, rep from * to last 17 sts, k3, p2, k6, p2, k3, p1.

Row 6: P3, *k2, [p3, k2] twice, p6, rep from * to last 15 sts, k2, [p3, k2] twice, p3.

Row 7: K2, *p2, k3, p4, k3, p2, k4, rep from * to last 16 sts, p2, k3, p4, k3, p2, k2.

Row 8: P1, *k2, [p5, k2] twice, p2; rep from * to last 17 sts, k2, [p5, k2] twice, p1.

Row 9: P2, *k14, p4; rep from * to last 16 sts, k14, p2.

Row 10: K1, *p16, k2; rep from * to last 17 sts, p16, k1.

Rep these 10 rows.

Tweed pattern

Multiple of 6 + 3.

Row 1 (RS): K3, *p3, k3; rep from *
to end.

Rep the last row twice more.

Row 4: Knit.

Row 5: Purl.

Row 6: Knit.

Row 7: K3, *p3, k3; rep from * to end.

Rep the last row twice more.

Row 10: Purl.

Row 11: Knit.

Row 12: Purl.

Rep these 12 rows.

Chain stitch rib

Multiple of 3 + 2.

Row 1 (WS): K2, *p1, k2; rep from *
to end.

Row 2: P2, *k1, p2; rep from * to end.

Row 3: As row 1.

Row 4: P2, *yb, insert needle through
centre of st 3 rows below next st on
needle and knit this in the usual way,
slipping st above off needle at the same
time, p2; rep from * to end.

Rep these 4 rows.

Diamond pattern

Multiple of 8 + 1.

Row 1 (RS): P1, *k7, p1; rep from *
to end.

Row 2: K2, p5, *k3, p5; rep from * to last
2 sts, k2.

Row 3: K1, *p2, k3, p2, k1; rep from *
to end.

Row 4: P2, k2, p1, k2, *p3, k2, p1, k2;
rep from * to last 2 sts, p2.

Row 5: K3, p3, *k5, p3; rep from * to last
3 sts, k3.

Row 6: P4, k1, *p7, k1; rep from * to last
4 sts, p4.

Row 7: As row 5.

Row 8: As row 4.

Row 9: As row 3.

Row 10: As row 2.

Rep these 10 rows.

Mock cable rib

Multiple of 7 + 2.

Row 1 (RS): P2, *C2B, k3, p2; rep from * to end.

Row 2 and every alt row: K2, *p5, k2; rep from * to end.

Row 3: P2, *k1, C2B, k2, p2; rep from * to end.

Row 5: P2, *k2, C2B, k1, p2; rep from * to end.

Row 7: P2, *k3, C2B, p2; rep from * to end.

Row 8: K2, *p5, k2; rep from * to end.

Rep these 8 rows.

Brick stitch

Multiple of 4 + 1.

Row 1 (RS): K4, *k1 winding yarn twice around needle, k3; rep from * to last st, k1.

Row 2: P4, *sl 1 purlwise dropping extra loop, p3; rep from * to last st, p1.

Row 3: K4, *sl 1 purlwise, k3; rep from * to last st, k1.

Row 4: K4, *yf, sl 1 purlwise, yb, k3; rep from * to last st, k1.

Row 5: K2, *k1 winding yarn twice around needle, k3; rep from * to last 3 sts, k1 winding yarn twice around needle, k2.

Row 6: P2, *sl 1 purlwise dropping extra loop, p3; rep from * to last 3 sts, sl 1 purlwise, p2.

Row 7: K2, *sl 1 purlwise, k3; rep from * to last 3 sts, sl 1 purlwise, k2.

Row 8: K2, *yf, sl 1 purlwise, yb, k3, rep from * to last 3 sts, yf, sl 1 purlwise, yb, k2.

Rep these 8 rows.

Pyramids II

Multiple of 8 + 1.

Row 1 (WS): P1, *k1, p1; rep from * to end.

Row 2: K1, *p1, k1; rep from * to end.

Rep these 2 rows once more.

Row 5: P2, *[k1, p1] twice, k1, p3; rep from * to last 7 sts, [k1, p1] twice, k1, p2.

Row 6: K2, *[p1, k1] twice, p1, k3; rep from * to last 7 sts, [p1, k1] twice, p1, k2.

Rep the last 2 rows once more.

Row 9: P3, *k1, p1, k1, p5; rep from * to last 6 sts, k1, p1, k1, p3.

Row 10: K3, *p1, k1, p1, k5; rep from * to last 6 sts, p1, k1, p1, k3.

Rep the last 2 rows once more.

Row 13: P4, *k1, p7; rep from * to last 5 sts, k1, p4.

Row 14: K4, *p1, k7; rep from * to last 5 sts, p1, k4.

Rep the last 2 rows once more.

Rep these 16 rows.

Zigzag stitch

Multiple of 6 sts.

Row 1 (RS): *K3, p3; rep from * to end.

Row 2 and every alt row: Purl.

Row 3: P1, *k3, p3; rep from * to last 5 sts, k3, p2.

Row 5: P2, *k3, p3; rep from * to last 4 sts, k3, p1.

Row 7: *P3, k3; rep from * to end.

Row 9: As row 5.

Row 11: As row 3.

Row 12: Purl.

Rep these 12 rows.

Spaced checks

Multiple of 10 + 1.

Row 1 (WS): Purl.

Row 2: K4, *p3, k7; rep from * to last 7 sts, p3, k4.

Row 3: P4, *k3, p7; rep from * to last 7 sts, k3, p4.

Row 4: As row 2.

Row 5: Purl.

Row 6: Knit.

Row 7: K2, *p7, k3; rep from * to last 9 sts, p7, k2.

Row 8: P2, *k7, p3; rep from * to last 9 sts, k7, p2.

Row 9: As row 7.

Row 10: Knit.

Rep these 10 rows.

Fancy diamond

Multiple of 15.

Row 1 (RS): K1, *p13, k2; rep from * to last 14 sts, p13, k1.

Row 2: P2, *k11, p4; rep from * to last 13 sts, k11, p2.

Row 3: K3, *p9, k6; rep from * to last 12 sts, p9, k3.

Row 4: P4, *k7, p8; rep from * to last 11 sts, k7, p4.

Row 5: K5, *p5, k10; rep from * to last 10 sts, p5, k5.

Row 6: K1, *p5, k3, p5, k2; rep from * to last 14 sts, p5, k3, p5, k1.

Row 7: P2, *k5, p1, k5, p4; rep from * to last 13 sts, k5, p1, k5, p2.

Row 8: As row 3.

Row 9: As row 7.

Row 10: As row 6.

Row 11: As row 5.

Row 12: As row 4.

Row 13: As row 3.

Row 14: As row 2.

Rep these 14 rows.

Berry ladder

Multiple of 20 + 10.

Row 1 (RS): P2, *k2, p2; rep from * to end.

Row 2: K2, *p2, k2; rep from * to end.

Row 3: [K2, p2] twice, *k4, p2, k2, p2; rep from * to last 2 sts, k2.

Row 4: [P2, k2] twice, *p4, k2, p2, k2; rep from * to last 2 sts, p2.

Rep the last 4 rows once more, then rows 1–2 again.

Row 11: As row 2.

Row 12: P2, *k2, p2; rep from * to end.

Row 13: [K2, p2] 3 times, [k4, p2] twice, *[k2, p2] twice, [k4, p2] twice; rep from * to last 6 sts, k2, p2, k2.

Row 14: [P2, k2] twice, *[p4, k2] twice, [p2, k2] twice; rep from * to last 2 sts, p2.

Rep the last 4 rows once more, then rows 11–12 again.

Rep these 20 rows.

Embossed lozenge stitch

Multiple of 8 + 1.

Row 1 (RS): P3, *KB1, p1, KB1, p5; rep from * to last 6 sts, KB1, p1, KB1, p3.

Row 2: K3, *PB1, k1, PB1, k5; rep from * to last 6 sts, PB1, k1, PB1, k3.

Rep the last 2 rows once more.

Row 5: P2, *KB1, p3; rep from * to last 3 sts, KB1, p2.

Row 6: K2, *PB1, k3; rep from * to last 3 sts, PB1, k2.

Row 7: P1, *KB1, p5, KB1, p1; rep from * to end.

Row 8: K1, *PB1, k5, PB1, k1; rep from * to end.

Row 9: As row 7.

Row 10: As row 8.

Row 11: As row 5.

Row 12: As row 6.

Rep these 12 rows.

Slanted bamboo

Multiple of 8.

Row 1 (RS): P1, k6, *p2, k6; rep from * to last st, p1.

Row 2: K1, p5, *k3, p5; rep from * to last 2 sts, k2.

Row 3: P3, k4, *p4, k4; rep from * to last st, p1.

Row 4: K1, p3, k2, p1, *k2, p3, k2, p1; rep from * to last st, k1.

Row 5: P1, k2, *p2, k2; rep from * to last st, p1.

Row 6: K1, p1, k2, p3, *k2, p1, k2, p3; rep from * to last st, k1.

Row 7: P1, k4, *p4, k4; rep from * to last 3 sts, p3.

Row 8: K2, p5, *k3, p5; rep from * to last st, k1.

Row 9: As row 1.

Row 10: K1, p6, *k2, p6; rep from * to last st, k1.

Rep these 10 rows.

Squares

Multiple of 10 + 2.

Row 1 (RS): Knit.

Row 2: Purl.

Row 3: K2, *p8, k2; rep from * to end.

Row 4: P2, *k8, p2; rep from * to end.

Row 5: K2, *p2, k4, p2, k2; rep from * to end.

Row 6: P2, *k2, p4, k2, p2; rep from * to end.

Rep the last 2 rows twice more.

Row 11: As row 3.

Row 12: As row 4.

Rep these 12 rows.

Crossroad squares

Multiple of 12 + 2.

Row 1 (RS): K4, p6, *k6, p6; rep from * to last 4 sts, k4.

Row 2: P4, k6, *p6, k6; rep from * to last 4 sts, p4.

Row 3: K2, *p2, k6, p2, k2; rep from * to end.

Row 4: P2, *k2, p6, k2, p2; rep from * to end.

Rep the last 2 rows 3 times more.

Rows 11–12: As rows 1–2.

Row 13: Knit.

Row 14: Purl.

Rep these 14 rows.

Triangle ribs

Multiple of 8.

Row 1 (RS): *P2, k6; rep from * to end.

Row 2: *P6, k2; rep from * to end.

Row 3: *P3, k5; rep from * to end.

Row 4: *P4, k4; rep from * to end.

Row 5: *P5, k3; rep from * to end.

Row 6: *P2, k6; rep from * to end.

Row 7: *P7, k1; rep from * to end.

Row 8: *P2, k6; rep from * to end.

Row 9: As row 5.

Row 10: As row 4.

Row 11: As row 3.

Row 12: As row 2.

Rep these 12 rows.

Ocean wave

Multiple of 12 + 1.

Row 1 and every alt row (RS): Knit.

Row 2: P5, k3, *p9, k3; rep from * to last 5 sts, p5.

Row 4: P4, k5, *p7, k5; rep from * to last 4 sts, p4.

Row 6: P3, k3, p1, k3, *p5, k3, p1, k3; rep from * to last 3 sts, p3.

Row 8: P2, k3, *p3, k3; rep from * to last 2 sts, p2.

Row 10: P1, *k3, p5, k3, p1; rep from * to end.

Row 12: Purl.

Rep these 12 rows.

Elongated chevron

Row 1 (RS): P1, *[k2, p2] twice, k1, [p2, k2] twice, p1; rep from * to end.

Row 2: K1, *[p2, k2] twice, p1, [k2, p2] twice, k1; rep from * to end.

Rep the last 2 rows once more.

Row 5: [P2, k2] twice, *p3, k2, p2, k2; rep from * to last 2 sts, p2.

Row 6: [K2, p2] twice, *k3, p2, k2, p2; rep from * to last 2 sts, k2.

Rep the last 2 rows once more.

Row 9: As row 2.

Row 10: As row 1.

Row 11: As row 2.

Row 12: As row 1.

Row 13: As row 6.

Row 14: As row 5.

Row 15: As row 6.

Row 16: As row 5.

Rep these 16 rows.

Moss stitch zigzag

Multiple of 9.

Row 1 (RS): *[K1, p1] twice, k4, p1; rep from * to end.

Row 2: *P4, [k1, p1] twice, k1; rep from * to end.

Row 3: [K1, p1] 3 times, *k4, [p1, k1] twice, p1; rep from * to last 3 sts, k3.

Row 4: P2, *[k1, p1] twice, k1, p4; rep from * to last 7 sts, [k1, p1] twice, k1, p2.

Row 5: K3, *[p1, k1] twice, p1, k4; rep from * to last 6 sts, [p1, k1] 3 times.

Row 6: *[K1, p1] twice, k1, p4; rep from * to end.

Row 7: As row 5.

Row 8: As row 4.

Row 9: As row 3.

Row 10: As row 2.

Rep these 10 rows.

Single eyelet rib

Multiple of 5 + 2.
Row 1 (RS): P2, *k3, p2; rep from *
to end.
Row 2 and every alt row: K2, *p3, k2;
rep from * to end.
Row 3: P2, *k2tog, yf, k1, p2; rep from *
to end.
Row 5: As row 1.
Row 7: P2, *k1, yf, sl 1, k1, psso, p2; rep
from * to end.
Row 8: As row 2.
Rep these 8 rows.

Double eyelet rib

Multiple of 7 + 2.
Row 1 (RS): P2, *k5, p2; rep from *
to end.
Row 2: K2, *p5, k2; rep from * to end.
Row 3: P2, *k2tog, yf, k1, yf, sl 1, k1,
psso, p2; rep from * to end.
Row 4: As row 2.
Rep these 4 rows.

Square rib

Multiple of 2 + 1.
Row 1 (RS): K2, p1, *k1, p1; rep from * to
last 2 sts, k2.
Row 2: K1, *p1, k1; rep from * to end.
Row 3: As row 1.
Row 4: K1, p1, *yb, insert needle through
centre of st 2 rows below next st on
needle and knit this in the usual way
slipping st above off needle at the same
time, p1; rep from * to last st, k1.
Rep these 4 rows.

Diagonal knot stitch

Multiple of 3 + 1.
Special abbreviation: Make Knot =
P3tog leaving sts on needle, yrn, then purl
same 3 sts together again.
Row 1 and every alt row (RS): Knit.
Row 2: *Make Knot; rep from * to last
st, p1.
Row 4: P2, *Make Knot; rep from * to last
2 sts, p2.
Row 6: P1, *Make Knot; rep from * to end.
Rep these 6 rows.

Close checks

Multiple of 6 + 3.
Row 1 (RS): K3, *p3, k3; rep from *
to end.
Row 2: P3, *k3, p3; rep from * to end.
Rep the last 2 rows once more.
Row 5: As row 2.
Row 6: As row 1.
Rep the last 2 rows once more.
Rep these 8 rows.

Mock cable – left

Multiple of 4 + 2.
Row 1 (RS): P2, *k2, p2; rep from *
to end.
Row 2: K2, *p2, k2; rep from * to end.
Row 3: P2, *C2B, p2; rep from * to end.
Row 4: As row 2.
Rep these 4 rows.

Small cable with grooves

Multiple of 12.

Row 1 (RS): *K2, p1, k6, p1, k2; rep from * to end.

Row 2: *P2, k1, p6, k1, p2; rep from * to end.

Rows 3, 5, 7 and 9: *K2, p2, k4, p2, k2; rep from * to end.

Rows 4, 6 and 8: *P2, k2, p4, k2, p2; rep from * to end.

Row 10: *P2, slip next 2 sts onto cable needle and hold at front of work, p2, k2 from cable needle, slip next 2 sts onto cable needle and hold at front of work, k2, p2 from cable needle, p2; rep from * to end.

Row 11: Knit.

Row 12: As row 2.

Rep these 12 rows.

Baby cable and garter ridges

Multiple of 25.

Row 1 (RS): *P9, k4, p12; rep from * to end.

Row 2: *[P3, k1] 3 times, p4, k1, [p3, k1] twice; rep from * to end.

Row 3: *[P1, k3] twice, p1, C4F, [p1, k3] 3 times; rep from * to end.

Row 4: As row 2.

Rep these 4 rows.

Twists with knotted pattern

Multiple of 20.

Row 1 (RS): *P2, k5, p5, k5, p3; rep from * to end.

Row 2 and every even row: *K3, p5, k5, p5, k2; rep from * to end.

Row 3: As row 1.

Row 5: *P2, using another ball of yarn k5, turn, p5, work another 12 rows in st st on these 5 sts, place on stitch holder, slip next 5 sts onto cable needle and hold at back of work, using another ball of yarn k5, turn, p5, work another 12 rows in st st on these 5 sts, place on stitch holder, knot the 2 strips as follows: put 2nd strip underneath 1st then over 1st, k5 sts from 2nd strip, p5 sts from cable needle, k5 sts from 1st strip, p3; rep from * to end.

Rows 7, 9, 11, 13 and 15: As row 1.

Row 16: As row 2.

Rep these 16 rows.

Sand wind

Multiple of 12 + 6 + 1 st for the rim on each edge.

Rows 1 (RS) and 5: Knit.

Row 2 and every even row: Purl.

Row 3: 1 edge st, *C6F, k6; rep from * to last st, 1 edge st.

Row 7: 1 edge st, *k6, C6B; rep from * to last st, 1 edge st.

Row 8: Knit.

Rep these 8 rows.

Rhombus

Panel of 12 sts on a background of st st.

Rows 1 (RS) and 5: Knit.

Row 2 and every even row: Purl.

Row 3: C4B, k4, C4F.

Row 7: K2, C4F, C4B, k2.

Row 8: Purl.

Rep these 8 rows.

20-stitch twisted candle

Panel of 20 sts on a background of rev st st.

Rows 1 (RS), 5, 7, 9 and 11: Knit.

Row 2 and all even rows: Purl.

Row 3: C10B, C10F.

Row 12: As row 2.

Rep these 12 rows.

Woven cable stitch

Multiple of 4.

Row 1 (RS): *C4F; rep from * to end.

Row 2: Purl.

Row 3: K2, *C4B; rep from * to last 2 sts, k2.

Row 4: Purl.

Rep these 4 rows.

Knotted cable

Panel of 6 sts on a background of rev st st.

Row 1 (RS): K2, p2, k2.

Row 2 and every alt row: P2, k2, p2.

Row 3: C6.

Rows 5, 7 and 9: K2, p2, k2.

Row 10: As row 2.

Rep these 10 rows.

Little pearl

Panel of 4 sts on a background of st st.

Row 1 (RS): C2F, C2B.

Row 2: Purl.

Row 3: C2B, C2F.

Row 4: Purl.

Rep these 4 rows.

Big twisted candle

Panel of 9 sts on a background of rev st st.

Row 1 (RS): Knit.

Row 2 and all even rows: Purl.

Rows 3, 5, 7, 11, 13, 15 and 17: Knit.

Row 9: C9 (slip next 4 sts onto cable needle and hold at front of work), k5, k4 sts from cable needle.

Row 18: As row 2.

Rep these 18 rows.

Sloping diamonds

Multiple of 10.

Row 1 (RS): *K2, p5, C3B; rep from * to end.

Row 2: *P3, k5, p2; rep from * to end.

Row 3: *K2, p4, C3B, k1; rep from * to end.

Row 4: *P4, k4, p2; rep from * to end.

Row 5: *K2, p3, T3B, k2; rep from * to end.

Row 6: *P2, k1, p2, k3, p2; rep from * to end.

Row 7: *K2, p2, T3B, p1, k2; rep from * to end.

Row 8: *P2, [k2, p2] twice; rep from * to end.

Row 9: *K2, p1, T3B, p2, k2; rep from * to end.

Row 10: *P2, k3, p2, k1, p2; rep from * to end.

Row 11: *K2, T3B, p3, k2; rep from * to end.

Row 12: *P2, k4, p4; rep from * to end.

Row 13: *K1, T3B, p4, k2; rep from * to end.

Row 14: *P2, k5, p3; rep from * to end.

Row 15: *T3B, p5, k2; rep from * to end.

Row 16: *P2, k6, p2; rep from * to end.

Rep these 16 rows.

Dramatic curves

Multiple of 47 sts on row 1; 62 sts thereafter.

Row 1 (RS): P8, *[k1, p1] in each of next 5 sts, p8; rep from * to end.

Row 2: K8 *p10, place point of left-hand needle into the st below needle of the last knit st just worked, knit it together with the next st on left-hand needle, k7; rep from * to end.

Row 3: P8, *k10, p8; rep from * to end.

Row 4: As row 2.

Rows 5–12: Rep last 2 rows 4 times more.

Row 13: P8, sl next 10 sts onto cable needle and hold at front, sl following 8 sts onto 2nd cable needle and hold at back, k10, p8 from sts held on 2nd cable needle, k10 from sts held on 1st cable needle, p8, k10, p8.

Row 14: As row 2.

Rows 15–24: Rep rows 3–4, 5 times.

Row 25: P8, k10, p8, sl next 10 sts onto cable needle and hold at back of work, sl following 8 sts onto 2nd cable needle and also hold at back, k10, p8 from sts held on 2nd cable needle, k10 from sts held on 1st cable needle, p8.

Row 26: As row 2.

Rep rows 3–26.

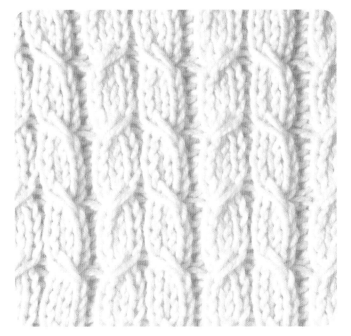

Alternating twists

Multiple of 9 + 2.

Row 1 (WS): K2, *p3, k1, p3, k2; rep from * to end.

Row 2: *P2, wyib sl 1, k2, p1, k2, wyib sl 1; rep from * to last 2 sts, p2.

Row 3: K2, *wyif sl 1, p2, k1, p2, wyif sl 1, k2; rep from * to end.

Row 4: *P2, drop sl st off needle to front of work, k2, pick up dropped st and knit it, p1, wyib sl next 2 sts, drop sl st off needle to front of work, sl same 2 sts back to left-hand needle, pick up dropped st and knit it; rep from * to last 2 sts, p2.

Row 5: K2, *p3, k1, p3, k2; rep from * to end.

Row 6: *P2, k3, p1, k3; rep from * to last 2 sts, p2.

Rep these 6 rows.

Twisted candles

Multiple of 18 + 8 + 1 st for the rim on each edge.

Row 1 (RS): Knit.

Row 2: Purl.

Rows 3 and 5: Knit.

Row 4: Purl.

Row 6: 1 edge st, k1, p6, k1, *k11, p6, k1; rep from * to last st, 1 edge st.

Row 7: Knit.

Row 8: As row 6.

Row 9: 1 edge st, *k1, C6F, k11; rep from * to last 9 sts, k1, C6F, k1, 1 edge st.

Row 10: As row 6.

Rows 11–21: As rows 1–2.

Row 22: 1 edge st, *k10, p6, k10; rep from * to last st, 1 edge st.

Row 23: As row 1.

Row 24: As row 22.

Row 25: 1 edge st, *k10, C6F, k10; rep from * to last st, 1 edge st.

Row 26: As row 22.

Rep these 26 rows.

Geometric twisted candles

Multiple of 10 + 6 + 1 st for the rim on each edge.

Row 1 (RS): 1 edge st, *p1, k4, p5; rep from * to last 7 sts, p1, k4, p1, 1 edge st.

Row 2 and every even row: Knit all k sts and purl all p sts.

Row 3: Knit all k sts and purl all p sts.

Row 5: 1 edge st, *p1, C4B, p5; rep from * to last 6 sts, p1, C4B, 1 edge st.

Row 7: As row 3.

Row 9: 1 edge st, *p6, k4; rep from * to last 7 sts, p6, 1 edge st.

Row 11: As row 3.

Row 13: 1 edge st, *p6, C4B; rep from * to last 7 sts, p6, 1 edge st.

Row 15: As row 3.

Row 16: As row 2.

Rep these 16 rows.

Crossed grooves

Multiple of 8 + 2 + 1 st for the rim on each edge.

Rows 1 (RS), 3, 5, 9, 11 and 13: 1 edge st *k2, p2; rep from * to last 3 sts, k2, 1 edge st.

Row 2 and all even rows: Knit all k sts and purl all p sts.

Row 7: 1 edge st, *C6 (slip next 4 sts onto cable needle and hold at back of work, k2, slip 3rd and 4th sts from cable needle onto left-hand needle, p2tbl, k2 sts from cable needle), p2; rep from * to last 3 sts, k2, 1 edge st.

Row 15: 1 edge st, k2, *p2, C6; rep from * to last st, 1 edge st.

Row 16: As row 2.

Rep these 16 rows.

Rhombus delight

Multiple of 10.

Row 1 (RS): *P1, k1tbl, p1, k1tbl, p1, T2B, k1, T2F; rep from * to end.

Row 2: *P5, k1, p1tbl, k1, p1tbl, k1; rep from * to end.

Row 3: *P1, k1tbl, p1, k1tbl, p1, T2B, k1, T2F; rep from * to end.

Row 4: *K1, p3, k2, p1tbl, k1, p1tbl, k1; rep from * to end.

Row 5: *P1, k1tbl, p1, k1tbl, p2, (k 3rd st on left-hand needle, k 2nd st on left-hand needle, k 1st st on left-hand needle, slip all 3 sts off together), p1; rep from * to end.

Row 6: As row 4.

Rep these 6 rows.

Floating snake pattern

Multiple of 10 + 5.

Special abbreviations:

3-st RC (3-stitch right cross): Sl 2 sts onto cable needle and hold to back, k1, k2 from cable needle.

3-st LC (3-stitch left cross): Sl 1 st onto cable needle and hold to front, k2, k1 from cable needle.

Row 1 (RS): *P2, k1, p2, k1tbl, 3-st RC, k1tbl; rep from * to last 5 sts, p2, k1, p2.

Rows 2 and 4: *K2, p1, k2, wyif sl 1, p3, wyif sl 1; rep from * to last 5 sts, k2, p1, k2.

Row 3: *P2, k1, p2, k1tbl, 3-st LC, k1tbl; rep from * to last 5 sts, p2, k1, p2.

Rep these 4 rows.

Open honeycomb

Multiple of 4 + 1 st for the rim on each edge.

Row 1 (RS): 1 edge st *T2B, T2F; rep from * to last st, 1 edge st.

Row 2 and all even rows: Purl.

Rows 3 and 7: Knit.

Row 5: 1 edge st, *T2F, T2B; rep from * to last st, 1 edge st; rep from * to end.

Row 8: As row 2.

Rep these 8 rows.

Ray of honey

Multiple of 4 + 1 st for the rim on each edge.

Row 1 (RS): 1 edge st *T2B, T2F; rep from * to last st, 1 edge st.

Rows 2 and 4: Purl.

Row 3: 1 edge st, *T2F, T2B; rep from * to last st, 1 edge st.

Rep these 4 rows.

Arched cables

Multiple of 24 + 2.

Row 1 (RS): Knit.

Row 2 and all even rows: K1, p to last st, k1.

Row 3: K1, *C4B, k4, C4F; rep from * to last st, k1.

Row 5: Knit.

Row 7: K3, C4F, C4B, *k4, C4F, C4B; rep from * to last 3 sts, k3.

Row 8: K1, p to last st, k1.

Rep these 8 rows.

Mock cable wide rib

Multiple of 13 + 8.

Row 1 (WS): P8, *k1, p3, k1, p8; rep from * to end.

Row 2: K8, *p1, slip 2 sts, k 3rd st on left-hand needle, k 2nd st, then k 1st st, then sl all 3 sts off left-hand needle, p1, k8; rep from * to end.

Rep these 2 rows.

Centred cables

Panel of 16 sts on a background of rev st st.

Special abbreviations:

T8B rib (twist 8 Back rib) = slip next 4 sts onto cable needle and hold at back of work, k1, p2, k1 from left-hand needle, then k1, p2, k1 from cable needle.

T8F rib (Twist 8 Front rib) = slip next 4 sts onto cable needle and hold at front of work, k1, p2, k1 from left-hand needle, then k1, p2, k1 from cable needle.

Row 1 (RS): K1, p2, [k2, p2] 3 times, k1.

Row 2: P1, k2, [p2, k2] 3 times, p1.

Row 3: T8B rib, T8F rib.

Row 4: As row 2.

Rows 5–14: Rep rows 1–2, 5 times.

Row 15: T8F rib, T8B rib.

Row 16: As row 2.

Rows 17–24: Rep rows 1–2, 4 times.

Rep these 24 rows.

Slipped three-stitch cable

Panel of 3 sts on a background of rev st st.

Slipped to the left:

Row 1 (RS): Sl 1 purlwise, k2.

Row 2: P2, sl 1 purlwise.

Row 3: C3L.

Row 4: Purl.

Rep these 4 rows.

Slipped to the right:

Row 1 (RS): K2, sl 1 purlwise.

Row 2: Sl 1 purlwise, p2.

Row 3: C3R.

Row 4: Purl.

Rep these 4 rows.

Divided circles

Multiple of 28 + 18.

Row 1 (RS): P6, k6, *p4, [k2, p4] 3 times, k6; rep from * to last 6 sts, p6.

Row 2: K6, p6, *k4, p14, k4, p6; rep from * to last 6 sts, k6.

Row 3: P4, T4B, k2, *[T4F, p2] twice, k2, [p2, T4B] twice, k2; rep from * to last 8 sts, T4F, p4.

Row 4: K4, *p10, k4; rep from * to end.

Row 5: P2, T4B, p2, k2, *[p2, T4F] twice, k2, [T4B, p2] twice, k2; rep from * to last 8 sts, p2, T4F, p2.

Row 6: K2, p14, *k4, p6, k4, p14; rep from * to last 2 sts, k2.

Row 7: P2, *[k2, p4] 3 times, k6, p4; rep from * to last 16 sts, k2, [p4, k2] twice, p2.

Row 8: As row 6.

Row 9: P2, T4F, p2, k2, *[p2, T4B] twice, k2, [T4F, p2] twice, k2; rep from * to last 8 sts, p2, T4B, p2.

Row 10: As row 4.

Row 11: P4, T4F, k2, *[T4B, p2] twice, k2, [p2, T4F] twice, k2; rep from * to last 8 sts, T4B, p4.

Row 12: As row 2.

Rep these 12 rows.

Sloping cable

Panel of 10 sts on a background of rev st st.

Note: Increases should be made by knitting into front and back of next st.

Row 1 (WS): K1, p8, k1.

Row 2: P1, yb, sl 1, k1, psso, k4, inc in next st, k1, p1.

Rows 3–9: Rep rows 1–2, 3 times more, then row 1 again.

Row 10: P1, C8F, p1.

Row 11: As row 1.

Row 12: P1, inc in next st, k5, k2tog, p1.

Rows 13–19: Rep rows 11–12, 3 times more, then row 11 again.

Row 20: P1, C8B, p1.

Rep these 20 rows.

Eight-stitch cable

Panel of 8 sts on a background of rev st st.

Row 1 (RS): Knit.

Row 2: Purl.

Row 3: C8B.

Row 4: Purl.

Rows 5–8: Rep rows 1–2 twice more.

Row 9: C8F.

Row 10: Purl.

Rows 11–12: Rep rows 1–2 once.

Rep these 12 rows.

Cable with bobbles

Panel of 9 sts on a background of
rev st st.

Row 1 (RS): P2, T5BP, p2.

Row 2: K2, p2, k1, p2, k2.

Row 3: P1, T3B, p1, T3F, p1.

Row 4: K1, p2, k3, p2, k1.

Row 5: T3B, p3, T3F.

Row 6: P2, k5, p2.

Row 7: K2, p2, MB, p2, k2.

Row 8: As row 6.

Row 9: T3F, p3, T3B.

Row 10: As row 4.

Row 11: P1, T3F, p1, T3B, p1.

Row 12: As row 2.

Rep these 12 rows.

Pillar cable

Panel of 5 sts on a background of
rev st st.

Row 1 (RS): K1, [C2F] twice.

Row 2: P1, [C2BW] twice.

Rep these 2 rows.

5-stitch panel

Horn cable

Panel of 16 sts on a background of
rev st st.

Row 1 (RS): K4, C4B, C4F, k4.

Row 2: P16.

Row 3: K2, C4B, k4, C4F, k2.

Row 4: P16.

Row 5: C4B, k8, C4F.

Row 6: P16.

Rep these 6 rows.

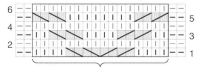

16-stitch panel

Textured cable

Panel of 13 sts on a background of rev st st.

Row 1 (RS): P3, C3B, p1, C3F, p3.

Row 2: K3, p3, k1, p3, k3.

Row 3: P2, C3B, p1, k1, p1, C3F, p2.

Row 4: K2, p3, k1, p1, k1, p3, k2.

Row 5: P1, C3B, p1, [k1, p1] twice, C3F, p1.

Row 6: K1, p3, k1, [p1, k1] twice, p3, k1.

Row 7: C3B, p1, [k1, p1] 3 times, C3F.

Row 8: P3, k1, [p1, k1] 3 times, p3.

Row 9: K2, p1, [k1, p1] 4 times, k2.

Row 10: P2, k1, [p1, k1] 4 times, p2.

Row 11: T3F, p1, [k1, p1] 3 times, T3B.

Row 12: K1, p2, k1, [p1, k1] 3 times, p2, k1.

Row 13: P1, T3F, p1, [k1, p1] twice, T3B, p1.

Row 14: K2, p2, k1, [p1, k1] twice, p2, k2.

Row 15: P2, T3F, p1, k1, p1, T3B, p2.

Row 16: K3, p2, k1, p1, k1, p2, k3.

Row 17: P3, T3F, p1, T3B, p3.

Row 18: K4, p2, k1, p2, k4.

Row 19: P4, C5B, p4.

Row 20: K4, p5, k4.

Rep these 20 rows.

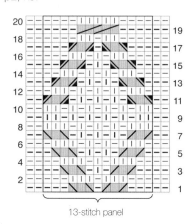

13-stitch panel

Crossroads cable

Panel of 12 sts on a background of rev st st.

Row 1 (RS): P3, T3B, T3F, p3.

Row 2: K3, p2, k2, p2, k3.

Row 3: P2, T3B, p2, T3F, p2.

Row 4: K2, p2, k4, p2, k2.

Row 5: P1, T3B, p4, T3F, p1.

Row 6: K1, p2, k6, p2, k1.

Row 7: T3B, p6, T3F.

Row 8: P2, k8, p2.

Row 9: T3F, p6, T3B.

Row 10: As row 6.

Row 11: P1, T3F, p4, T3B, p1.

Row 12: As row 4.

Row 13: P2, T3F, p2, T3B, p2.

Row 14: As row 2.

Row 15: P3, T3F, T3B, p3.

Row 16: K4, p4, k4.

Row 17: P4, C4B, p4.

Row 18: K4, p4, k4.

Rep these 18 rows.

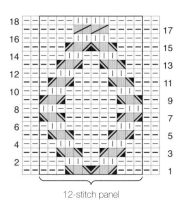

12-stitch panel

Framed cross cable

Panel of 16 sts on a background of rev st st.

Row 1 (RS): K2, p3, T3B, T3F, p3, k2.
Row 2: P2, k3, p2, k2, p2, k3, p2.
Row 3: K2, p2, T3B, p2, T3F, p2, k2.
Row 4: P2, k2, p2, k4, p2, k2, p2.
Row 5: K2, p1, T3B, p4, T3F, p1, k2.
Row 6: P2, k1, p2, k6, p2, k1, p2.
Row 7: K2, T3B, p6, T3F, k2.
Row 8: P4, k8, p4.
Row 9: C4F, p8, C4B.
Row 10: As row 8.
Row 11: K2, T3F, p6, T3B, k2.
Row 12: As row 6.
Row 13: K2, p1, T3F, p4, T3B, p1, k2.
Row 14: As row 4.
Row 15: K2, p2, T3F, p2, T3B, p2, k2.
Row 16: As row 2.
Row 17: K2, p3, T3F, T3B, p3, k2.
Row 18: P2, k4, p4, k4, p2.
Row 19: K2, p4, C4B, p4, k2.
Row 20: As row 18.
Rep these 20 rows.

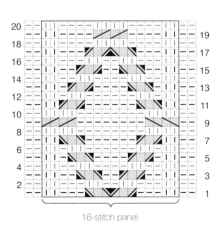

16-stitch panel

Open and closed cable I

Panel of 8 sts on a background of rev st st.

Special abbreviations:
T6F rib (Twist 6 Front rib) = slip next 3 sts onto cable needle and hold at front of work, k1, p1, k1 from left-hand needle, then k1, p1, k1 from cable needle.
T4R rib (Twist 4 Right rib) = slip next st onto cable needle and hold at back of work, k1, p1, k1 from left-hand needle, then p1 from cable needle.
T4L rib (Twist 4 Left rib) = slip next 3 sts onto cable needle and hold at front of work, p1 from left-hand needle, then k1, p1, k1 from cable needle.

Row 1 (RS): P1, k1, p1, k2, p1, k1, p1.
Row 2: K1, p1, k1, p2, k1, p1, k1.
Row 3: P1, T6F rib, p1.
Row 4: As row 2.
Row 5: T4R rib, T4L rib.
Row 6: P1, k1, p1, k2, p1, k1, p1.
Row 7: K1, p1, k1, p2, k1, p1, k1.
Rows 8–12: Rep the last 2 rows twice more, then row 6 again.
Row 13: T4L rib, T4R rib.
Rows 14–16: As rows 2–4.
Rows 17–18: As rows 1–2.
Rep these 18 rows.

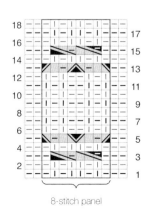

8-stitch panel

Smocking stitch pattern

Multiple of 8 + 7.

Row 1 (RS): P1, k1, *p3, k1; rep from * to last st, p1.

Row 2: K1, p1, *k3, p1; rep from * to last st, k1.

Row 3 (smocking row): P1, slip next 5 sts onto cable needle and hold at front of work, wind yarn twice around sts on cable needle in an anti-clockwise direction then work the sts from the cable needle as follows: k1, p3, k1 (this will now be called 'smock 5'), *p3, smock 5; rep from * to last st, p1.

Rows 4–8: Rep row 2, then rows 1–2 twice more.

Row 9: P1, k1, p3, *smock 5, p3; rep from * to last 2 sts, k1, p1.

Row 10: As row 2.

Rows 11–12: As rows 1–2.

Repeat these 12 rows.

Note: This method creates a small gap in the work at either side of the smocked stitches. The technique can be adapted to any rib pattern, provided the stitches on the cable needle begin and end with a knit stitch. The number of rows between the smocked stitches can also be varied as required.

Fuchsia stitch

Multiple of 6.

Note: Stiches should only be counted after rows 11–12.

Row 1 (RS): P2, *k2, yf, p4; rep from * to last 4 sts, k2, yf, p2.

Row 2: K2, *p3, k4; rep from * to last 5 sts, p3, k2.

Row 3: P2, *k3, yf, p4; rep from * to last 5 sts, k3, yf, p2.

Row 4: K2, *p4, k4; rep from * to last 6 sts, p4, k2.

Row 5: P2, *k4, yf, p4; rep from * to last 6 sts, k4, yf, p2.

Row 6: K2, *p5, k4; rep from * to last 7 sts, p5, k2.

Row 7: P2, *k3, k2tog, p4; rep from * to last 7 sts, k3, k2tog, p2.

Row 8: As row 4.

Row 9: P2, *k2, k2tog, p4; rep from * to last 6 sts, k2, k2tog, p2.

Row 10: As row 2.

Row 11: P2, *k1, k2tog, p4; rep from * to last 5 sts, k1, k2tog, p2.

Row 12: K2, *p2, k4; rep from * to last 4 sts, p2, k2.

Rep these 12 rows.

Defined diamonds

Multiple of 8 + 10.

Row 1 (RS): P3, C4B, *p4, C4B; rep from * to last 3 sts, p3.

Row 2: K3, p4, *k4, p4; rep from * to last 3 sts, k3.

Row 3: P1, *T4B, T4F; rep from * to last st, p1.

Row 4: K1, p2, k4, *p4, k4; rep from * to last 3 sts, p2, k1.

Row 5: P1, k2, p4, *C4B, p4; rep from * to last 3 sts, k2, p1.

Row 6: As row 4.

Row 7: P1, *T4F, T4B; rep from * to last st, p1.

Row 8: As row 2.

Rep these 8 rows.

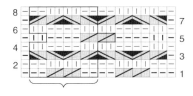

8-stitch repeat

Cable with stripes

Multiple of 13 + 1.

Row 1 (RS): P1, [k1, p1] twice, T2B, T2F, *p1, [k1, p1] 4 times, T2B, T2F; rep from * to last 5 sts, p1, [k1, p1] twice.

Row 2: [K1, p1] 3 times, k2, *p1, [k1, p1] 5 times, k2; rep from * to last 6 sts, [p1, k1] 3 times.

Row 3: P1, [k1, p1] twice, T2F, T2B, *p1, [k1, p1] 4 times, T2F, T2B; rep from * to last 5 sts, p1, [k1, p1] twice.

Row 4: [K1, p1] twice, k2, p2, k2, *p1, [k1, p1] 3 times, k2, p2, k2; rep from * to last 4 sts, [p1, k1] twice.

Row 5: [P1, k1] twice, p2, C2B, p2, *k1, [p1, k1] 3 times, p2, C2B, p2; rep from * to last 4 sts, [k1, p1] twice.

Row 6: As row 4.

Rep these 6 rows.

13-stitch repeat

Four-section cable

Panel of 7 sts on a background of rev st st.

Special abbreviation:

T7B rib (Twist 7 Back rib) = slip next 4 sts onto cable needle and hold at back of work, k1, p1, k1 from left-hand needle, then [p1, k1] twice from cable needle.

Row 1 (RS): K1, [p1, k1] 3 times.

Row 2: PB1, [k1, PB1] 3 times.

Row 3: T7B rib.

Row 4: As row 2.

Rows 5–10: Rep rows 1–2, 3 times.

Rep these 10 rows.

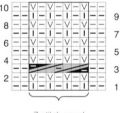

7-stitch panel

Medallion moss cable

Panel of 13 sts on a background of rev st st.

Row 1 (RS): K4, [p1, k1] 3 times, k3.

Row 2: P3, [k1, p1] 4 times, p2.

Rows 3–4: Rep rows 1–2 once more.

Row 5: C6F, k1, C6B.

Row 6: Purl.

Row 7: Knit.

Rep last 2 rows twice.

Row 12: Purl.

Row 13: C6B, k1, C6F.

Row 14: As row 2.

Row 15: As row 1.

Row 16: As row 2.

Rep these 16 rows.

Bold cable

Panel of 6 sts on a background of rev st st.

Row 1 (RS): K6.

Row 2: P6.

Row 3: C6B.

Row 4: P6.

Rows 5–8: Rep rows 1–2 twice.

Row 9: C6F.

Row 10: P6.

Rows 11–12: As rows 1–2.

Rep these 12 rows.

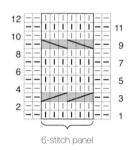

6-stitch panel

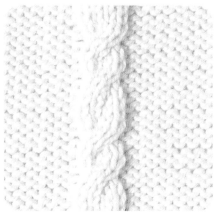

Six-stitch spiral cable

Panel of 6 sts on a background of rev st st.

Row 1 (RS): [C2F] 3 times.

Row 2: Purl.

Row 3: K1, [C2F] twice, k1.

Row 4: Purl.

Rep these 4 rows.

Climbing cable

Panel of 4 sts on a background of rev st st.

Row 1 (RS): K4.

Row 2: P4.

Row 3: C4B.

Row 4: P4.

Rows 5–8: Rep rows 1–4 once more.

Rows 9–12: Rep rows 1–2 twice.

Rep these 12 rows.

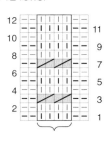

4-stitch panel

Alternated cable

Worked over 10 sts on a background of rev st st.

Row 1 (RS): P1, k8, p1.

Row 2: K1, p8, k1.

Row 3: P1, C4B, C4F, p1.

Row 4: K1, p2, k4, p2, k1.

Row 5: T3B, p4, T3F.

Row 6: P2, k6, p2.

Row 7: K2, p6, k2.

Rows 8–10: Rep rows 6–7 once more, then row 6 again.

Row 11: T3F, p4, T3B.

Row 12: As row 4.

Row 13: P1, C4F, C4B, p1.

Row 14: K1, p8, k1.

Row 15: P1, C4B, C4F, p1.

Row 16: K1, p8, k1.

Row 17: P1, k8, p1.

Rows 18–20: Rep rows 14–16 once more.

Rep these 20 rows.

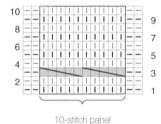

Honeycomb pattern

Worked over a multiple of 8 sts. The example shown is worked over 24 sts.

Row 1 (RS): *C4B, C4F; rep from * to end of panel.
Row 2: Purl.
Row 3: Knit.
Row 4: Purl.
Row 5: *C4F, C4B; rep from * to end of panel.
Row 6: Purl.
Row 7: Knit.
Row 8: Purl.
Rep these 8 rows.

Chunky cable

Panel of 10 sts on a background of rev st st.

Row 1 (RS): K10.
Row 2: P10.
Row 3: C10F.
Row 4: P10.
Rows 5–10: Rep rows 1–2, 3 times.
Rep these 10 rows.

10-stitch panel

Slipped double chain

Worked over 7 sts.

Row 1 (RS): Sl 1 purlwise, k5, sl 1 purlwise.
Row 2: Sl 1 purlwise, p5, sl 1 purlwise.
Row 3: C3L, k1, C3R.
Row 4: Purl.
Row 5: K2, sl 1 purlwise, k1, sl 1 purlwise, k2.
Row 6: P2, sl 1 purlwise, p1, sl 1 purlwise, p2.
Row 7: C3R, k1, C3L.
Row 8: Purl.
Rep these 8 rows.

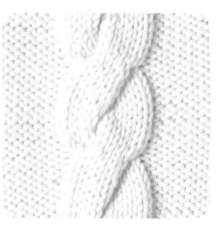

Small moss stitch cable

Panel of 5 sts on a background of rev st st.

Row 1 (WS): [P1, k1] twice, p1.

Row 2: K2, p1, k2.

Rows 3–5: Rep rows 1–2 once more, then row 1 again.

Row 6: Slip next st onto cable needle and hold at front of work, slip next 3 sts onto 2nd cable needle and hold at back of work, knit next st from left-hand needle, knit the 3 sts from 2nd cable needle, then knit st from 1st cable needle.

Rows 7–11: Work 5 rows in st st, starting with purl.

Row 12: As row 6.

Rows 13–16: Work rows 1–2 twice more.

Rep these 16 rows.

Roman cable

Panel of 4 sts on a background of rev st st.

Row 1 (RS): C2B, C2F.

Row 2: P4.

Rep these 2 rows.

4-stitch panel

Tulip cable

Panel of 12 sts on a background of rev st st.

Row 1 (RS): K12.

Row 2: P12.

Row 3: C12B.

Row 4: P12.

Rows 5–12: Rep rows 1–2, 4 times.

Rep these 12 rows.

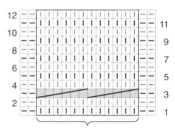

12-stitch panel

Garden path cable

Panel of 6 sts on a background of
rev st st.

Row 1 (RS): K2, C4F.

Row 2: P6.

Row 3: K6.

Row 4: P6.

Rows 5–6: As rows 1–2.

Row 7: C4B, k2.

Row 8: P6.

Rows 9–10: As rows 3–4.

Rows 11–12: As rows 7–8.

Rep these 12 rows.

Country lane cable

Panel of 10 sts on a background of
rev st st.

Row 1 (RS): K10.

Row 2: P10.

Row 3: C10F.

Row 4: P10.

Rows 5–12: Rep rows 1–2, 4 times.

Row 13: C10B.

Row 14: P10.

Rows 15–20: Rep rows 1–2, 3 times.

Rep these 20 rows.

Stacked cable

Panel of 8 sts on a background of
rev st st.

Row 1 (RS): K8.

Row 2: P8.

Row 3: C4B, C4F.

Row 4: P8.

Rep these 4 rows.

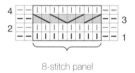

8-stitch panel

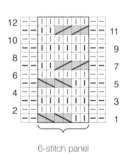

6-stitch panel

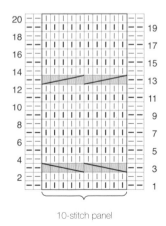

10-stitch panel

Cabled moss stitch

Panel of 13 sts on a background of rev st st.

Row 1 (RS): P3, T3B, k1, T3F, p3.
Row 2: K3, p2, k1, p1, k1, p2, k3.
Row 3: P2, T3B, k1, p1, k1, T3F, p2.
Row 4: K2, p2, [k1, p1] twice, k1, p2, k2.
Row 5: P1, T3B, [k1, p1] twice, k1, T3F, p1.
Row 6: K1, p2, [k1, p1] 3 times, k1, p2, k1.
Row 7: T3B, [k1, p1] 3 times, k1, T3F.
Row 8: P2, [k1, p1] 4 times, k1, p2.
Row 9: K3, [p1, k1] 3 times, p1, k3.
Row 10: P3, [k1, p1] 3 times, k1, p3.
Row 11: T3F, [k1, p1] 3 times, k1, T3B.
Row 12: K1, p3, [k1, p1] twice, k1, p3, k1.
Row 13: P1, T3F, [k1, p1] twice, k1, T3B, p1.
Row 14: K2, p3, k1, p1, k1, p3, k2.
Row 15: P2, T3F, k1, p1, k1, T3B, p2.
Row 16: K3, p3, k1, p3, k3.
Row 17: P3, T3F, k1, T3B, p3.
Row 18: K4, p5, k4.
Row 19: P4, T5R, p4.
Row 20: K4, p2, k1, p2, k4.
Row 21: P3, T3B, p1, T3F, p3.
Row 22: [K3, p2] twice, k3.
Row 23: [P3, k2] twice, p3.
Row 24: As row 22.
Row 25: P3, T3F, p1, T3B, p3.
Row 26: As row 20.
Row 27: As row 19.
Row 28: As row 20.
Rep these 28 rows.

Open and closed cable II

Panel of 18 sts on a background of rev st st.

Row 1 (RS): P5, C4B, C4F, p5.
Row 2: K5, p2, k4, p2, k5.
Row 3: P4, T3B, p4, T3F, p4.
Row 4: K4, p2, k6, p2, k4.
Row 5: P3, T3B, p6, T3F, p3.
Row 6: K3, p2, k8, p2, k3.
Row 7: P2, T3B, p8, T3F, p2.
Row 8: K2, p2, k10, p2, k2.
Row 9: P1, T3B, p10, T3F, p1.
Row 10: K1, p2, k12, p2, k1.
Row 11: T3B, p12, T3F.
Row 12: P2, k14, p2.
Row 13: K2, p14, k2.
Rows 14–16: Rep rows 12–13 once more, then row 12 again.
Row 17: T3F, p12, T3B.
Row 18: As row 10.
Row 19: P1, T3F, p10, T3B, p1.
Row 20: As row 8.
Row 21: P2, T3F, p8, T3B, p2.
Row 22: As row 6.
Row 23: P3, T3F, p6, T3B, p3.
Row 24: As row 4.
Row 25: P4, T3F, p4, T3B, p4.
Row 26: As row 2.
Row 27: P5, C4F, C4B, p5.
Row 28: K5, p8, k5.
Row 29: P5, C4B, C4F, p5.
Row 30: As row 28.
Row 31: P5, k8, p5.
Rows 32–39: Rep rows 28–31 twice more.
Row 40: As row 28.
Rep these 40 rows.

Twisted eyelet cable

Panel of 8 sts on a background of rev st st.

Row 1 (RS): Knit.

Row 2 and every alt row: Purl.

Row 3: K2, yf, slip next 2 sts onto cable needle and hold at front of work, k2tog from left-hand needle, then k2tog from cable needle, yf, k2.

Row 5: Knit.

Row 7: C3F, k2, C3B.

Row 9: K1, C3F, C3B, k1.

Row 10: Purl.

Rep these 10 rows.

Cable with horn detail

Panel of 6 sts on a background of rev st st.

Row 1 (RS): K1, C2B, C2F, k1.

Row 2: P6.

Row 3: C2B, k2, C2F.

Row 4: P6.

Rep these 4 rows.

6-stitch panel

Large woven cable

Panel of 20 sts on a background of rev st st.

Row 1 (RS): K20.

Row 2: P20.

Row 3: K4, [C8F] twice.

Row 4: P20.

Rows 5–8: Rep rows 1–2 twice.

Row 9: [C8B] twice, k4.

Row 10: P20.

Rows 11–12: As rows 1–2.

Rep these 12 rows.

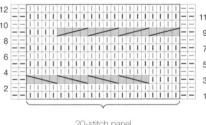

20-stitch panel

Cable and dot

Panel of 15 sts on a background of rev st st.

Row 1 (WS): K2, k into front, back, front, back and front of next st (bobble made), k2, p2, k1, p2, k2, make bobble in next st as before, k2.
Row 2: P2, k5tog tbl (completing bobble), p2, C5F, p2, k5tog tbl, p2.
Row 3: K5, p2, k1, p2, k5.
Row 4: P4, T3B, p1, T3F, p4.
Row 5: K4, p2, k3, p2, k4.
Row 6: P3, T3B, p3, T3F, p3.
Row 7: K3, p2, k2, make bobble in next st (as on row 1), k2, p2, k3.
Row 8: P2, T3B, p2, k5tog tbl, p2, T3F, p2.
Row 9: K2, p2, k7, p2, k2.
Row 10: P1, T3B, p7, T3F, p1.
Row 11: K1, p2, k2, make bobble in next st, k3, make bobble in next st, k2, p2, k1.
Row 12: T3B, p2, k5tog tbl, p3, k5tog tbl, p2, T3F.
Row 13: P2, k11; p2.
Row 14: K2, p11, k2.
Row 15: P2, k3, make bobble in next st, k3, make bobble in next st, k3, p2.
Row 16: T3F, p2, k5tog tbl, p3, k5tog tbl, p2, T3B.
Row 17: K1, p2, k9, p2, k1.
Row 18: P1, T3F, p7, T3B, p1.
Row 19: K2, p2, k3, make bobble in next st, k3, p2, k2.
Row 20: P2, T3F, p2, k5tog tbl, p2, T3B, p2.
Row 21: K3, p2, k5, p2, k3.
Row 22: P3, T3F, p3, T3B, p3.
Row 23: K4, p2, k3, p2, k4.
Row 24: P4, T3F, p1, T3B, p4.
Rep these 24 rows.
Note: The cable as given here twists to the left. To work the cable twisted to the right, work C5B instead of C5F on row 2.

Free cable

Panel of 7 sts on a background of rev st st.

Row 1 (RS): [T2F] twice, p3.
Row 2: K3, [PB1, k1] twice.
Row 3: P1, [T2F] twice, p2.
Row 4: K2, PB1, k1, PB1, k2.
Row 5: P2, [T2F] twice, p1.
Row 6: [K1, PB1] twice, k3.
Row 7: P3, [T2F] twice.
Row 8: PB1, k1, PB1, k4.
Row 9: P4, k1, p1, k1.
Row 10: As row 8.
Row 11: P3, [T2B] twice.
Row 12: As row 6.
Row 13: P2, [T2B] twice, p1.
Row 14: As row 4.
Row 15: P1, [T2B] twice, p2.
Row 16: As row 2.
Row 17: [T2B] twice, p3.
Row 18: K4, PB1, k1, PB1.
Row 19: K1, p1, k1, p4.
Row 20: As row 18.
Rep these 20 rows.

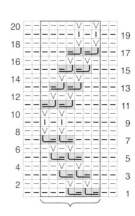

7-stitch panel

Raised circle cable

Panel of 4 sts on a background of rev st st.

Row 1 (RS): C2B, C2F.

Row 2: P4.

Row 3: C2F, C2B.

Row 4: P4.

Rep these 4 rows.

4-stitch panel

Small raised circle cable

Panel of 4 sts on a background of rev st st.

Row 1 (RS): C2B, C2F.

Row 2: P4.

Rows 3–4: Rep rows 1–2 once more.

Row 5: C2F, C2B.

Row 6: P4.

Rows 7–8: Rep rows 5–6 once more.

Rep these 8 rows.

4-stitch panel

Tip

When working on complex patterns, you may find it helpful to place markers to denote the beginning and end of pattern repeats (or every 20 stitches or so if a single repeat contains a lot of stiches). This may be particularly helpful, for example, when setting a cable panel against an otherwise plain knitted background.

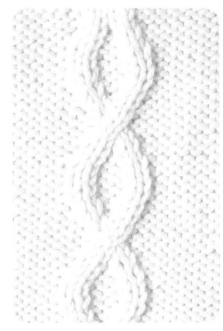

Tight braid cable

Panel of 10 sts on a background of rev st st.

Row 1 (WS): Purl.
Row 2: K2, [C4F] twice.
Row 3: Purl.
Row 4: [C4B] twice, k2.
Rep these 4 rows.

Folded cable

Panel of 10 sts on a background of rev st st.

Row 1 (RS): K10.
Row 2: P10.
Row 3: C10B.
Row 4: P10.
Rows 5–8: Rep rows 1–2 twice.
Row 9: K2, C6B, k2.
Row 10: P10.
Rows 11–14: Rep rows 1–2 twice.
Rows 15–16: As rows 9–10.
Rows 17–18: As rows 1–2.
Rep these 18 rows.

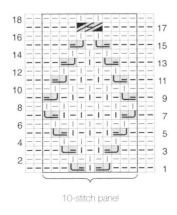

10-stitch panel

Linking ovals

Panel of 8 sts on a background of rev st st.

Row 1 (RS): P2, C4B, p2.
Row 2: K2, p4, k2.
Row 3: P1, T3B, T3F, p1.
Row 4: K1, p2, k2, p2, k1.
Row 5: T3B, p2, T3F.
Row 6: P2, k4, p2.
Row 7: K2, p4, k2.
Row 8: P2, k4, p2.
Row 9: T3F, p2, T3B.
Row 10: K1, p2, k2, p2, k1.
Row 11: P1, T3F, T3B, p1.
Row 12: K2, p4, k2.
Rep these 12 rows.

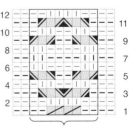

8-stitch panel

Propellor cable

Panel of 6 sts on a background of
rev st st.

Row 1 (RS): K6.

Row 2: P6.

Row 3: C6F.

Row 4: P6.

Rows 5–10: Rep rows 1–2 once, then rep
rows 1–4 once.

Rows 11–20: Rep rows 1–2, 5 times.

Rep these 20 rows.

Lace cable pattern

Panel of 8 sts on a background of
rev st st.

Row 1 (RS): K2, yf, sl 1, k1, psso, k4.

Row 2 and every alt row: Purl.

Row 3: K3, yf, sl 1, k1, psso, k3.

Row 5: K4, yf, sl 1, k1, psso, k2.

Row 7: K5, yf, sl 1, k1, psso, k1.

Row 9: C6B, yf, sl 1, k1, psso.

Row 10: Purl.

Rep these 10 rows.

Cable with braid

Panel of 6 sts on a background of
rev st st.

Row 1 (RS): K2, C4F.

Row 2: P6.

Row 3: C4B, k2.

Row 4: P6.

Rep these 4 rows.

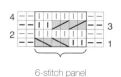

6-stitch panel

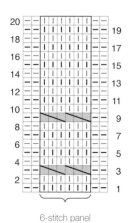

6-stitch panel

Cable fabric

Multiple of 6.

Row 1: Knit.

Row 2 and every alt row: Purl.

Row 3: *K2, C4B; rep from * to end.

Row 5: Knit.

Row 7: *C4F, k2; rep from * to end.

Row 8: Purl.

Rep these 8 rows.

Sweeping cable

Panel of 8 sts on a background of rev st st.

Row 1 (RS): K8.

Row 2: P8.

Row 3: C8B.

Row 4: P8.

Rows 5–8: Rep rows 1–2 twice.

Rep these 8 rows.

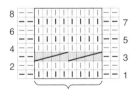

8-stitch panel

Tip

Cable patterns are very attractive, so why not make your tension
swatches into a feature by framing them? Cast on an additional 8
stitches to your swatch, keeping 4 stitches at the beginning and end of
each row in garter stitch. This will will give a border to the swatch and
prevent it from rolling. It also makes measuring the swatch easier.

Open cable

Panel of 7 sts on a background of rev st st.

Row 1 (RS): K7.

Row 2: P7.

Row 3: C3R, k1, C3L.

Row 4: P7.

Rep these 4 rows.

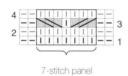

7-stitch panel

Medium circle cable

Panel of 8 sts on a background of rev st st.

Row 1 (RS): K8.

Row 2 and every alt row: P8.

Row 3: C4B, C4F.

Row 5: K8.

Row 7: C4F, C4B.

Row 8: P8.

Rep these 8 rows.

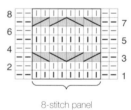

8-stitch panel

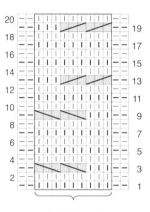

Vine cable

Panel of 9 sts on a background of rev st st.

Row 1 (RS): K9.
Row 2: P9.
Row 3: K3, C6F.
Row 4: P9.
Rows 5–10: Rep rows 1–2 twice, then rep rows 3–4 once.
Rows 11–12: As rows 1–2.
Row 13: C6B, k3.
Row 14: P9.
Rows 15–18: Rep rows 1–2 twice.
Rows 19–20: As rows 13–14.
Rep these 20 rows.

9-stitch panel

Divided cable I

Panel of 12 sts on a background of rev st st.

Row 1 (RS): [K1, p1] 4 times, T4B.
Row 2: K1, p3, [k1, p1] 4 times.
Row 3: [K1, p1] 3 times, T4B, T2F.
Row 4: P1, k2, p3, [k1, p1] 3 times.
Row 5: [K1, p1] twice, T4B, T2F, T2B.
Row 6: K1, C2BW, k2, p3, [k1, p1] twice.
Row 7: K1, p1, T4B, T2F, T2B, T2F.
Row 8: P1, k2, C2FW, k2, p3, k1, p1.
Row 9: T4B, [T2F, T2B] twice.
Row 10: K1, C2BW, k2, C2BW, k3, p2.
Row 11: T4FP, [T2B, T2F] twice.
Row 12: As row 8.
Row 13: K1, p1, T4FP, T2B, T2F, T2B.
Row 14: As row 6.
Row 15: [K1, p1] twice, T4FP, T2B, T2F.
Row 16: As row 4.
Row 17: [K1, p1] 3 times, T4FP, T2B.
Row 18: As row 2.
Row 19: [K1, p1] 4 times, T4FP.
Row 20: P2, [k1, p1] 5 times.
Rep these 20 rows.

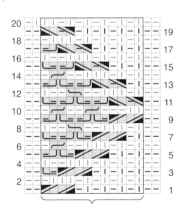

12-stitch panel

Overlapping cable

Panel of 6 sts on a background of rev st st.

Row 1 (RS): K6.

Row 2: P6.

Row 3: C6B.

Row 4: P6.

Rows 5–6: As rows 1–2.

Row 7: K1, C4B, k1.

Row 8: P6.

Rows 9–12: Rep the last 4 rows once more.

Rep these 12 rows.

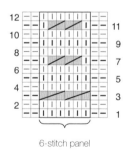

6-stitch panel

Raised curve cable

Panel of 4 sts on a background of rev st st.

Row 1 (RS): K4.

Row 2 and every alt row: P4.

Row 3: C4B.

Row 5: K4.

Row 7: C4F.

Row 8: P4.

Rep these 8 rows.

4-stitch panel

Large circle cable

Panel of 12 sts on a background of rev st st.

Row 1 (RS): K12.

Row 2: P12.

Row 3: C6B, C6F.

Row 4: P12.

Rows 5–8: Rep rows 1–2 twice.

Row 9: C6F, C6B.

Row 10: P12.

Rows 11–12: As rows 1–2.

Rep these 12 rows.

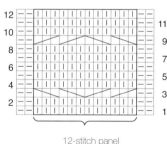

12-stitch panel

Disappearing cable

Panel of 18 sts on a background of rev st st.

Row 1 (RS): P6, k6, p6.
Row 2: K6, p6, k6.
Row 3: P3, k3, C6F, k3, p3.
Row 4: K3, p12, k3.
Row 5: P3, k12, p3.
Rows 6–8: Rep rows 4–5 once more, then row 4 again.
Row 9: K3, T6B, T6F, k3.
Row 10: P6, k6, p6.
Row 11: K6, p6, k6.
Rows 12–14: Rep rows 10–11 once more, then row 10 again.
Row 15: T6B, p6, T6F.
Row 16: P3, k12, p3.
Row 17: K3, p12, k3.
Rows 18–20: Rep rows 16–17 once more, then row 16 again.
Row 21: C6F, p6, C6B.
Rows 22–26: Rep rows 10–11 twice, then row 10 again.
Row 27: P3, C6F, C6B, p3.
Rows 28–32: Rep rows 4–5 twice, then row 4 again.
Row 33: P6, C6F, p6.
Row 34: As row 2.
Row 35: As row 1.
Row 36: As row 2.
Rep these 36 rows.

Divided cable II

Panel of 12 sts on a background of rev st st.

Row 1 (RS): T4F, [p1, k1] 4 times.
Row 2: [P1, k1] 4 times, p3, k1.
Row 3: T2B, T4F, [p1, k1] 3 times.
Row 4: [P1, k1] 3 times, p3, k2, p1.
Row 5: T2F, T2B, T4F, [p1, k1] twice.
Row 6: [P1, k1] twice, p3, k2, C2FW, k1.
Row 7: T2B, T2F, T2B, T4F, p1, k1.
Row 8: P1, k1, p3, k2, C2BW, k2, p1.
Row 9: [T2F, T2B] twice, T4F.
Row 10: P2, k3, C2FW, k2, C2FW, k1.
Row 11: [T2B, T2F] twice, T4BP.
Row 12: As row 8.
Row 13: T2F, T2B, T2F, T4BP, p1, k1.
Row 14: As row 6.
Row 15: T2B, T2F, T4BP, [p1, k1] twice.
Row 16: As row 4.
Row 17: T2F, T4BP, [p1, k1] 3 times.
Row 18: As row 2.
Row 19: T4BP, [p1, k1] 4 times.
Row 20: [P1, k1] 5 times, p2.
Rep these 20 rows.

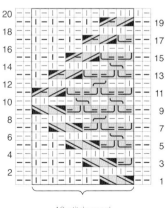

12-stitch panel

Bulky cable

Panel of 6 sts on a background of rev st st.

Row 1 (RS): K6.
Row 2: P6.
Row 3: C6B.
Row 4: P6.
Rep these 4 rows.

6-stitch panel

Twelve-stitch braid

Panel of 12 sts on a background of rev st st.

Row 1 (RS): K12.
Row 2: P12.
Row 3: K4, C8B.
Row 4: P12.
Rows 5–6: As rows 1–2.
Row 7: C8F, k4.
Row 8: P12.
Rep these 8 rows.

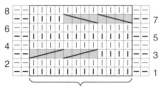

12-stitch panel

Checkered cable

Panel with a multiple of 4 + 2.
Example shown is worked over 10 sts on a background of rev st st.

Row 1 (RS): K2, *C4F; rep from * to end.
Row 2: Purl.
Row 3: *C4B; rep from * to last 2 sts, k2.
Row 4: Purl.
Rep these 4 rows.

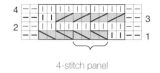

4-stitch panel

Tip

You will probably find a cable needle a very useful item when working with cable or aran stitches (although you can make do with a straight double-pointed needle if you don't have a dedicated cable needle). The cable needle should be about the same size or smaller than the working needles; don't use a larger size as this makes it difficult to knit from after the stitches are crossed.

Lattice pattern I

Multiple of 4 + 6.

Row 1 (RS): P1, *T2F, T2B; rep from * to last st, p1.

Row 2: K2, *C2BW, k2; rep from * to end.

Row 3: P1, *T2B, T2F; rep from * to last st, p1.

Row 4: K1, p1, k2, *C2FW, k2; rep from * to last 2 sts, p1, k1.

Rep these 4 rows.

4-stitch repeat

Trophy cable I

Panel of 16 sts on a background of rev st st.

Row 1 (RS): K16.

Row 2: P16.

Row 3: C8B, C8F.

Row 4: P16.

Rows 5–8: Rep rows 1–2 twice.

Rep these 8 rows.

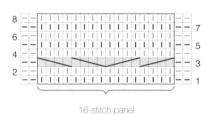

16-stitch panel

Open bobble pattern

Multiple of 4 +2.

Row 1 (RS): Purl.

Row 2: K1, *M3, k3tog; rep from * to last st, k1.

Row 3: Purl.

Row 4: K1, *k3tog, M3; rep from * to last st, k1.

Rep these 4 rows.

4-stitch repeat

Filled oval cable

Panel of 8 sts on a background of rev st st.

Row 1 (RS): K8.

Row 2: P8.

Row 3: C8B.

Row 4: P8.

Rows 5–6: As rows 1–2.

Row 7: K2, C4B, k2.

Row 8: P8.

Rows 9–12: Rep the last 4 rows once more.

Rep these 12 rows.

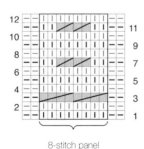

8-stitch panel

Bell cable

Worked over 26 sts on a background of rev st st.

Row 1 (RS): K2, [p3, k2] twice, p2, [k2, p3] twice, k2.

Row 2: P2, [k3, p2] twice, k2, p2, [k3, p2] twice.

Rows 3–10: Rep rows 1–2, 4 times more.

Row 11: T5L, k2, T5R, p2, T5L, k2, T5R.

Row 12: K3, p6, k8, p6, k3.

Row 13: P3, k6, p8, k6, p3.

Rows 14–18: Rep rows 12–13 twice more, then row 12 again.

Row 19: P3, C6F, p8, C6B, p3.

Row 20: K3, p6, k8, p6, k3.

Rep these 20 rows.

Trophy cable II

Panel of 20 sts on a background of rev st st.

Row 1 (RS): K20.

Row 2: P20.

Row 3: C10B, C10F.

Row 4: P20.

Rows 5–12: Rep rows 1–2, 4 times.

Rep these 12 rows.

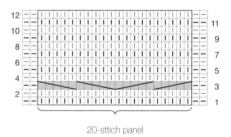

20-sttich panel

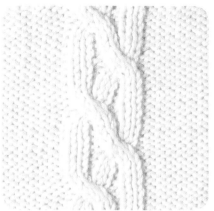

Touching paths

Panel of 9 sts on a background of rev st st.

Row 1 (RS): P3, T4B, k2.
Row 2: P2, k2, p2, k3.
Row 3: P1, T4B, p1, T3B.
Row 4: K1, p2, k3, p2, k1.
Row 5: T3B, p1, T4B, p1.
Row 6: K3, p2, k2, p2.
Row 7: K2, T4B, p3.
Row 8: K5, p4.
Row 9: C4B, p5.
Row 10: K5, p4.
Row 11: K2, T4F, p3.
Row 12: As row 6.
Row 13: T3F, p1, T4F, p1.
Row 14: As row 4.
Row 15: P1, T4F, p1, T3F.
Row 16: As row 2.
Row 17: P3, T4F, k2.
Row 18: P4, k5.
Row 19: P5, C4B.
Row 20: P4, k5.
Rep these 20 rows.

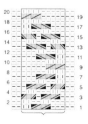

9-stitch panel

Crossing paths

Panel of 10 sts on a background of rev st st.

Special abbreviation:

T6L rib (Twist 6 Left rib) = slip next 4 sts onto cable needle and hold at front of work, knit next 2 sts from left-hand needle, slip the 2 purl sts from cable needle back to left-hand needle and purl them, then knit 2 sts from cable needle.

Row 1 (RS): K2, [p2, k2] twice.
Row 2: P2, [k2, p2] twice.
Row 3: T6L rib, p2, k2.
Row 4: As row 2.
Rows 5–8: Rep rows 1–2 twice.
Row 9: K2, p2, T6L rib.
Row 10: As row 2.
Rows 11–12: As rows 1–2.
Rep these 12 rows.

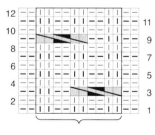

10-stitch panel

Interlocking cable

Panel of 12 sts on a background of rev st st.

Row 1 (RS): K12.
Row 2: P12.
Row 3: C6B, C6F.
Row 4: P12.
Rows 5–8: Rep rows 1–2 twice.
Rows 9–10: As rows 3–4 rows.
Rows 11–14: Rep rows 1–2 twice.
Row 15: C6F, C6B.
Row 16: P12.
Rows 17–20: Rep rows 1–2 twice.
Rows 21–22: As rows 15–16.
Rows 23–24: As rows 1–2.
Rep these 24 rows.

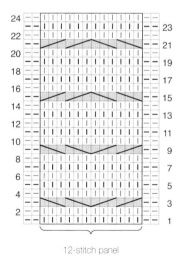

12-stitch panel

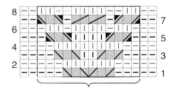

Inserted cable

Panel of 14 sts on a background of rev st st.

Row 1 (WS): K5, p4, k5.
Row 2: P5, C4F, p5.
Row 3: K5, p4, k5.
Row 4: P4, T3B, T3F, p4.
Row 5: K4, p2, k2, p2, k4.
Row 6: P3, T3B, p2, T3F, p3.
Row 7: K3, p2, k4, p2, k3.
Row 8: P2, T3B, p4, T3F, p2.
Row 9: K2, p2, k6, p2, k2.
Row 10: P1, [T3B] twice, [T3F] twice, p1.
Row 11: [K1, p2] twice, k2, [p2, k1] twice.
Row 12: [T3B] twice, p2, [T3F] twice.
Row 13: P2, k1, p2, k4, p2, k1, p2.
Row 14: K1, T2F, T3F, p2, T3B, T2B, k1.
Row 15: [P1, k1] twice, p2, k2, p2, [k1, p1] twice.
Row 16: K1, p1, T2F, T3F, T3B, T2B, p1, k1.
Row 17: P1, k2, p1, k1, p4, k1, p1, k2, p1.
Row 18: T2F, T2B, p1, C4F, p1, T2F, T2B.
Row 19: K1, C2B, k2, p4, k2, C2F, k1.
Rows 20–35: Rep rows 4–18.
Rep these 35 rows.

Dancing cable

Panel of 16 sts on a background of rev st st.

Row 1 (RS): P2, C4F, p4, C4F, p2.
Row 2: K2, p4, k4, p4, k2.
Row 3: P2, k4, p4, k4, p2.
Row 4: As row 2.
Rows 5–6: As rows 1–2.
Row 7: [T4B, T4F] twice.
Row 8: P2, k4, p4, k4, p2.
Row 9: K2, p4, C4F, p4, k2.
Row 10: As Row 8.
Row 11: K2, p4, k4, p4, k2.
Row 12: As row 8.
Rows 13–22: Rep rows 9–12 twice more, then rows 9–10 again.
Row 23: [T4F, T4B] twice.
Row 24: As row 2.
Rep these 24 rows.

Open V-stitch

Panel of 12 sts on a background of rev st st.

Row 1 (RS): P3, C3B, C3F, p3.
Row 2: K3, p6, k3.
Row 3: P2, C3B, k2, C3F, p2.
Row 4: K2, p8, k2.
Row 5: P1, T3B, k4, T3F, p1.
Row 6: K1, p2, k1, p4, k1, p2, k1.
Row 7: T3B, p1, C4B, p1, T3F.
Row 8: P2, k2, p4, k2, p2.
Rep these 8 rows.

12-stitch panel

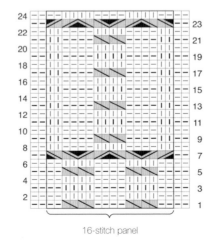

16-stitch panel

Moss stitch hearts

Worked over 19 sts.

Row 1 (RS): P6, T3B, k1, T3F, p6.

Row 2: K6, p3, k1, p3, k6.

Row 3: P5, C3B, p1, k1, p1, C3F, p5.

Row 4: K5, p2, [k1, p1] twice, k1, p2, k5.

Row 5: P4, T3B, [k1, p1] twice, k1, T3F, p4.

Row 6: K4, p3, [k1, p1] twice, k1, p3, k4.

Row 7: P3, C3B, [p1, k1] 3 times, p1, C3F, p3.

Row 8: K3, p2, [k1, p1] 4 times, k1, p2, k3.

Row 9: P2, T3B, [k1, p1] 4 times, k1, T3F, p2.

Row 10: K2, p3, [k1, p1] 4 times, k1, p3, k2.

Row 11: P1, C3B, [p1, k1] 5 times, p1, C3F, p1.

Row 12: K1, p2, [k1, p1] 6 times, k1, p2, k1.

Row 13: T3B, [k1, p1] 6 times, k1, T3F.

Row 14: P3, [k1, p1] 6 times, k1, p3.

Row 15: K2, [p1, k1] 7 times, p1, k2.

Row 16: As row 14.

Row 17: T4F, [p1, k1] 5 times, p1, T4B.

Row 18: K2, p3, [k1, p1] 4 times, k1, p3, k2.

Row 19: P2, T4F, [p1, k1] 3 times, p1, T4B, p2.

Row 20: K7, p2, k1, p2, k7.

Rep these 20 rows.

Note: Bobbles may be knitted into this pattern by working row 19 as follows: P2, T4F, p1, k1, p1, MB, p1, k1, p1, T4B, p2.

Bobble with cable

Panel of 9 sts on a background of rev st st.

Special abbreviation:

MB (Make Bobble) = (K1, p1) twice all into next st (turn and p4, turn and k4) twice, turn and p4, turn and sl 2, k2tog, p2sso (bobble completed).

Row 1 (RS): P1, T3B, p1, T3F, p1.

Row 2: K1, p2, k3, p2, k1.

Row 3: T3B, p3, T3F.

Row 4: P2, k5, p2.

Row 5: K2, p2, MB, p2, k2.

Row 6: P2, k5, p2.

Row 7: T3F, p3, T3B.

Row 8: As row 2.

Row 9: P1, T3F, p1, T3B, p1.

Row 10: K2, p5, k2.

Row 11: P2, T5BP, p2.

Row 12: K2, p5, k2.

Rep these 12 rows.

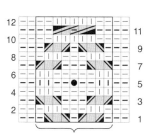

9-stitch panel

Double diamonds

Panel of 20 sts on a background of rev st st.

Row 1 (RS): P6, T4BP, T4FP, p6.
Row 2: K6, [p2, k1] twice, p2, k6.
Row 3: P4, T4B, p1, k2, p1, T4F, p4.
Row 4: K4, [p2, k3] twice, p2, k4.
Row 5: P2, T4B, p2, C2B, C2F, p2, T4F, p2.
Row 6: K2, p2, k4, p4, k4, p2, k2.
Row 7: T4B, p2, C4B, C4F, p2, T4F.
Row 8: P2, k4, p8, k4, p2.
Row 9: T4F, C4B, k4, C4F, T4B.
Row 10: K2, p16, k2.
Row 11: P2, C4B, k8, C4F, p2.
Row 12: K2, p16, k2.
Row 13: T4B, T4F, k4, T4B, T4F.
Row 14: As row 8.
Row 15: T4F, p2, T4F, T4B, p2, T4B.
Row 16: As row 6.
Row 17: P2, T4F, p2, T2F, T2B, p2, T4B, p2.
Row 18: As row 4.
Row 19: P4, T4F, p1, k2, p1, T4B, p4.
Row 20: As row 2.
Row 21: P6, T4F, T4B, p6.
Row 22: K8, p4, k8.
Row 23: P8, k4, p8.
Row 24: K8, p4, k8.
Rep these 24 rows.

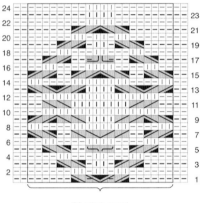

20-stitch panel

Cable with swirl

Panel of 22 sts on a background of rev st st.

Special abbreviations:

Work 5tog (Work 5 sts together) = with yarn at back of work, slip 3 sts purlwise, *pass 2nd st on right-hand needle over 1st (centre) st, slip centre st back to left-hand needle, pass 2nd st on left-hand needle over*, slip centre st back to right-hand needle; rep from * to * once more, purl centre st. (Note: Stitch referred to as 'centre st' is centre one of 5 sts.)

Row 1 (RS): T4B, p1, T4F, T4B, p9.
Row 2: K11, p4, k5, p2.
Row 3: K2, p5, C4B, p11.
Row 4: As row 2.
Row 5: T4F, p1, T4B, T4F, p9.
Row 6: K9, p2, k4, p2, k1, p2, k2.
Row 7: P2, work 5tog, p4, T4F, p4, M5K, p2.
Row 8: K2, p2, k1, p2, k4, p2, k9.
Row 9: P9, T4F, T4B, p1, T4F.
Row 10: P2, k5, p4, k11.
Row 11: P11, C4F, p5, k2.
Row 12: As row 10.
Row 13: P9, T4B, T4F, p1, T4B.
Row 14: As row 8.
Row 15: P2, M5K, p4, T4B, p4, work 5tog, p2.
Row 16: As row 6.
Rep these 16 rows.

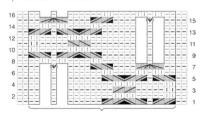

22-stitch panel

Slanting stripes

Multiple of 6 + 4.

Row 1 (RS): P1, *T3F, p3; rep from * to last 3 sts, p3.

Row 2: K6, p2, *k4, p2; rep from * to last 2 sts, k2.

Row 3: P2, *T3F, p3; rep from * to last 2 sts, p2.

Row 4: K5, p2, *k4, p2; rep from * to last 3 sts, k3.

Row 5: *P3, T3F; rep from * to last 4 sts, p4.

Row 6: K4, *p2, k4; rep from * to end.

Row 7: P4, *T3F, p3; rep from * to end.

Row 8: K3, *p2, k4; rep from * to last st, k1.

Row 9: P5, T3F, *p3, T3F; rep from * to last 2 sts, p2.

Row 10: K2, *p2, k4; rep from * to last 2 sts, k2.

Row 11: P6, T3F, *p3, T3F; rep from * to last st, p1.

Row 12: K1, *p2, k4; rep from * to last 3 sts, k3.

Rep these 12 rows.

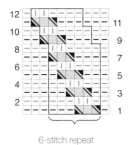

6-stitch repeat

Loose V stitch

Panel of 12 sts on a background of rev st st.

Row 1 (RS): P3, T3B, T3F, p3.

Row 2: K3, p2, k2, p2, k3.

Row 3: P2, T3B, p2, T3F, p2.

Row 4: K2, p2, k4, p2, k2.

Row 5: P1, T3B, p4, T3F, p1.

Row 6: K1, p2, k6, p2, k1.

Row 7: T3B, p6, T3F.

Row 8: P2, k8, p2.

Rep these 8 rows.

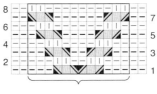

12-stitch panel

Woven cable

Worked over a multiple of 8 + 4 sts on a background of rev st st
(minimum 20 sts).

The example shown is worked over 28 sts.

Row 1 (RS): Knit.

Row 2 and every alt row: K2, purl to 2 sts before end of
panel, k2.

Row 3: Knit.

Row 5: K2, *C8B; rep from * to 2 sts before end of panel, k2.

Row 7: Knit.

Row 9: Knit.

Row 11: K6, *C8F; rep from * to 6 sts before end of panel, k6.

Row 12: As row 2.

Rep these 12 rows.

Zigzag cable

Multiple of 4 + 2.

Row 1 (RS): P3, T2B, *p2, T2B; rep from * to last st, p1.

Row 2: K2, *p1, k3; rep from * to end.

Row 3: P2, *T2B, p2; rep from * to end.

Row 4: *K3, p1; rep from * to last 2 sts, k2.

Row 5: P1, T2B, *p2, T2B; rep from * to last 3 sts, p3.

Row 6: K4, p1, *k3, p1; rep from * to last st, k1.

Row 7: P1, T2F, *p2, T2F; rep from * to last 3 sts, p3.

Row 8: As row 4.

Row 9: P2, *T2F, p2; rep from * to end.

Row 10: As row 2.

Row 11: P3, T2F, *p2, T2F; rep from * to last st, p1.

Row 12: K1, p1, *k3, p1; rep from * to last 4 sts, k4.

Rep these 12 rows.

Note: This stitch is also very effective when worked as a panel of
4 sts on a background of rev st st.

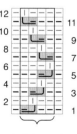

4-stitch repeat

Rippled diamonds

Panel of 11 sts on a background of rev st st.

Special abbreviation:

T3RP (Twist 3 Right Purl) = slip next 2 sts onto cable needle and hold at back of work, knit next st from left-hand needle, then p1, k1 from cable needle.

Row 1 (RS): P3, T2B, k1, T2F, p3.

Row 2: K3, p1, [k1, p1] twice, k3.

Row 3: P2, T2B, k1, p1, k1, T2F, p2.

Row 4: K2, p1, [k1, p1] 3 times, k2.

Row 5: P1, T2B, k1, [p1, k1] twice, T2F, p1.

Row 6: K1, [p1, k1] 5 times.

Row 7: T2B, k1, [p1, k1] 3 times, T2F.

Row 8: P1, [k1, p1] 5 times.

Row 9: T2F, p1, [k1, p1] 3 times, T2B.

Row 10: As row 6.

Row 11: P1, T2F, p1, [k1, p1] twice, T2B, p1.

Row 12: As row 4.

Row 13: P2, T2F, p1, k1, p1, T2B, p2.

Row 14: As row 2.

Row 15: P3, T2F, p1, T2B, p3.

Row 16: K4, p1, k1, p1, k4.

Row 17: P4, T3RP, p4.

Row 18: As row 16.

Rep these 18 rows.

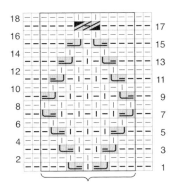

11-stitch panel

Lattice pattern II

Worked over a multiple of 16 + 1 (minimum 33) on a background of rev st st.

The example shown is worked over 33 sts.

Row 1 (RS): K1, *yf, k2, sl 1, k1, psso, p7, k2tog, k2, yf, k1; rep from * to end.

Row 2: P5, *k7, p9; rep from * to last 12 sts, k7, p5.

Row 3: K2, *yf, k2, sl 1, k1, psso, p5, k2tog, k2, yf, k2tog, yf, k1; rep from * to last 15 sts, yf, k2, sl 1, k1, psso, p5, k2tog, k2, yf, k2.

Row 4: P6, *k5, p11; rep from * to last 11 sts, k5, p6.

Row 5: *K2tog, yf, k1, yf, k2, sl 1, k1, psso, p3, k2tog, k2, yf, k2tog, yf; rep from * to last st, k1.

Row 6: P7, *k3, p13; rep from * to last 10 sts, k3, p7.

Row 7: K1, *k2tog, yf, k1, yf, k2, sl 1, k1, psso, p1, k2tog, k2, yf, [k2tog, yf] twice; rep from * to last 16 sts, k2tog, yf, k1, yf, k2, sl 1, k1, psso, p1, k2tog, k2, yf, k2tog, yf, k2.

Row 8: P8, *k1, p15; rep from * to last 9 sts, k1, p8.

Row 9: P5, *C7B, p9; rep from * to last 12 sts, C7B, p5.

Row 10: K5, *p3, k1, p3, k9; rep from * to last 12 sts, p3, k1, p3, k5.

Row 11: P4, *k2tog, k2, yf, k1, yf, k2, sl 1, k1, psso, p7; rep from * to last 13 sts, k2tog, k2, yf, k1, yf, k2, sl 1, k1, psso, p4.

Row 12: K4, *p9, k7; rep from * to last 13 sts, p9, k4.

Row 13: P3, *k2tog, k2, yf, k2tog, yf, k1, yf, k2, sl 1, k1, psso, p5; rep from * to last 14 sts, k2tog, k2, yf, k2tog, yf, k1, yf, k2, sl 1, k1, psso, p3.

Row 14: K3, *p11, k5; rep from * to last 14 sts, p11, k3.

Row 15: P2, *k2tog, k2, yf, [k2tog, yf] twice, k1, yf, k2, sl 1, k1, psso, p3; rep from * to last 15 sts, k2tog, k2, yf, [k2tog,

yf] twice, k1, yf, k2, sl 1, k1, psso, p2.

Row 16: K2, *p13, k3; rep from * to last 15 sts, p13, k2.

Row 17: P1, *k2tog, k2, yf, [k2tog, yf] 3 times, k1, yf, k2, sl 1, k1, psso, p1; rep from * to end.

Row 18: K1, *p15, k1; rep from * to end.

Row 19: P1, k3, *p9, C7F; rep from * to last 13 sts, p9, k3, p1.

Row 20: K1, p3, *k9, p3, k1, p3; rep from * to last 13 sts, k9, p3, k1.

Rep these 20 rows.

Chunky braid

Panel with a multiple of 6 + 9.

Example shown is worked over 15 sts on a background of rev st st.

Row 1 (RS): Knit.

Row 2: Purl.

Row 3: K3, *C6F; rep from * to end.

Row 4: Purl.

Rows 5–6: As rows 1–2.

Row 7: *C6B; rep from * to last 3 sts, k3.

Row 8: Purl.

Rep these 8 rows.

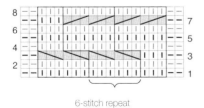

6-stitch repeat

Little cable fabric

Multiple of 4 + 1.

Row 1 (RS): K1, *sl 1 purlwise, k3; rep from * to end.

Row 2: *P3, sl 1 purlwise; rep from * to last st, p1.

Row 3: K1, *C3L, k1; rep from * to end.

Row 4: Purl.

Row 5: K5, *sl 1, k3; rep from * to end.

Row 6: *P3, sl 1; rep from * to last 5 sts, p5.

Row 7: K3, *C3R, k1; rep from * to last 2 sts, k2.

Row 8: Purl.

Rep these 8 rows.

Cable with segments

Panel of 16 sts on a background of rev st st.

Special abbreviations:

T8B rib (Twist 8 Back rib) = slip next 4 sts onto cable needle and hold at back of work, k1, p2, k1 from left-hand needle, then k1, p2, k1 from cable needle.

T8F rib (Twist 8 Front rib) = slip next 4 sts onto cable needle and hold at front of work, k1, p2, k1 from left-hand needle, then k1, p2, k1 from cable needle.

Row 1 (RS): K1, p2, [k2, p2] 3 times, k1.

Row 2: P1, k2, [p2, k2] 3 times, p1.

Row 3: T8B rib, T8F rib.

Row 4: As row 2.

Rows 5–12: Rep rows 1–2, 4 times.

Rep these 12 rows.

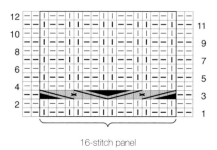

16-stitch panel

Bobbles and waves

Worked over 26 sts on a background of rev st st.

Row 1 (RS): P2, T3B, p5, C6B, p5, T3F, p2.

Row 2: K2, p2, k6, p6, k6, p2, k2.

Row 3: P1, T3B, p4, T5B, T5F, p4, T3F, p1.

Row 4: K1, p2, k5, p3, k4, p3, k5, p2, k1.

Row 5: T3B, p3, T5B, p4, T5F, p3, T3F.

Row 6: P2, k1, make bobble as follows: knit into front, back and front of next st, [turn and knit these 3 sts] 3 times, then turn and sl 1, k2tog, psso (bobble completed), k2, p3, k8, p3, k2, make bobble as before, k1, p2.

Row 7: T3F, p3, k3, p8, k3, p3, T3B.

Row 8: K1, p2, k3, p3, k8, p3, k3, p2, k1.

Row 9: P1, T3F, p2, T5F, p4, T5B, p2, T3B, p1.

Row 10: K2, p2, [k4, p3] twice, k4, p2, k2.

Row 11: P2, T3F, p3, T5F, T5B, p3, T3B, p2.

Row 12: K1, make bobble as before, k1, p2, k5, p6, k5, p2, k1, make bobble, k1.

Rep these 12 rows.

Internal diamonds

Panel of 14 sts on a background of rev st st.

Row 1 (RS): P4, C3B, C3F, p4.

Row 2: K4, [PB1] 6 times, k4.

Row 3: P3, T3B, C2B, T3F, p3.

Row 4: K3, *[PB1] twice, k1; rep from * twice more, k2.

Row 5: P2, T3B, p1, C2B, p1, T3F, p2.

Row 6: *K2, [PB1] twice; rep from * twice more, k2.

Row 7: P1, T3B, p1, T2B, T2F, p1, T3F, p1.

Row 8: K1, [PB1] twice, k2, [PB1, k2] twice, [PB1] twice, k1.

Row 9: T3B, p1, T2B, p2, T2F, p1, T3F.

Row 10: [PB1] twice, k2, PB1, k4, PB1, k2, [PB1] twice.

Row 11: K2, p2, k1, p4, k1, p2, k2.

Row 12: As row 10.

Row 13: T3F, p1, T2F, p2, T2B, p1, T3B.

Row 14: As row 8.

Row 15: P1, T3F, p1, T2F, T2B, p1, T3B, p1.

Row 16: As row 6.

Row 17: P2, T3F, p1, C2B, p1, T3B, p2.

Row 18: As row 4.

Row 19: P3, T3F, C2B, T3B, p3.

Row 20: As row 2.

Row 21: P4, T3F, T3B, p4.

Row 22: K5, [PB1] 4 times, k5.

Row 23: P5, C4B, p5.

Row 24: As row 22.

Rep these 24 rows.

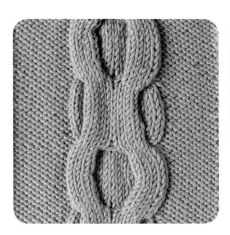

Criss-cross cable with twists

Panel of 16 sts on a background of rev st st.

Row 1 (RS): P2, C4F, p4, C4F, p2.

Row 2: K2, p4, k4, p4, k2.

Row 3: P2, k4, p4, k4, p2.

Row 4: As row 2.

Row 5: As row 1.

Row 6: As row 2.

Row 7: [T4B, T4F] twice.

Row 8: As row 3.

Row 9: K2, p4, C4F, p4, k2.

Row 10: As row 3.

Row 11: As row 2.

Row 12: As row 3.

Row 13: As row 9.

Rows 14–21: Rep rows 10–14 twice more.

Row 22: As row 3.

Row 23: [T4F, T4B] twice.

Row 24: As row 2.

Rep these 24 rows.

Wide cable panel

Panel of 20 sts on a background of rev st st.

Row 1 and every alt row (WS): Purl.

Row 2: K6, C4B, C4F, k6.

Row 4: K4, C4B, k4, C4F, k4.

Row 6: K2, C4B, k8, C4F, k2.

Row 8: C4B, k12, C4F.

Rep these 8 rows.

Padded cable

Panel of 20 sts on a background of rev st st.

Row 1 (RS): K20.

Row 2: P20.

Row 3: C10B, C10F.

Row 4: P20.

Rows 5–14: Rep rows 1–2, 5 times.

Row 15: C10F, C10B.

Row 16: P20.

Rows 17–24: Rep rows 1–2, 4 times.

Rep these 24 rows.

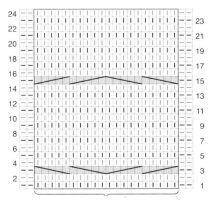

20-stitch panel

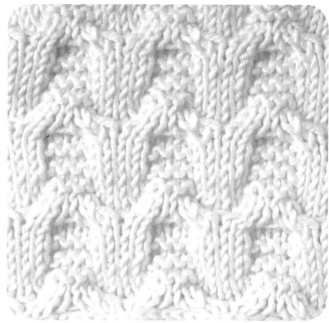

Cable stitch

Multiple of 12.

Row 1 (RS): *K2, p1, k6, p1, k2; rep from * to end.

Row 2: *P2, k1, p6, k1, p2; rep from * to end.

Row 3 and every alt row: *K2, p2, k4, p2, k2; rep from * to end.

Row 4 and every alt row: *P2, k2, p4, k2, p2; rep from * to end.

Row 10: *P2, T4F, T4B, p2; rep from * to end.

Row 11: Knit.

Row 12: As row 2.

Rep these 12 rows.

Forked cable

Multiple of 8 + 2.

Row 1 (WS): Purl.

Row 2: P3, k4, *p4, k4; rep from * to last 3 sts, p3.

Rows 3–7: Rep rows 1–2 twice more, then row 1 again.

Row 8: K3, p4, *k4, p4; rep from * to last 3 sts, k3.

Row 9: Purl.

Row 10: K1, *C4F, C4B; rep from * to last st, k1.

Rep these 10 rows.

Tip

To avoid having to have a knot in the middle of the row where you have joined a new ball of yarn, check that you have enough yarn to complete the next row – you will need approximately three times the width of the swatch or garment. If you do not have sufficient yarn, tie the yarn off at the end of the row and join in the new ball. Weave the yarn tail into the seam at the end of the project.

Vine and twist

Worked over 17 sts on a background of rev st st.

Row 1 (RS): P6, C5, p6.
Row 2: K6, p5, k6.
Row 3: P5, T3B, k1, T3F, p5.
Row 4: K5, p2, k1, p1, k1, p2, k5.
Row 5: P4, T3B, p1, k1, p1, T3F, p4.
Row 6: K4, p2, k2, p1, k2, p2, k4.
Row 7: P3, k2tog, k1, p2, yon, k1, yf, p2, k1, sl 1, k1, psso, p3.
Row 8: K3, p2, k2, p3, k2, p2, k3.
Row 9: P2, k2tog, k1, p2, [k1, yf] twice, k1, p2, k1, sl 1, k1, psso, p2.
Row 10: K2, p2, k2, p5, k2, p2, k2.
Row 11: P1, k2tog, k1, p2, k2, yf, k1, yf, k2, p2, k1, sl 1, k1, psso, p1.
Row 12: K1, p2, k2, p7, k2, p2, k1.
Row 13: Purl into front and back of next st (called inc 1), k2, p2, k2, insert needle into next 2 sts on left-hand needle as if to

k2tog, then slip both sts onto right-hand needle without knitting them (called sl 2tog knitwise), k1, pass 2 slipped sts over (called p2sso), k2, p2, k2, inc 1.
Row 14: As row 10.
Row 15: P1, inc 1, k2, p2, k1, sl 2tog knitwise, k1, p2sso, k1, p2, k2, inc 1, p1.
Row 16: As row 8.
Row 17: P2, inc 1, k2, p2, sl 2tog knitwise, k1, p2sso, p2, k2, inc 1, p2.
Row 18: As row 6.
Row 19: P4, T3F, p1, k1, p1, T3B, p4.
Row 20: As row 4.
Row 21: P5, T3F, k1, T3B, p5.
Row 22: As row 2.
Row 23: As row 1.
Row 24: As row 2.
Row 25: P6, k5, p6.
Row 26: As row 2.
Rep these 26 rows.

Double spiral cable

Panel of 22 sts worked on a background of rev st st. The number of sts within the panel varies.

Special abbreviation:

Work 5tog (Work 5 sts together) = with yarn at back of work, slip 3 sts purlwise, *pass 2nd st on right-hand needle over

1st (centre) st, slip centre st back to left-hand needle, pass 2nd st on left-hand needle over*, slip centre st back to right-hand needle; rep from * to * once more, purl centre st. (Note: Stitch referred to as 'centre st' is centre 1 of 5 sts.)

Row 1 (RS): P9, k4, p9.
Row 2: K9, p4, k9.
Row 3: P9, C4B, p9.
Row 4: K9, p4, k9.
Row 5: P2, M5K, p4, T4B, T4F, p4, M5K, p2.
Row 6: K2, p2, k1, [p2, k4] 3 times, p2, k1, p2, k2.
Row 7: T4B, p1, T4F, T4B, p4, T4F, T4B, p1, T4F.
Row 8: P2, k5, p4, k8, p4, k5, p2.
Row 9: K2, p5, C4F, p8, C4B, p5, k2.
Row 10: As row 8.
Row 11: T4F, p1, T4B, T4F, p4, T4B, T4F, p1, T4B.
Row 12: As row 6.

Row 13: P2, work 5tog, p4, T4F, T4B, p4, work 5tog, p2.
Rows 14–16: As rows 2–4.
Rep these 16 rows.

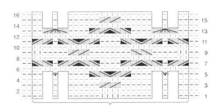

22-stitch panel

Ornamental cable

Panel of 30 sts on a background of rev st st.

Row 1 (RS): K9, C6B, C6F, k9.
Row 2 and every alt row: P30.
Row 3: K6, C6B, k6, C6F, k6.
Row 5: K3, C6B, k12, C6F, k3.
Row 7: C6B, k18, C6F.
Row 8: P30.
Rep these 8 rows.

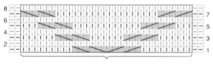

30-stitch panel

Small wavy cable

Multiple of 3 + 1.
Row 1 (RS): P1, *C2B, p1; rep from * to end.
Row 2: K1, *p2, k1; rep from * to end.
Row 3: P1, *C2F, p1; rep from * to end.
Row 4: As row 2.
Rep these 4 rows.

3-stitch repeat

Diagonal ripple

Multiple of 4 + 3.
Row 1 (RS): P4, T2B, *p2, T2B; rep from * to last st, p1.
Row 2: K2, p1, *k3, p1; rep from * to last 4 sts, k4.
Row 3: P3, *T2B, p2; rep from * to end.
Row 4: K3, *p1, k3; rep from * to end.
Row 5: *P2, T2B; rep from * to last 3 sts, p3.
Row 6: K4, p1, *k3, p1; rep from * to last 2 sts, k2.
Row 7: P1, T2B, *p2, T2B; rep from * to last 4 sts, p4.
Row 8: K5, p1, *k3, p1; rep from * to last st, k1.
Rep these 8 rows.

4-stitch repeat

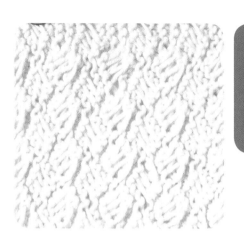

Eyelet cable

Multiple of 8 + 1.

Special abbreviation:

C3tog (Cross 3 together) = slip next 2 sts onto cable needle and hold at back of work, knit next st from left-hand needle, then k2tog from cable needle.

Row 1 (RS): P1, *C3tog, p1, k3, p1; rep from * to end.

Row 2: K1, *p3, k1, p1, yrn, p1, k1; rep from * to end.

Row 3: P1, *k3, p1, C3tog, p1; rep from * to end.

Row 4: K1, *p1, yrn, p1, k1, p3, k1; rep from * to end.

Rep these 4 rows.

Lace and cables

Multiple of 11 + 7.

Row 1 (RS): K1, *yf, sl 1, k1, psso, k1, k2tog, yf, k6; rep from * to last 6 sts, yf, sl 1, k1, psso, k1, k2tog, yf, k1.

Row 2 and every alt row: Purl.

Row 3: K2, *yf, sl 1, k2tog, psso, yf, k8; rep from * to last 5 sts, yf, sl 1, k2tog, psso, yf, k2.

Row 5: As row 1.

Row 7: K2, *yf, sl 1, k2tog, psso, yf, k1, C6B, k1; rep from * to last 5 sts, yf, sl 1, k2tog, psso, yf, k2.

Row 8: Purl.

Rep these 8 rows.

Loose woven cables

Multiple of 6 + 2.

Row 1 (RS): Knit.

Row 2: K1, knit to last st wrapping yarn twice around needle for each st, k1.

Row 3: K1, *C6B (dropping extra loops); rep from * to last st, k1.

Rows 4–5: Work 2 rows in garter st.

Row 6: K4, *knit to last 4 sts, wrapping yarn twice around needle for each st, k4.

Row 7: K4, *C6F (dropping extra loops); rep from * to last 4 sts, k4.

Row 8: Knit.

Rep these 8 rows.

Diagonal tramline cable

Panel of 18 sts on a background of rev st st.

Row 1 (RS): K2, p3, k2, p4, k2, p3, k2.
Row 2: P2, k3, p2, k4, p2, k3, p2.
Row 3: As row 1.
Row 4: As row 2.
Row 5: [T3F, p2] twice, T3B, p2, T3B.
Row 6: K1, p2, k3, p2, k2, p2, k3, p2, k1.
Row 7: P1, T3F, p2, T3F, T3B, p2, T3B, p1.
Row 8: K2, p2, k3, p4, k3, p2, k2.
Row 9: P2, T3F, p2, C4B, p2, T3B, p2.
Row 10: K3, p2, k2, p4, k2, p2, k3.
Row 11: P3, [T3F, T3B] twice, p3.
Row 12: K4, p4, k2, p4, k4.
Row 13: P4, C4F, p2, C4F, p4.
Row 14: K4, p4, k2, p4, k4.
Row 15: P3, [T3B, T3F] twice, p3.
Row 16: K3, p2, k2, p4, k2, p2, k3.
Row 17: P2, T3B, p2, C4B, p2, T3F, p2.
Row 18: K2, p2, k3, p4, k3, p2, k2.
Row 19: P1, T3B, p2, T3B, T3F, p2, T3F, p1.
Row 20: K1, p2, k3, p2, k2, p2, k3, p2, k1.
Row 21: [T3B, p2] twice, T3F, p2, T3F.
Row 22: As row 2.
Row 23: As row 1.
Rows 24–26: Rep rows 22–23 once more, then row 22 again.
Rep these 26 rows.

Simple cable

Panel of 2 sts on a background of rev st st.
Row 1 (RS): C2B
Row 2: P2.
Rep these 2 rows.

2-stitch panel

Twisted and crossed cable

Panel of 16 sts on a background of rev st st.
Row 1 (RS): P2, C4B, p4, C4F, p2.
Row 2: K2, p4, k4, p4, k2.
Row 3: P1, T3B, T3F, p2, T3B, T3F, p1.
Row 4: K1, [p2, k2] 3 times, p2, k1.
Row 5: [T3B, p2, T3F] twice.
Row 6: P2, k4, p4, k4, p2.
Row 7: K2, p4, C4B, p4, k2.
Row 8: As row 6.
Row 9: K2, p4, k4, p4, k2.
Row 10: As row 6.
Row 11: As row 7.
Row 12: As row 6.
Row 13: [T3F, p2, T3B] twice.
Row 14: As row 4.
Row 15: P1, T3F, T3B, p2, T3F, T3B, p1.
Row 16: As row 2.
Row 17: As row 1.
Row 18: As row 2.
Row 19: As row 3.
Row 20: As row 4.
Row 21: P1, [k2, p2] twice, k2, slip last 6 sts worked onto cable needle and wrap yarn 4 times anti-clockwise around these 6 sts, then slip the 6 sts back onto right-hand needle, p2, k2, p1.
Row 22: As row 4.
Row 23: As row 15.
Row 24: As row 2.
Rep these 24 rows.

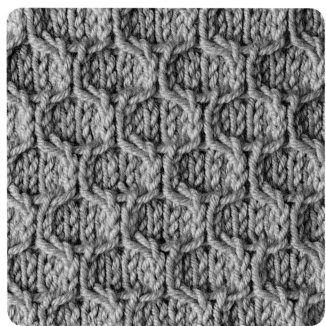

Repeated ovals

Multiple of 8 + 1.

Special abbreviation:

Work 5tog (Work 5 sts together) = with yarn at front (WS), slip 3 sts purlwise, k2tog, p3sso.

Row 1 (RS): K1, *p5, k1, p1, k1; rep from * to end.

Row 2: P1, *k1, p1, k5, p1; rep from * to end.

Row 3: As row 1.

Row 4: P1, *M5K, p1, work 5tog, p1; rep from * to end.

Row 5: K1, *p1, k1, p5, k1; rep from * to end.

Row 6: P1, *k5, p1, k1, p1; rep from * to end.

Rows 7–9: Rep rows 5–6 once more, then row 5 again.

Row 10: P1, *work 5tog, p1, M5K, p1; rep from * to end.

Rows 11–12: As rows 1–2.

Rep these 12 rows.

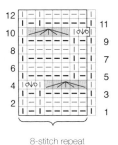

8-stitch repeat

Repeated circles

Multiple of 6 + 2.

Row 1 (RS): Knit.

Row 2: Purl.

Row 3: K1, *C3R, C3L; rep from * to last st, k1.

Row 4: Purl.

Rows 5–6: As rows 1–2.

Row 7: K1, *C3L, C3R; rep from * to last st, k1.

Row 8: Purl.

Rep these 8 rows.

Note: This stitch is also very effective when worked as a panel with a multiple of 6 sts on a background of rev st st.

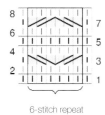

6-stitch repeat

Small circle cable

Multiple of 6 + 2.

Row 1 (RS): P2, *C2B, C2F, p2; rep from * to end.

Row 2: K2, *p4, k2; rep from * to end.

Row 3: P2, *C2F, C2B, p2; rep from * to end.

Row 4: As row 2.

Rep these 4 rows.

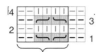

6-stitch repeat

Slanting diagonals

Multiple of 6 + 4.

Row 1 (RS): P6, T3B, *p3, T3B; rep from * to last st, p1.

Row 2: K2, *p2, k4; rep from * to last 2 sts, k2.

Row 3: P5, T3B, *p3, T3B; rep from * to last 2 sts, p2.

Row 4: K3, *p2, k4; rep from * to last st, k1.

Row 5: P4, *T3B, p3; rep from * to end.

Row 6: K4, *p2, k4; rep from * to end.

Row 7: *P3, T3B; rep from * to last 4 sts, p4.

Row 8: K5, p2, *k4, p2; rep from * to last 3 sts, k3.

Row 9: P2, *T3B, p3; rep from * to last 2 sts, p2.

Row 10: K6, p2, *k4, p2; rop from * to last 2 sts, k2.

Row 11: P1, *T3B, p3; rep from * to last 3 sts, p3.

Row 12: K7, p2, *k4, p2; rep from * to last st, k1.

Rep these 12 rows.

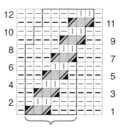

6-stitch repeat

Crossed cables

Multiple of 12 + 14.

Row 1 (RS): P3, T4B, T4F, *p4, T4B, T4F; rep from * to last 3 sts, p3.

Row 2: K3, p2, *k4, p2; rep from * to last 3 sts, k3.

Row 3: P1, *T4B, p4, T4F; rep from * to last st, p1.

Row 4: K1, p2, k8, *p4, k8; rep from * to last 3 sts, p2, k1.

Row 5: P1, k2, p8, *C4B, p8; rep from * to last 3 sts, k2, p1.

Row 6: As row 4.

Row 7: P1, *T4F, p4, T4B; rep from * to last st, p1.

Row 8: As row 2.

Row 9: P3, T4F, T4B, *p4, T4F, T4B; rep from * to last 3 sts, p3.

Row 10: K5, p4, *k8, p4; rep from * to last 5 sts, k5.

Row 11: P5, C4F, *p8, C4F; rep from * to last 5 sts, p5.

Row 12: As row 10.

Rep these 12 rows.

Rose garden

Multiple of 9 + 5.

Row 1 (RS): P2, KB1, p2, *k4, p2, KB1, p2; rep from * to end.

Row 2: K2, PB1, k2, *p4, k2, PB1, k2; rep from * to end.

Row 3: P2, KB1, p2, *C4B, p2, KB1, p2; rep from * to end.

Row 4: As row 2.

Rep these 4 rows.

9-stitch repeat

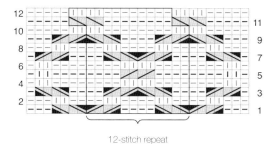

12-stitch repeat

Leafy trellis

Multiple of 10 + 3.

Row 1: Edge st, *k1 twisted, p1, k1, K1B, p1, k1 twisted, p1, k1 twisted, p1, k1 twisted, p1; rep from * to last 2 sts, k1 twisted, edge st.

Row 2: Edge st, p1 twisted, *k1, p1 twisted, k1, p1 twisted, k1, p1 twisted, k1, p3, p1 twisted; rep from * to last st, edge st.

Row 3: Edge st, *k1 twisted, K1B, sl 1 as if to p with thread behind work, k2tog and draw sl st over, through, p1, k1 twisted, p1, k1 twisted, p1, k1 twisted, p1; rep from * to last 2 sts, k1 twisted, edge st.

Row 4: As row 2.

Row 5: As row 3.

Row 6: As row 2.

Row 7: As row 3.

Rep these 7 rows.

Eyelet rib variation

Multiple of 8 + 2.

Eyelet openwork is worked on WS rows to clearly indent the rib pattern.

Row 1 (RS): P2, *k6, p2; rep from * to end.

Row 2 (WS): K2, *p6, yo, k2tog; rep from * to last 8 sts, p6, k2.

Rep these 2 rows until desired length, end with a RS row.

Next row (WS): K2, *p2, yo, k2tog; rep from * to last 4 sts, p2, k2.

Next row (RS): P2, *k2, p2; rep from * to end.

Rep these last 2 rows to cont patt, or work in a variation as desired.

Extended open-work stitches

Multiple of 6 + 2 st for the rim on each edge.

Row 1 (RS): Knit.

Row 2: 1 edge st, *knit each st wrapping yarn around needle 3 times; rep from * to last st, k1.

Row 3: 1 edge st, *slip next 3 sts onto cable needle and leave at back of work, k3, k3 sts from cable needle; rep from * to last st, 1 edge st.

Row 4: Knit.

Rep these 4 rows.

Slanting openwork stitch

Even number of sts.
Row 1 (RS): Edge st, *yf, k2tog; rep from * to last st, edge st.
Rows 2 and 4: Purl.
Row 3: K2, * yf, k2tog; rep from * to last 2 sts, k2tog.
Rep these 4 rows.

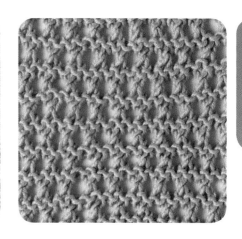

Eyelet quadrants

Multiple of 6 + 2.
Row 1 (RS): 1 edge st, *k1, k2tog, yo, k1, yo, ssk; rep from * to last st, 1 edge st.
Row 2 and every alt row: 1 edge st, purl to last st, 1 edge st.
Row 3, 7, 9 and 11: 1 edge st, knit to last st, 1 edge st.
Row 5: As row 1.
Rep these 12 rows.

Ridged eyelet stitch

Multiple of 2.
Rows 1–3: Knit.
Row 4 (WS): P1, *yrn, p2tog; rep from * to last st, p1.
Rows 5–7: Knit.
Row 8: P1, *p2tog, yrn; rep from * to last st, p1.
Rep these 8 rows.

Feather openwork

Multiple of 5 + 2.
Row 1 (RS): K1, *k2tog, yf, k1, yf, sl 1, k1, psso; rep from * to last st, k1.
Row 2: Purl.
Rep these 2 rows.

Single lace rib

Multiple of 4 + 1.
Row 1 (RS): K1, *yf, k2tog, p1, k1; rep from * to end.
Row 2: P1, *yrn, p2tog, k1, p1; rep from * to end.
Rep these 2 rows.

Purse stitch

Multiple of 2.
Row 1: P1, *yrn, p2tog; rep from * to last st, p1.
Rep this row.

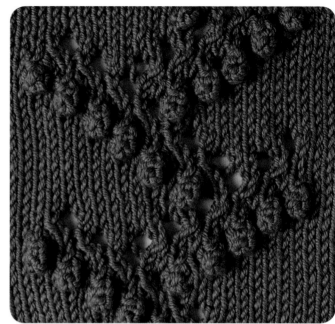

Angel wings lace panel

Worked over 19 sts.

Row 1 (RS): P2, sl 1, k1, psso, k5, yo, k1, yo, k5, k2tog, p2.

Row 2: K2, p2tog, p5, yo, p1, yo, p5, p2tog tbl, k2.

Row 3: P2, sl 1, k1, psso, k4, yo, k3, yo, k4, k2tog, p2.

Row 4: K2, p2tog, p4, yo, p3, yo, p4, p2tog tbl, k2.

Row 5: P2, sl 1, k1, psso, k3, yo, k5, yo, k3, k2tog, p2.

Row 6: K2, p2tog, p3, yo, p5, yo, p3, p2tog tbl, k2.

Row 7: P2, sl 1, k1, psso, k2, yo, k7, yo, k2, k2tog, p2.

Row 8: K2, p2tog, p2, yo, p7, yo, p2, p2tog tbl, k2.

Row 9: P2, sl 1, k1, psso, k1, yo, k9, yo, k1, k2tog, p2.

Row 10: K2, p2tog, p1, yo, p9, yo, p1, p2tog tbl, k2.

Rep these 10 rows.

Mimosa shoot

Multiple of 20.

Row 1 (RS): K6, yf, sl 1, k1, psso, k2, MB [k1, p1, k1, p1 into next st, turn, k4, turn, sl st purlwise, p3tog, psso], k9.

Row 2 and every alt row: Purl.

Row 3: K8, yf, sl 1, k1, psso, k2, MB, k7.

Row 5: K10, yf, sl 1, k1, psso, k2, MB, k5.

Row 7: K9, MB, k2, yf, sl 1, k1, psso, k2, MB, k3.

Row 9: K7, MB, k2, k2tog, yf, k2, yf, sl 1, k1, psso, k2, MB, k1.

Row 11: K5, MB, k2, k2tog, yf, k6, yf, sl 1, k1, psso, k2.

Row 13: K3, MB, k2, k2tog, yf, k12.

Row 15: K1, MB, k2, k2tog, yf, k2, MB, k11.

Row 17: K2, k2tog, yf, k2, yf, sl 1, k1, psso, k2, MB, k9.

Row 19: K8, yf, sl 1, k1, psso, k2, MB, k7.

Row 20: Purl.

Rep rows 5–20.

Papyrus lace

Multiple of 8 + 1.

Row 1 (RS): K1, * yf, sl 1, k1, psso, k3, k2tog, yf, k1; rep from * to end.

Row 2 and even rows: Purl.

Row 3: K1, *k1, yf, sl 1, k1, psso, k1, k2tog, yf, k2; rep from * to end.

Row 5: K1, *k2, yf, sl 1, k2tog, psso, yo, k3; rep from * to end.

Row 7: Knit.

Rows 9–11: K1, *k1, k2tog, yf, k1, yf, sl 1, k1, psso, k2; rep from * to end.

Row 13: As row 1.

Row 15: As row 3.

Row 17: As row 5.

Rows 19–21: As row 9.

Row 22: P1, *yrn, p2tog, p3, p2tog tbl, yrn, p1; rep from * to end.

Row 23: K1, *k1, yrn, sl 1, k1, psso, k1, k2tog, yrn, k2; rep from * to end.

Row 24: P1, *yrn, p2tog, yrn, p3tog, yrn, p2tog tbl, yrn, pl; rep from * to end.

Row 25: K1, *k1, sl 1 k1 psso, yrn, k1, yrn, k2tog, k2; rep from * to end.

Row 26: P1, *p1, p2tog, yrn, p1, yrn, p2tog tbl, p2; rep from * to end.

Rep rows 23–26.

Rep these 30 rows.

Lace and moss stitch

Multiple of 8 + 1.

Work 8 rows in moss st.

Lace pattern:

Row 1: K1, *yfon, sl 1, k1, psso, k3, k2tog, yfon, k1; rep from * to end.

Row 2 and every alt row: Purl.

Row 3: *K2, yfon, sl 1, k1, psso, k1, k2tog, yfon, k1; rep from * to last st, k1.

Row 5: *K3, yfon, sl 1, k2tog, psso, yfon, k2; rep from * to last st, k1.

Row 6: Purl.

Rep these 14 rows.

Slanting eyelet rib

Multiple of 10.

Row 1: K3, p2, k2tog, yfon, C2B, p1.
Row 2: K2, p3, k2, p3.
Row 3: K3, p1, k2tog, yfon, C2B, p2.
Row 4: K2, p4, k1, p3.
Row 5: K3, k2tog, yfon, C2B, k1, p2.
Row 6: K2, p8.
Row 7: K2, k2tog, yfon, C2B, k2, p2.
Row 8: K2, p8.
Row 9: K1, k2tog, yfon, C2B, k3, p2.
Row 10: K2, p3, k1, p4.
Row 11: K2tog, yfon, C2B, p1, k3, p2.
Row 12: K2, p3, k2, p3.

Rep these 12 rows.

Embossed leaf pattern

Multiple of 7 + 6.

Note: sts should be counted only after rows 15 and 16 of this pattern.

Row 1 (RS): P6, *yon, k1, yfrn, p6; rep from * to end.

Row 2: K6, *p3, k6; rep from * to end.

Row 3: P6, *[k1, yf] twice, k1, p6; rep from * to end.

Row 4: K6, *p5, k6; rep from * to end.

Row 5: P6, *k2, yf, k1, yf, k2, p6; rep from * to end.

Row 6: K6, *p7, k6; rep from * to end.

Row 7: P6, *k3, yf, k1, yf, k3, p6; rep from * to end.

Row 8: K6, *p9, k6; rep from * to end.

Row 9: P6, *sl 1, k1, psso, k5, k2tog, p6; rep from * to end.

Row 10: K6, *p7, k6; rep from * to end.

Row 11: P6, *sl 1, k1, psso, k3, k2tog, p6; rep from * to end.

Row 12: K6, *p5, k6; rep from * to end.

Row 13: P6, *sl 1, k1, psso, k1, k2tog, p6; rep from * to end.

Row 14: K6, *p3, k6; rep from * to end.

Row 15: P6, *sl 1, k2tog, psso, p6; rep from * to end.

Row 16: Knit.

Row 17: Purl.

Rows 18–20: Rep the last 2 rows once more, then row 16 again.

Rep these 20 rows.

Falling leaves

Multiple of 10 + 3.

Row 1 (RS): K1, k2tog, k3, *yf, k1, yf, k3, sl 1, k2tog, psso, k3; rep from * to last 7 sts, yf, k1, yf, k3, sl 1, k1, psso, k1.

Row 2 and every alt row: Purl.

Row 3: K1, k2tog, k2, *yf, k3, yf, k2, sl 1, k2tog, psso, k2; rep from * to last 8 sts, yf, k3, yf, k2, sl 1, k1, psso, k1.

Row 5: K1, k2tog, k1, *yf, k5, yf, k1, sl 1, k2tog, psso, k1; rep from * to last 9 sts, yf, k5, yf, k1, sl 1, k1, psso, k1.

Row 7: K1, k2tog, yf, k7, *yf, sl 1, k2tog, psso, yf, k7; rep from * to last 3 sts, yf, sl 1, k1, psso, k1.

Row 9: K2, yf, k3, *sl 1, k2tog, psso, k3, yf, k1, yf, k3; rep from * to last 8 sts, sl 1, k2tog, psso, k3, yf, k2.

Row 11: K3, yf, k2, *sl 1, k2tog, psso, k2, yf, k3, yf, k2; rep from * to last 8 sts, sl 1, k2tog, psso, k2, yf, k3.

Row 13: K4, yf, k1, *sl 1, k2tog, psso, k1, yf, k5, yf, k1; rep from * to last 8 sts, sl 1, k2tog, psso, k1, yf, k4.

Row 15: K5, *yf, sl 1, k2tog, psso, yf, k7; rep from * to last 8 sts, yf, sl 1, k2tog, psso, yf, k5.

Row 16: Purl.

Rep these 16 rows.

Bluebell insertion

Multiple of 8.

Row 1 (RS): P2, [k1, p2] twice.

Row 2: K2, [p1, k2] twice.

Rows 3–4: Rep the last 2 rows once more.

Row 5: P1, yon, sl 1, k1, psso, p2, k2tog, yfrn, p1.

Row 6: K1, p2, k2, p2, k1.

Row 7: P2, yon, sl 1, k1, psso, k2tog, yfrn, p2.

Row 8: K2, p4, k2.

Rep these 8 rows.

Eyelet twist panel

Multiple of 13.

Row 1 and every alt row (WS): Purl.

Row 2: K1, [yf, sl 1, k1, psso] twice, k3, [k2tog, yf] twice, k1.

Row 4: K2, [yf, sl 1, k1, psso] twice, k1, [k2tog, yf] twice, k2.

Row 6: K3, yf, sl 1, k1, psso, yf, sl 1, k2tog, psso, yf, k2tog, yf, k3.

Row 8: K4, yf, sl 1, k2tog, psso, yf, k2tog, yf, k4.

Row 10: K4, [k2tog, yf] twice, k5.

Row 12: K3, [k2tog, yf] twice, k1, yf, sl 1, k1, psso, k3.

Row 14: K2, [k2tog, yf] twice, k1, [yf, sl 1, k1, psso] twice, k2.

Row 16: K1, [k2tog, yf] twice, k3, [yf, sl 1, k1, psso] twice, k1.

Row 18: [K2tog, yf] twice, k5, [yf, sl 1, k1, psso] twice.

Rep these 18 rows.

Filigree cables pattern lace

Multiple of 12 + 8.

Row 1 (RS): P2, *k2, yf, k2tog, p2; rep from * to end.

Row 2: K2, *p2, yrn, p2tog, k2; rep from * to end.

Rep the last 2 rows twice more.

Row 7: P2, k2, yf, k2tog, p2, *C4F, p2, k2, yf, k2tog, p2; rep from * to end.

Row 8: As row 2.

Rep rows 1–2, 3 times more.

Row 15: P2, C4F, p2, *k2, yf, k2tog, p2, C4F, p2; rep from * to end.

Row 16: As row 2.

Rep these 16 rows.

Tip

It is quite a common error when working lace or eyelet stitches to forget to make a yarnover. If you realize that you have forgotten to pass a slipped stitch, you can remedy this by working it on the wrong-side row when you come to the decreased stitch.

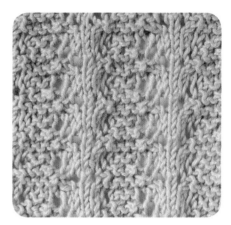

Lacy stars

Multiple of 8 sts + 5.

Row 1 and all odd-numbered rows (WS): Purl.

Row 2: K4, *ssk, yf, k1, yf, k2tog, k3; rep from *, end k1.

Row 4: K5, *yf, sl2, k1, p2sso, yf, k5; rep from *.

Row 6: Rep row 2.

Row 8: Ssk, yf, k1, yf, k2tog, *k3, ssk, yf, k1, yf, k2tog; rep from *.

Row 10: K1, *yf, sl2, k1, p2sso, yf, k5; rep from *, end last rep k1.

Row 12: Rep row 8.

Rep these 12 rows.

Dewdrop pattern

Multiple of 6 + 1.

Row 1 (WS): K2, *p3, k3; rep from * to last 5 sts, p3, k2.

Row 2: P2, *k3, p3; rep from * to last 5 sts, k3, p2.

Row 3: As row 1.

Row 4: K2, *yf, sl 1, k2tog, psso, yf, k3; rep from * to last 5 sts, yf, sl 1, k2tog, psso, yf, k2.

Row 5: As row 2.

Row 6: K2, *p3, k3; rep from * to last 5 sts, p3, k2.

Row 7: As row 2.

Row 8: K2tog, *yf, k3, yf, sl 1, k2tog, psso; rep from * to last 5 sts, yf, k3, yf, sl 1, k1, psso.

Rep these 8 rows.

Garter stitch eyelet chevron

Multiple of 9 + 1.

Row 1 (RS): K1, *yf, sl 1, k1, psso, k4, k2tog, yf, k1; rep from * to end.

Row 2: P2, *k6, p3; rep from * to last 8 sts, k6, p2.

Row 3: K2, *yf, sl 1, k1, psso, k2, k2tog, yf, k3; rep from * to last 8 sts, yf, sl 1, k1, psso, k2, k2tog, yf, k2.

Row 4: P3, *k4, p5; rep from * to last 7 sts, k4, p3.

Row 5: K3, *yf, sl 1, k1, psso, k2tog, yf, k5; rep from * to last 7 sts, yf, sl 1, k1, psso, k2tog, yf, k3.

Row 6: P4, *k2, p7; rep from * to last 6 sts, k2, p4.

Rep these 6 rows.

Fern lace

Multiple of 9 + 4.
Row 1 (WS): Purl.
Row 2: K3, *yf, k2, sl 1, k1, psso, k2tog, k2, yf, k1; rep from * to last st, k1.
Row 3: Purl.
Row 4: K2, *yf, k2, sl 1, k1, psso, k2tog, k2, yf, k1; rep from * to last 2 sts, k2.
Rep these 4 rows.

Cell stitch

Multiple of 4 + 3.
Row 1 (RS): K2, *yf, sl 1, k2tog, psso, yf, k1; rep from * to last st, k1.
Row 2: Purl.
Row 3: K1, k2tog, yf, k1, *yf, sl 1, k2tog, psso, yf, k1; rep from * to last 3 sts, yf, sl 1, k1, psso, k1.
Row 4: Purl.
Rep these 4 rows.

Little arrowhead

Multiple of 6 + 1.
Row 1 (RS): K1, *yf, sl 1, k1, psso, k1, k2tog, yf, k1; rep from * to end.
Row 2: Purl.
Row 3: K2, *yf, sl 1, k2tog, psso, yf, k3; rep from * to last 5 sts, yf, sl 1, k2tog, psso, yf, k2.
Row 4: Purl.
Rep these 4 rows.

Crowns I

Multiple of 5.
Work 4 rows in garter st.
Row 5: K1, *k1 winding yarn around needle 3 times; rep from * to end.
Row 6: *Sl 5 sts purlwise dropping extra loops, return these 5 sts to left-hand needle then work into these 5 sts together as follows: k1, [p1, k1] twice; rep from * to end.
Work 2 rows in garter st.
Rep these 8 rows.

Foaming waves

Multiple of 12 + 1.
Rows 1–4: Knit 4 rows.
Row 5 (RS): K1, *[k2tog] twice, [yf, k1] 3 times, yf, [sl 1, k1, psso] twice, k1; rep from * to end.
Row 6: Purl.
Rows 7–12: Rep the last 2 rows 3 times more.
Rep these 12 rows.

Eyelets

Multiple of 3 + 2.
Rows 1–2: Work 2 rows in st st, starting with knit.
Row 3 (RS): K2, *yf, k2tog, k1; rep from * to end.
Row 4: Purl.
Rep these 4 rows.

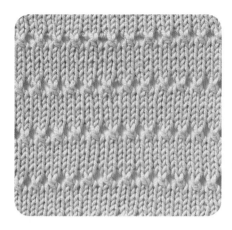  

Eyelet rows

Multiple of 2 + 2.

Row 1 (RS): 1 edge st, knit to last st, 1 edge st.

Row 2 and every alt row: 1 edge st, purl to last st, 1 edge st.

Row 3: 1 edge st, *yo, ssk; rep from * to last st, 1 edge st.

Row 5, 7, 9, 13 and 15: As row 1.

Row 11: 1 edge st, k1, *yo, ssk; rep from * to last 2 sts, k1, 1 edge st.

Rep these 16 rows.

Spiral and eyelet panel

Worked across 24 sts on a background of rev st st.

Row 1 (RS): K3, k2tog, k4, yfrn, p2, yon, k2tog, p2, yon, k4, sl 1, k1, psso, k3.

Row 2 and every alt row: P9, k2, p2, k2, p9.

Row 3: K2, k2tog, k4, yf, k1, p2, k2tog, yfrn, p2, k1, yf, k4, sl 1, k1, psso, k2.

Row 5: K1, k2tog, k4, yf, k2, p2, yon, k2tog, p2, k2, yf, k4, sl 1, k1, psso, k1.

Row 7: K2tog, k4, yf, k3, p2, k2tog, yfrn, p2, k3, yf, k4, sl 1, k1, psso.

Row 8: P9, k2, p2, k2, p9.

Rep these 8 rows.

Candelabra panel

Worked over 13 sts on a background of st st.

Row 1 (RS): Knit.

Row 2 and every alt row: Purl.

Row 3: Knit.

Row 5: K4, k2tog, yf, k1, yf, sl 1, k1, psso, k4.

Row 7: K3, k2tog, yf, k3, yf, sl 1, k1, psso, k3.

Row 9: K2, [k2tog, yf] twice, k1, [yf, sl 1, k1, psso] twice, k2.

Row 11: K1, [k2tog, yf] twice, k3, [yf, sl 1, k1, psso] twice, k1.

Row 13: [K2tog, yf] 3 times, k1, [yf, sl 1, k1, psso] 3 times.

Row 14: Purl.

Rep these 14 rows.

Zigzag panel

Worked over 9 sts on a background of st st.

Row 1 (RS): K3, sl 1, k1, psso, yf, k2tog, yf, k2.

Row 2 and every alt row: Purl.

Row 3: K2, sl 1, k1, psso, yf, k2tog, yf, k3.

Row 5: K1, sl 1, k1, psso, yf, k2tog, yf, k4.

Row 7: Sl 1, k1, psso, yf, k2tog, yf, k5.

Row 9: K2, yf, sl 1, k1, psso, yf, k2tog, k3.

Row 11: K3, yf, sl 1, k1, psso, yf, k2tog, k2.

Row 13: K4, yf, sl 1, k1, psso, yf, k2tog, k1.

Row 15: K5, yf, sl 1, k1, psso, yf, k2tog.

Row 16: Purl.

Rep these 16 rows.

Eyelet fan panel

Worked over 13 sts on a background of st st.

Work 4 rows in garter st (row 1 is RS).

Row 5: Sl 1, k1, psso, k4, yf, k1, yf, k4, k2tog.

Rows 6, 8, 10 and 12: Purl.

Row 7: Sl 1, k1, psso, [k3, yf] twice, k3, k2tog.

Row 9: Sl 1, k1, psso, k2, yf, k2tog, yf, k1, yf, sl 1, k1, psso, yf, k2, k2tog.

Row 11: Sl 1, k1, psso, k1, yf, k2tog, yf, k3, yf, sl 1, k1, psso, yf, k1, k2tog.

Row 13: Sl 1, k1, psso, [yf, k2tog] twice, yf, k1, [yf, sl 1, k1, psso] twice, yf, k2tog.

Row 14: Purl.

Rep these 14 rows.

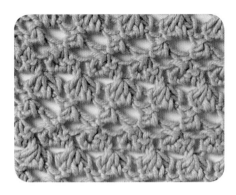

Grand eyelets

Multiple of 4.

Note: Sts should not be counted after row 1.

Row 1: P2, *yrn, p4tog; rep from * to last 2 sts, p2.

Row 2: K3, [k1, p1, k1] into next st, *k1, [k1, p1, k1] into next st; rep from * to last 2 sts, k2.

Row 3: Knit.

Rep these 3 rows.

Bluebell ribs

Multiple of 5 + 2.

Row 1 (RS): P2, *k3, p2; rep from * to end.

Row 2: K2, *p3, k2; rep from * to end. Rep the last 2 rows once more.

Row 5: P2, *yon, sl 1, k2tog, psso, yfrn, p2; rep from * to end.

Row 6: As row 2.

Rep these 6 rows.

Knotted openwork

Multiple of 3.

Row 1 (WS): Purl.

Row 2: K2, *yf, k3, with left-hand needle lift first of the 3 sts just knitted over the last 2; rep from * to last st, k1.

Row 3: Purl.

Row 4: K1, *k3, with left-hand needle lift first of the 3 sts just knitted over the last 2, yf; rep from * to last 2 sts, k2.

Rep these 4 rows.

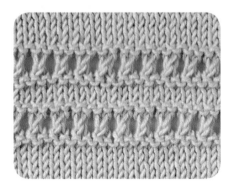

Ridged eyelet border

Multiple of 2 + 1.

Worked on a background of st st.

Rows 1–3: Knit.

Row 4 (WS): *P2tog, yrn; rep from * to last st, p1.

Rows 5–7: Knit.

Row 8: Purl.

Rep the first 6 rows once more.

Simple garter stitch lace

Multiple of 4 + 2.

Row 1: K2, *yfrn, p2tog, k2; rep from * to end.

Rep this row.

Chevron and feather

Multiple of 13 + 1.

Row 1 (RS): *K1, yf, k4, k2tog, sl 1, k1, psso, k4, yf; rep from * to last st, k1.

Row 2: Purl.

Rep these 2 rows.

Little flowers

Multiple of 6 + 3.

Row 1 (RS): Knit.

Row 2 and every alt row: Purl.

Row 3: Knit.

Row 5: *K4, yf, sl 1, k1, psso; rep from * to last 3 sts, k3.

Row 7: K2, k2tog, yf, k1, yf, sl 1, k1, psso, *k1, k2tog, yf, k1, yf, sl 1, k1, psso; rep from * to last 2 sts, k2.

Rows 9–11: Knit.

Row 13: K1, yf, sl 1, k1, psso, *k4, yf, sl 1, k1, psso; rep from * to end.

Row 15: K2, yf, sl 1, k1, psso, k1, k2tog, yf, *k1, yf, sl 1, k1, psso, k1, k2tog, yf; rep from * to last 2 sts, k2.

Row 16: Purl.

Rep these 16 rows.

Little fountain pattern

Multiple of 4 + 1.

Note: Sts should only be counted after rows 3–4.

Row 1 (RS): K1, *yf, k3, yf, k1; rep from * to end.

Row 2: Purl.

Row 3: K2, sl 1, k2tog, psso, *k3, sl 1, k2tog, psso; rep from * to last 2 sts, k2.

Row 4: Purl.

Rep these 4 rows.

Butterfly lace

Multiple of 8 + 7.

Row 1 (RS): K1, *k2tog, yf, k1, yf, sl 1, k1, psso, k3; rep from * to last 6 sts, k2tog, yf, k1, yf, sl 1, k1, psso, k1.

Row 2: P3, *sl 1 purlwise, p7; rep from * to last 4 sts, sl 1 purlwise, p3.

Rep the last 2 rows once more.

Row 5: K5, *k2tog, yf, k1, yf, sl 1, k1, psso, k3; rep from * to last 2 sts, k2.

Row 6: P7, *sl 1 purlwise, p7; rep from * to end.

Rep the last 2 rows once more.

Rep these 8 rows.

Tip

When slipping the first and last stitch of each row, be careful when you turn your work to avoid having a slipped loop down the side of your project.

Cable and lace check

Multiple of 12 + 8.

Row 1 (WS): K2, p2tog, yrn, p2, k2, *p4, k2, p2tog, yrn, p2, k2; rep from * to end.

Row 2: P2, k2tog, yf, k2, p2, *k4, p2, k2tog, yf, k2, p2; rep from * to end.

Row 3: As row 1.

Row 4: P2, k2tog, yf, k2, p2, *C4B, p2, k2tog, yf, k2, p2; rep from * to end.

Rows 5–7: As rows 1–3.

Row 8: P2, *C4B, p2; rep from * to end.

Row 9: K2, p4, k2, *p2tog, yrn, p2, k2, p4, k2; rep from * to end.

Row 10: P2, k4, p2, *k2tog, yf, k2, p2, k4, p2; rep from * to end.

Row 11: As row 9.

Row 12: P2, C4B, p2, *k2tog, yf, k2, p2, C4B, p2; rep from * to end.

Rows 13–15: As rows 9–11.

Row 16: As row 8.

Rep these 16 rows.

Leafy lace

Multiple of 10 + 1.

Row 1 (RS): KB1, *p9, KB1; rep from * to end.

Row 2: P1, *k9, p1; rep from * to end.
Rep the last 2 rows once more.

Row 5: KB1, *p2, p2tog, yon, KB1, yfrn, p2tog, p2, KB1; rep from * to end.

Row 6: P1, *k4, PB1, k4, p1; rep from * to end.

Row 7: KB1, *p1, p2tog, yon, [KB1] 3 times, yfrn, p2tog, p1, KB1; rep from * to end.

Row 8: P1, *k3, [PB1] 3 times, k3, p1; rep from * to end.

Row 9: KB1, *p2tog, yon, [KB1] 5 times, yfrn, p2tog, KB1; rep from * to end.

Row 10: P1, *k2, [PB1] 5 times, k2, p1; rep from * to end.

Row 11: KB1, *p1, yon, [KB1] twice, sl 1, k2tog, psso, [KB1] twice, yfrn, p1, KB1; rep from * to end.

Row 12: As row 10.

Row 13: KB1, *p2, yon, KB1, sl 1, k2tog, psso, KB1, yfrn, p2, KB1; rep from * to end.

Row 14: As row 8.

Row 15: KB1, *p3, yon, sl 1, k2tog, psso, yfrn, p3, KB1; rep from * to end.

Row 16: As row 6.
Rep these 16 rows.

Cockleshells

Worked over 19 sts on a background of garter st.

Row 1 (RS): Knit.

Row 2: Knit.

Row 3: K1, yfrn, yrn, p2tog tbl, k13, p2tog, yrn, yon, k1.

Row 4: K2, p1, k15, p1, k2.

Rows 5–6: Knit.

Row 7: K1, yfrn, yrn, p2tog tbl, [yrn] twice, p2tog tbl, k11, p2tog, [yrn] twice, p2tog, yrn, yon, k1.

Row 8: [k2, p1] twice, k13, [p1, k2] twice.

Row 9: Knit.

Row 10: K5, k15 wrapping yarn 3 times around needle for each st, k5.

Row 11: K1, yfrn, yrn, p2tog tbl, [yrn] twice, p2tog tbl, [yrn] twice, pass next 15 sts to right-hand needle dropping extra loops, pass same 15 sts back to left-hand needle and purl all 15 sts tog, [yrn] twice, p2tog, [yrn] twice, p2tog, yrn, yon, k1.

Row 12: K1, p1, [k2, p1] twice, k3, [p1, k2] twice, p1, k1.
Rep these 12 rows.

Eyelet panes

Multiple of 6 + 3.

Note: Sts should not be counted after rows 3, 4, 9 or 10 of this pattern.

Row 1 (RS): K2, *yf, sl 1, k1, psso, k1, k2tog, yf, k1; rep from * to last st, k1.

Row 2 and every alt row: Purl.

Row 3: K3, *yf, k3; rep from * to end.

Row 5: K1, k2tog, *yf, sl 1, k1, psso, k1, k2tog, yf, sl 1, k2tog, psso; rep from * to last 8 sts, yf, sl 1, k1, psso, k1, k2tog, yf, sl 1, k1, psso, k1.

Row 7: K2, *k2tog, yf, k1, yf, sl 1, k1, psso, k1; rep from * to last st, k1.

Row 9: As row 3.

Row 11: K2, *k2tog, yf, sl 1, k2tog, psso, yf, sl 1, k1, psso, k1; rep from * to last st, k1.

Row 12: Purl.

Rep these 12 rows.

Fern diamonds

Multiple of 10 + 1.

Row 1 (RS): K3, *k2tog, yf, k1, yf, sl 1, k1, psso, k5; rep from * to last 8 sts, k2tog, yf, k1, yf, sl 1, k1, psso, k3.

Row 2 and every alt row: Purl.

Row 3: K2, *k2tog, [k1, yf] twice, k1, sl 1, k1, psso, k3; rep from * to last 9 sts, k2tog, [k1, yf] twice, k1, sl 1, k1, psso, k2.

Row 5: K1, *k2tog, k2, yf, k1, yf, k2, sl 1, k1, psso, k1; rep from * to end.

Row 7: K2tog, *k3, yf, k1, yf, k3, sl 1, k2tog, psso; rep from * to last 9 sts, k3, yf, k1, yf, k3, sl 1, k1, psso.

Row 9: K1, *yf, sl 1, k1, psso, k5, k2tog, yf, k1; rep from * to end.

Row 11: K1, *yf, k1, sl 1, k1, psso, k3, k2tog, k1, yf, k1; rep from * to end.

Row 13: K1, *yf, k2, sl 1, k1, psso, k1, k2tog, k2, yf, k1; rep from * to end.

Row 15: K1, *yf, k3, sl 1, k2tog, psso, k3, yf, k1; rep from * to end.

Row 16: Purl.

Rep these 16 rows.

Clover pattern

Multiple of 12 + 1.

Row 1 (RS): K2tog, k4, yf, k1, yf, k4, *sl 1, k2tog, psso, k4, yf, k1, yf, k4; rep from * to last 2 sts, sl 1, k1, psso.

Row 2 and every alt row: Purl.

Row 3: K2tog, k3, [yf, k3] twice, *sl 1, k2tog, psso, k3, [yf, k3] twice; rep from * to last 2 sts, sl 1, k1, psso.

Row 5: K2tog, k2, yf, k5, yf, k2, *sl 1, k2tog, psso, k2, yf, k5, yf, k2; rep from * to last 2 sts, sl 1, k1, psso.

Row 7: K1, *yf, k4, sl 1, k2tog, psso, k4, yf, k1; rep from * to end.

Row 9: K2, yf, k3, sl 1, k2tog, psso, k3, *[yf, k3] twice, sl 1, k2tog, psso, k3; rep from * to last 2 sts, yf, k2.

Row 11: K3, yf, k2, sl 1, k2tog, psso, k2, *yf, k5, yf, k2, sl 1, k2tog, psso, k2; rep from * to last 3 sts, yf, k3.

Row 12: Purl.

Rep these 12 rows.

Lace diamond border

Multiple of 8.

Row 1 (RS): *K1, yf, k3, pass 3rd st on right-hand needle over first 2 sts; rep from * to end.

Row 2 and every alt row: Purl.

Row 3: Knit.

Row 5: K3, *yf, sl 1, k1, psso, k6; rep from * to last 5 sts, yf, sl 1, k1, psso, k3.

Row 7: K2, *[yf, sl 1, k1, psso] twice, k4; rep from * to last 6 sts, [yf, sl 1, k1, psso] twice, k2.

Row 9: K1, *[yf, sl 1, k1, psso] 3 times, k2; rep from * to last 7 sts, [yf, sl 1, k1, psso] 3 times, k1.

Row 11: As row 7.

Row 13: As row 5.

Row 15: Knit.

Row 17: As row 1.

Row 18: Purl.

Rep these 18 rows.

Bead stitch

Multiple of 7.

Row 1 (RS): K1, k2tog, yf, k1, yf, sl 1, k1, psso, *k2, k2tog, yf, k1, yf, sl 1, k1, psso; rep from * to last st, k1.

Row 2: *P2tog tbl, yrn, p3, yrn, p2tog; rep from * to end.

Row 3: K1, yf, sl 1, k1, psso, k1, k2tog, yf, *k2, yf, sl 1, k1, psso, k1, k2tog, yf; rep from * to last st, k1.

Row 4: P2, yrn, p3tog, yrn, *p4, yrn, p3tog, yrn; rep from * to last 2 sts, p2.

Rep these 4 rows.

Lacy lattice stitch

Multiple of 6 + 1.

Row 1 (RS): K1, *yfrn, p1, p3tog, p1, yon, k1; rep from * to end.

Row 2 and every alt row: Purl.

Row 3: K2, yf, sl 1, k2tog, psso, yf, *k3, yf, sl 1, k2tog, psso, yf; rep from * to last 2 sts, k2.

Row 5: P2tog, p1, yon, k1, yfrn, p1, *p3tog, p1, yon, k1, yfrn, p1; rep from * to last 2 sts, p2tog.

Row 7: K2tog, yf, k3, yf, *sl 1, k2tog, psso, yf, k3, yf; rep from * to last 2 sts, sl 1, k1, psso.

Row 8: Purl.

Rep these 8 rows.

Parasol stitch

Worked over 17 sts on a background of st st.

Note: Sts should only be counted after rows 11 and 12 of this pattern.

Row 1 (RS): Yf, k1, [p3, k1] 4 times, yf.

Row 2 and every alt row: Purl.

Row 3: K1, yf, k1, [p3, k1] 4 times, yf, k1.

Row 5: K2, yf, k1, [p3, k1] 4 times, yf, k2.

Row 7: K3, yf, k1, [p2tog, p1, k1] 4 times, yf, k3.

Row 9: K4, yf, k1, [p2tog, k1] 4 times, yf, k4.

Row 11: K5, yf, k1, [k3tog, k1] twice, yf, k5.

Row 12: Purl.

Rep these 12 rows.

Diagonal openwork

Multiple of 4 + 2.

Row 1 (RS): *K1, yf, sl 1, k2tog, psso, yf; rep from * to last 2 sts, k2.

Row 2 and every alt row: Purl.

Row 3: K2, *yf, sl 1, k2tog, psso, yf, k1; rep from * to end.

Row 5: K2tog, yf, k1, yf, *sl 1, k2tog, psso, yf, k1, yf; rep from * to last 3 sts, sl 1, k1, psso, k1.

Row 7: K1, k2tog, yf, k1, yf, *sl 1, k2tog, psso, yf, k1, yf; rep from * to last 2 sts, sl 1, k1, psso.

Row 8: Purl.

Rep these 8 rows.

Little shell pattern

Multiple of 7 + 2.
Row 1 (RS): Knit.
Row 2: Purl.
Row 3: K2, *yfrn, p1, p3tog, p1, yon, k2; rep from * to end.
Row 4: Purl.
Rep these 4 rows.

Zigzag eyelet columns

Multiple of 6 + 4.
Row 1 (RS): *K4, yo, ssk; rep from * to last 4 sts, k4.
Row 2: Purl.
Row 3: *K4, k2tog, yo; rep from * to last 4 sts, k4.
Row 4: Purl.
Rep these 4 rows.

Faggoted panel

Worked over 9 sts on a st st background.
Row 1 (RS): P1, k1, k2tog, yf, k1, yf, k2tog tbl, k1, p1.
Row 2: K1, p7, k1.
Row 3: P1, k2tog, yf, k3, yf, k2tog tbl, p1.
Row 4: As row 2.
Rep these 4 rows.

Astrakhan bobbles

Multiple of 12 + 3.
Either side of this stitch may be used.
Row 1: K2, *yf, k4, p3tog, k4, yf, k1; rep from * to last st, k1.
Rep this row 5 times more.
Row 7: K1, p2tog, *k4, yf, k1, yf, k4, p3tog; rep from * to last 12 sts, k4, yf, k1, yf, k4, p2tog, k1.
Rep this row 5 times more.
Rep these 12 rows.

Pillar openwork

Multiple of 3 + 2.
Row 1 (RS): K1, *yf, sl 1 purlwise, k2, psso the k2; rep from * to last st, k1.
Row 2: Purl.
Rep these 2 rows.

Ridged lace

Multiple of 2.
Row 1 (RS): K1, *yf, k2tog tbl; rep from * to last st, k1.
Row 2: P1, *yrn, p2tog; rep from * to last st, p1.
Rep these 2 rows.

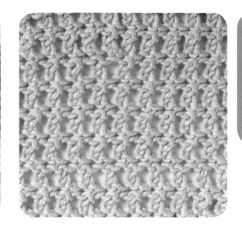

Crowns II

Multiple of 10 + 7.

Special abbreviations:

KW5 = knit 5 sts wrapping yarn 3 times around needle for each st.

Twist 5 = slip 5 sts purlwise dropping extra loops, return these 5 sts to left-hand needle, then k1, [p1, k1] twice into same 5 sts tog.

Row 1: K6, KW5, *k5, KW5; rep from * to last 6 sts, k6.

Row 2: P6, Twist 5, *p5, Twist 5; rep from * to last 6 sts, p6.

Row 3: Knit.

Row 4: K6, p5, *k5, p5; rep from * to last 6 sts, k6.

Row 5: K1, KW5, *k5, KW5; rep from * to last st, k1.

Row 6: P1, Twist 5, *p5, Twist 5; rep from * to last st, p1.

Row 7: Knit.

Row 8: K1, p5, *k5, p5; rep from * to last st, k1.

Rep these 8 rows.

King Charles lace

Worked over 11 sts on a background of st st.

Row 1 (RS): P2, k2tog, [k1, yf] twice, k1, sl 1, k1, psso, p2.

Row 2 and every alt row: K2, p7, k2.

Row 3: P2, k2tog, yf, k3, yf, sl 1, k1, psso, p2.

Row 5: P2, k1, yf, sl 1, k1, psso, k1, k2tog, yf, k1, p2.

Row 7: P2, k2, yf, sl 1, k2tog, psso, yf, k2, p2.

Row 8: As row 2.

Rep these 8 rows.

Ridge and hole pattern

Multiple of 2 + 1.

Note: Sts should only be counted after rows 1, 3 or 4 of this pattern.

Row 1 (RS): Purl.

Row 2: *P2tog; rep from * to last st, p1.

Row 3: P1, *purl through horizontal strand of yarn lying between stitch just worked and next st, p1; rep from * to end.

Row 4: P1, *yrn, p2tog; rep from * to end.

Rep these 4 rows.

Bear paw panel

Worked over 23 sts on a background of st st.

Row 1 (RS): K2, [p4, k1] 3 times, p4, k2.

Row 2: P2, [k4, p1] 3 times, k4, p2.

Row 3: K1, yf, k1, p2, p2tog, [k1, p4] twice, k1, p2tog, p2, k1, yf, k1.

Row 4: P3, k2, p2, k4, p1, k4, p2, k2, p3.

Row 5: K2, yf, k1, p3, k1, p2, p2tog, k1, p2tog, p2, k1, p3, k1, yf, k2.

Row 6: P4, k3, p1, k2, p3, k2, p1, k3, p4.

Row 7: K3, yf, k1, p1, p2tog, [k1, p3] twice, k1, p2tog, p1, k1, yf, k3.

Row 8: P5, k1, p2, k3, p1, k3, p2, k1, p5.

Row 9: K4, yf, k1, p2, k1, p1, p2tog, k1, p2tog, p1, k1, p2, k1, yf, k4.

Row 10: P6, k2, p1, k1, p3, k1, p1, k2, p6.

Row 11: K5, yf, k1, p2tog, [k1, p2] twice, k1, p2tog, k1, yf, k5.

Row 12: P9, k2, p1, k2, p9.

Row 13: K6, yf, k1, p1, k1, [p2tog, k1] twice, p1, k1, yf, k6.

Row 14: P8, k1, p5, k1, p8.

Rep these 14 rows.

Arched windows

Worked over 13 sts on a background of rev st st.

Note: Sts should not be counted after rows 3, 4, 7 or 8.

T5R (Twist 5 Right) = slip next 3 sts onto cable needle and hold at back of work, knit next 2 sts from left-hand needle, then p1, k2 from cable needle.

Row 1 (RS): K2, p2, k2tog, yf, k1, yf, sl 1, k1, psso, p2, k2.

Row 2: P2, k2, p5, k2, p2.

Row 3: K2, p2, k1, yf, k3, yf, k1, p2, k2.

Row 4: P2, k2, p7, k2, p2.

Row 5: K2, p2, yb, sl 1, k1, psso, yf, sl 1, k2tog, psso, yf, k2tog, p2, k2.

Row 6: As row 2.

Row 7: T3F, p1, k1, yf, k3, yf, k1, p1, T3B.

Row 8: K1, p2, k1, p7, k1, p2, k1.

Row 9: P1, T3F, sl 1, k1, psso, yf, sl 1, k2tog, psso, yf, k2tog, T3B, p1.

Row 10: K2, p9, k2.

Row 11: P2, T3F, p3, T3B, p2.

Row 12: [K3, p2] twice, k3.

Row 13: P3, T3F, p1, T3B, p3.

Row 14: K4, p2, k1, p2, k4.

Row 15: P4, T5R, p4.

Row 16: Knit.

Rep these 16 rows.

Peacock plume

Multiple of 16 sts + 1.

Rows 1–3 (WS): Purl.

Row 2: Knit.

Row 4: [K1, yf] 3 times, [sl 1, k1, psso] twice, sl 2, k1, p2sso, [k2tog] twice, *yf, [k1, yf] 5 times, [sl 1, k1, psso] twice, sl 2, k1, p2sso, [k2tog] twice; rep from * to last 3 sts, [yf, k1] 3 times.

Rows 5–16: Rep the last 4 rows 3 times more.

Rows 17 and 19: Purl.

Row 18: Knit.

Row 20: [K2tog] 3 times, [yf, k1] 5 times, *yf, [sl 1, k1, psso] twice, sl 2, k1, p2sso, [k2tog] twice, [yf, k1] 5 times; rep from * to last 6 sts, yf, [sl 1, k1, psso] 3 times.

Rows 21–32: Rep the last 4 rows 3 times more.

Rep these 32 rows.

Canterbury bells

Multiple of 5.

Note: Sts should only be counted after rows 1, 2 and 10.

Row 1 (RS): P2, KB1, *p4, KB1; rep from * to last 2 sts, p2.

Row 2: K2, PB1, *k4, PB1; rep from * to last 2 sts, k2.

Row 3: P2, KB1, *p2, turn, cast on 8 sts cable method, turn, p2, KB1; rep from * to last 2 sts, p2.

Row 4: K2, PB1, *k2, p8, k2, PB1; rep from * to last 2 sts, k2.

Row 5: P2, KB1, *p2, k8, p2, KB1; rep from * to last 2 sts, p2.

Row 6: As row 4.

Row 7: P2, KB1, *p2, yb, sl 1, k1, psso, k4, k2tog, p2, KB1; rep from * to last 2 sts, p2.

Row 8: K2, PB1, *k2, p2tog, p2, p2tog tbl, k2, PB1; rep from * to last 2 sts, k2.

Row 9: P2, KB1, *p2, yb, sl 1, k1, psso, k2tog, p2, KB1; rep from * to last 2 sts, p2.

Row 10: K2, PB1, *k1, sl 1, k1, psso, k2tog, k1, PB1; rep from * to last 2 sts, k2.

Rep these 10 rows.

Leaf panel

Worked over 24 sts on a background of st st.

Row 1 (RS): Sl 1, k2tog, psso, k7, yf, k1, yfrn, p2, yon, k1, yf, k7, k3tog.

Row 2 and every alt row: P11, k2, p11.

Row 3: Sl 1, k2tog, psso, k6, [yf, k1] twice, p2, [k1, yf] twice, k6, k3tog.

Row 5: Sl 1, k2tog, psso, k5, yf, k1, yf, k2, p2, k2, yf, k1, yf, k5, k3tog.

Row 7: Sl 1, k2tog, psso, k4, yf, k1, yf, k3, p2, k3, yf, k1, yf, k4, k3tog.

Row 9: Sl 1, k2tog, psso, k3, yf, k1, yf, k4, p2, k4, yf, k1, yf, k3, k3tog.

Row 10: As row 2.

Rep these 10 rows.

Crowns of glory

Multiple of 14 + 1.

Note: Sts should only be counted after rows 7, 8, 9, 10, 11 and 12.

Row 1 (RS): K1, *sl 1, k1, psso, k9, k2tog, k1; rep from * to end.

Row 2: P1, *p2tog, p7, p2tog tbl, p1; rep from * to end.

Row 3: K1, *sl 1, k1, psso, k2, [yf] 3 times, k3, k2tog, k1; rep from * to end.

Row 4: P1, *p2tog, p2, [k1, p1, k1, p1, k1] into [yf] 3 times making 5 sts, p1, p2tog tbl, p1; rep from * to end.

Row 5: K1, *sl 1, k1, psso, k6, k2tog, k1; rep from * to end.

Row 6: P1, *p2tog, p7; rep from * to end.

Row 7: K2, [yf, k1] 5 times, yf, *k3, [yf, k1] 5 times, yf; rep from * to last 2 sts, k2.

Row 8: Purl.

Rows 9–10: Knit.

Row 11: Purl.

Row 12: Knit.

Rep these 12 rows.

Garter stitch lacy diamonds

Multiple of 10 + 1.

Row 1 and every alt row (RS): Knit.

Row 2: K3, *k2tog, yf, k1, yf, k2tog, k5; rep from * to last 8 sts, k2tog, yf, k1, yf, k2tog, k3.

Row 4: K2, *k2tog, yf, k3, yf, k2tog, k3; rep from * to last 9 sts, k2tog, yf, k3, yf, k2tog, k2.

Row 6: K1, *k2tog, yf, k5, yf, k2tog, k1; rep from * to end.

Row 8: K1, *yf, k2tog, k5, k2tog, yf, k1; rep from * to end.

Row 10: K2, *yf, k2tog, k3, k2tog, yf, k3; rep from * to last 9 sts, yf, k2tog, k3, k2tog, yf, k2.

Row 12: K3, *yf, k2tog, k1, k2tog, yf, k5; rep from * to last 8 sts, yf, k2tog, k1, k2tog, yf, k3.

Rep these 12 rows.

Moss lace diamonds

Multiple of 8 + 1.

Row 1 (RS): K1, *p1, k1; rep from * to end.

Row 2: K1, *p1, K1; rep from * to end.
Rep the last 2 rows once more.

Row 5: K1, *yf, sl 1, k1, psso, k3, k2tog, yf, k1; rep from * to end.

Row 6: Purl.

Row 7: K2, *yf, sl 1, k1, psso, k1, k2tog, yf, k3; rep from * to last 7 sts, yf, sl 1, k1, psso, k1, k2tog, yf, k2.

Row 8: Purl.

Row 9: K3, *yf, sl 1, k2tog, psso, yf, k5; rep from * to last 6 sts, yf, sl 1, k2tog, psso, yf, k3.

Row 10: Purl.

Row 11: K1, *p1, k1; rep from * to end.
Rep the last row 3 times more.

Row 15: K2, *k2tog, yf, k1, yf, sl 1, k1, psso, k3; rep from * to last 7 sts, k2tog, yf, k1, yf, sl 1, k1, psso, k2.

Row 16: Purl.

Row 17: *K1, k2tog, yf, k3, yf, sl 1, k1, psso; rep from * to last st, k1.

Row 18: Purl.

Row 19: K2tog, *yf, k5, yf, sl 1, k2tog, psso; rep from * to last 7 sts, yf, k5, yf, sl 1, k1, psso.

Row 20: Purl.
Rep these 20 rows.

Lace check

Multiple of 18 + 9.

Row 1 (WS): Purl.

Row 2: K1, *[yf, k2tog] 4 times, k10; rep from * to last 8 sts, [yf, k2tog] 4 times.

Row 3: Purl.

Row 4: *[Sl 1, k1, psso, yf] 4 times, k10; rep from * to last 9 sts, [sl 1, k1, psso, yf] 4 times, k1.
Rep the last 4 rows twice more.

Row 13: Purl.

Row 14: *K10, [yf, k2tog] 4 times; rep from * to last 9 sts, k9.

Row 15: Purl.

Row 16: K9, *[sl 1, k1, psso, yf] 4 times, k10; rep from * to end.
Rep the last 4 rows twice more.
Rep these 24 rows.

Twisted openwork pattern

Multiple of 4 + 1.

Row 1 (RS): P1, *k3, p1; rep from * to end.

Row 2: K1, *p3, k1; rep from * to end.

Row 3: As row 1.

Row 4: K1, *yfrn, p3tog, yon, k1; rep from * to end.

Row 5: K2, p1, *k3, p1; rep from * to last 2 sts, k2.

Row 6: P2, k1, *p3, k1; rep from * to last 2 sts, p2.

Row 7: As row 5.

Row 8: P2tog, yon, k1, yfrn, *p3tog, yon, k1, yfrn; rep from * to last 2 sts, p2tog.

Rep these 8 rows.

Knotted boxes I

Multiple of 8 + 5.

Row 1 (RS): Knit.

Row 2: Purl.

Row 3: K1, p3, *k5, p3; rep from * to last st, k1.

Row 4: P1, k3, *p5, k3; rep from * to last st, p1.

Row 5: K1, yf, k3tog, yf, *k5, yf, k3tog, yf; rep from * to last st, k1.

Work 3 rows in st st, starting purl.

Row 9: K5, *p3, k5; rep from * to end.

Row 10: P5, *k3, p5; rep from * to end.

Row 11: K5, *yf, k3tog, yf, k5; rep from * to end.

Row 12: Purl.

Rep these 12 rows.

Fishtail lace

Multiple of 8 + 1.

Row 1 (RS): K1, *yf, k2, sl 1, k2tog, psso, k2, yf, k1; rep from * to end.

Row 2: Purl.

Row 3: K2, *yf, k1, sl 1, k2tog, psso, k1, yf, k3; rep from * to last 7 sts, yf, k1, sl 1, k2tog, psso, k1, yf, k2.

Row 4: Purl.

Row 5: K3, *yf, sl 1, k2tog, psso, yf, k5; rep from * to last 6 sts, yf, sl 1, k2tog, psso, yf, k3.

Row 6: Purl.

Rep these 6 rows.

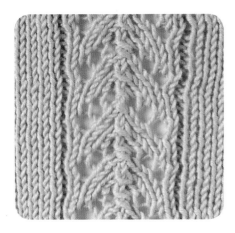

Fishtail lace panel

Worked over 11 sts on a background of st st.

Row 1 (RS): P1, k1, yf, k2, sl 1, k2tog, psso, k2, yf, k1, p1.

Row 2: K1, p9, k1.

Row 3: P1, k2, yf, k1, sl 1, k2tog, psso, k1, yf, k2, p1.

Row 4: As row 2.

Row 5: P1, k3, yf, sl 1, k2tog, psso, yf, k3, p1.

Row 6: As row 2.

Rep these 6 rows.

Knotted boxes II

Multiple of 6 + 5.

Row 1 (RS): K1, p3, *k3, p3; rep from * to last st, k1.

Row 2: P1, k3, *p3, k3; rep from * to last st, p1.

Row 3: K1, yf, k3tog, yf, *k3, yf, k3tog, yf; rep from * to last st, k1.

Row 4: Purl.

Row 5: K4, p3, *k3, p3; rep from * to last 4 sts, k4.

Row 6: P4, k3, *p3, k3; rep from * to last 4 sts, p4.

Row 7: K4, yf, k3tog, yf, *k3, yf, k3tog, yf; rep from * to last 4 sts, k4.

Row 8: Purl.

Rep these 8 rows.

Vandyke lace panel I

Worked over 17 sts on a background of st st.

Row 1 (RS): *K2tog, yf, k1, yf, sl 1, k1, psso*, k3, yf, sl 1, k1, psso, k2, rep from * to * once more.

Row 2: Purl.

Row 3: [K2tog, yf, k1, yf, sl 1, k1, psso, k1] twice, k2tog, yf, k1, yf, sl 1, k1, psso.

Row 4: Purl.

Row 5: *K2tog, yf, k1, yf, sl 1, k1, psso*, k2tog, yf, k3, yf, sl 1, k1, psso, rep from * to * once more.

Row 6: Purl.

Rep these 6 rows.

Vandyke lace panel II

Worked over 9 sts on a background
of st st.

Row 1 (RS): K4, yf, sl 1, k1, psso, k3.

Row 2 and every alt row: Purl.

Row 3: K2, k2tog, yf, k1, yf, sl 1, k1,
psso, k2.

Row 5: K1, k2tog, yf, k3, yf, sl 1, k1,
psso, k1.

Row 7: K2tog, yf, k5, yf, sl 1, k1, psso.

Row 8: Purl.

Rep these 8 rows.

Eyelet V-stitch

Multiple of 12 + 1.

Row 1 (RS): Knit.

Row 2 and every alt row: Purl.

Row 3: K4, yf, sl 1, k1, psso, k1, k2tog,
yf, *k7, yf, sl 1, k1, psso, k1, k2tog, yf; rep
from * to last 4 sts, k4.

Row 5: K5, yf, sl 1, k2tog, psso, yf, *k9,
yf, sl 1, k2tog, psso, yf; rep from * to last
5 sts, k5.

Row 7: Knit.

Row 9: K1, *k2tog, yf, k7, yf, sl 1, k1,
psso, k1; rep from * to end.

Row 11: K2tog, yf, k9, *yf, sl 1, k2tog,
psso, yf, k9; rep from * to last 2 sts, yf, sl
1, k1, psso.

Row 12: Purl.

Rep these 12 rows.

Diamond lace I

Multiple of 8 + 7.

Row 1 (RS): Knit.

Row 2 and every alt row: Purl.

Row 3: K3, *yf, sl 1, k1, psso, k6; rep
from * to last 4 sts, yf, sl 1, k1, psso, k2.

Row 5: K2, *yf, sl 1, k2tog, psso, yf, k5;
rep from * to last 5 sts, yf, sl 1, k2tog,
psso, yf, k2.

Row 7: As row 3.

Row 9: Knit.

Row 11: K7, *yf, sl 1, k1, psso, k6; rep
from * to end.

Row 13: K6, *yf, sl 1, k2tog, psso, yf, k5;
rep from * to last st, k1.

Row 15: As row 11.

Row 16: Purl.

Rep these 16 rows.

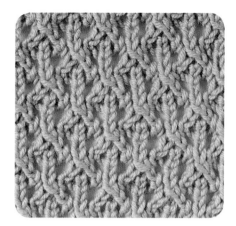

Ridged lace pattern

Multiple of 2 + 1.

Purl 3 rows.

Row 4 (RS): K1, *yf, sl 1, k1, psso; rep from * to end.

Purl 3 rows.

Row 8: K1, *yf, k2tog; rep from * to end.

Rep these 8 rows.

Pine cone pattern

Multiple of 10 + 1.

Row 1 (RS): Knit.

Row 2 and every alt row: Purl.

Row 3: K3, k2tog, yf, k1, yf, sl 1, k1, psso, *k5, k2tog, yf, k1, yf, sl 1, k1, psso; rep from * to last 3 sts, k3.

Row 5: K2, k2tog, yf, k3, yf, sl 1, k1, psso, *k3, k2tog, yf, k3, yf, sl 1, k1, psso; rep from * to last 2 sts, k2.

Rows 7 and 9: As row 3.

Row 11: Knit.

Row 13: K1, *yf, sl 1, k1, psso, k5, k2tog, yf, k1; rep from * to end.

Row 15: K2, yf, sl 1, k1, psso, k3, k2tog, yf, *k3, yf, sl 1, k1, psso, k3, k2tog, yf; rep from * to last 2 sts, k2.

Rows 17 and 19: As row 13.

Row 20: Purl.

Rep these 20 rows.

Feather lace

Multiple of 6 + 1.

Row 1 (RS): K1, *yf, k2tog tbl, k1, k2tog, yf, k1; rep from * to end.

Row 2 and every alt row: Purl.

Row 3: K1, *yf, k1, sl 1, k2tog, psso, k1, yf, k1; rep from * to end.

Row 5: K1, *k2tog, yf, k1, yf, k2tog tbl, k1; rep from * to end.

Row 7: K2tog, *[k1, yf] twice, k1, sl 1, k2tog, psso; rep from * to last 5 sts, [k1, yf] twice, k1, k2tog tbl.

Row 8: Purl.

Rep these 8 rows.

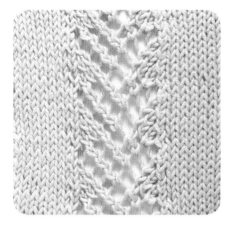

Fan lace panel

Worked over 11 sts on a background of st st.

Row 1 (RS): Sl 1, k1, psso, [KB1] 3 times, yf, k1, yf, [KB1] 3 times, k2tog.

Row 2 and every alt row: Purl.

Row 3: Sl 1, k1, psso, [KB1] twice, yf, k1, yf, sl 1, k1, psso, yf, [KB1] twice, k2tog.

Row 5: Sl 1, k1, psso, KB1, yf, k1, [yf, sl 1, k1, psso] twice, yf, KB1, k2tog.

Row 7: Sl 1, k1, psso, yf, k1, [yf, sl 1, k1, psso] 3 times, yf, k2tog.

Row 8: Purl.

Rep these 8 rows.

Raindrops

Multiple of 6 + 5.

Row 1 (RS): P5, *yrn, p2tog, p4; rep from * to end.

Row 2: K5, *p1, k5; rep from * to end.

Row 3: P5, *k1, p5; rep from * to end.

Rep the last 2 rows once more, then row 2 again.

Row 7: P2, yrn, p2tog, *p4, yrn, p2tog; rep from * to last st, p1.

Row 8: K2, p1, *k5, p1; rep from * to last 2 sts, k2.

Row 9: P2, k1, *p5, k1; rep from * to last 2 sts, p2.

Rep the last 2 rows once more, then row 8 again.

Rep these 12 rows.

Lozenge lace panel

Worked over 11 sts on a background of st st.

Row 1 (RS): K1, yf, sl 1, k1, psso, k5, k2tog, yf, k1.

Row 2 and every alt row: Purl.

Row 3: K2, yf, sl 1, k1, psso, k3, k2tog, yf, k2.

Row 5: K3, yf, sl 1, k1, psso, k1, k2tog, yf, k3.

Row 7: K4, yf, sl 1, k2tog, psso, yf, k4.

Row 9: K3, k2tog, yf, k1, yf, sl 1, k1, psso, k3.

Row 11: K2, k2tog, yf, k3, yf, sl 1, k1, psso, k2.

Row 13: K1, k2tog, yf, k5, yf, sl 1, k1, psso, k1.

Row 15: K2tog, yf, k7, yf, sl 1, k1, psso.

Row 16: Purl.

Rep these 16 rows.

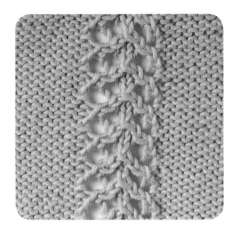

Lace rib panel

Worked over 7 sts on a background of rev st st.

Row 1 (RS): P1, yon, sl 1, k1, psso, k1, k2tog, yfrn, p1.
Row 2: K1, p5, k1.
Row 3: P1, k1, yf, sl 1, k2tog, psso, yf, k1, p1.
Row 4: K1, p5, k1.
Rep these 4 rows.

Bobble tree panel

Worked over 17 sts on a background of rev st st.

Row 1 (RS): P6, k2tog, yfrn, p1, yon, sl 1, k1, psso, p6.
Row 2: K6, p1, k3, p1, k6.
Row 3: P5, k2tog, yfrn, p3, yon, sl 1, k1, psso, p5.
Row 4: [K5, p1] twice, k5.
Row 5: P4, k2tog, yfrn, [p1, k1] twice, p1, yon, sl 1, k1, psso, p4.
Row 6: K4, p1, k2, p1, k1, p1, k2, p1, k4.
Row 7: P3, k2tog, yfrn, p2, k1, p1, k1, p2, yon, sl 1, k1, psso, p3.
Row 8: [K3, p1] twice, k1, [p1, k3] twice.
Row 9: P2, k2tog, yfrn, p2, k2tog, yfrn, p1, yon, sl 1, k1, psso, p2, yon, sl 1, k1, psso, p2.
Row 10: K2, [p1, k3] 3 times, p1, k2.
Row 11: P2, [k1, p1] twice into next st, turn and p4, turn and k4, turn and p4, turn and sl 1, k1, psso, k2tog, turn and p2tog, turn and slip bobble st onto right-hand needle (bobble completed), p2, k2tog, yfrn, p3, yon, sl 1, k1, psso, p2, make bobble, p2.
Row 12: [K5, p1] twice, k5.
Rep these 12 rows.

Lace and cable pattern

Worked over 21 sts on a st st background.

Special abbreviation:
CB4F or CB4B (Cable 4 Front or Back) = slip next 2 sts onto a cable needle and hold at front (or back) of work, knit into the back of next 2 sts on left-hand needle, then knit into the back of sts on cable needle.

Row 1 (RS): P2, [KB1] 4 times, k1, yf, k2tog tbl, k3, k2tog, yf, k1, [KB1] 4 times, p2.
Row 2 and every alt row: K2, [PB1] 4 times, k1, p7, k1, [PB1] 4 times, k2.
Row 3: P2, [KB1] 4 times, k2, yf, k2tog tbl, k1, k2tog, yf, k2, [KB1] 4 times, p2.
Row 5: P2, CB4F, k3, yf, sl 1, k2tog, psso, yf, k3, CB4B, p2.
Row 7: P2, [KB1] 4 times, k9, [KB1] 4 times, p2.
Row 8: As row 2.
Rep these 8 rows.

Catherine wheels

Worked over 13 sts on a background of st st.

Special abbreviations:

Inc 1 (increase 1) = knit into front and back of next st.

Inc 2 (increase 2) = knit into front, back and front of next st.

Work 5tog = sl 1, k1, psso, k3tog, pass the st resulting from sl 1, k1, psso over the st resulting from k3tog.

Row 1 and every alt row (WS): Purl.

Row 2: K5, sl 3, yf, pass same slipped sts back to left-hand needle, yb, knit 3 slipped sts, k5.

Row 4: K3, k3tog, yf, inc 2, yf, k3tog tbl, k3.

Row 6: K1, k3tog, yf, k2tog, yf, inc 2, yf, sl 1, k1, psso, yf, k3tog tbl, k1.

Row 8: [K2tog, yf] 3 times, KB1, [yf, sl 1, k1, psso] 3 times.

Row 10: K1, [yf, k2tog] twice, yf, sl 1, k2tog, psso, [yf, sl 1, k1, psso] twice, yf, k1.

Row 12: [Sl 1, k1, psso, yf] 3 times, KB1, [yf, k2tog] 3 times.

Row 14: K1, inc 1, yf, sl 1, k1, psso, yf, Work 5tog, yf, k2tog, yf, inc 1, k1.

Row 16: K3, inc 1, yf, Work 5tog, yf, inc 1, k3.

Rep these 16 rows.

Fishtails

Worked over 15 sts on a background of st st.

Row 1 (RS): K6, yf, sl 1, k2tog, psso, yf, k6.

Row 2 and every alt row: Purl.

Rep these 2 rows 3 times more.

Row 9: [K1, yf] twice, sl 1, k1, psso, k2, sl 1, k2tog, psso, k2, k2tog, [yf, k1] twice.

Row 11: K2, yf, k1, yf, sl 1, k1, psso, k1, sl 1, k2tog, psso, k1, k2tog, yf, k1, yf, k2.

Row 13: K3, yf, k1, yf, sl 1, k1, psso, sl 1, k2tog, psso, k2tog, yf, k1, yf, k3.

Row 15: K4, yf, sl 1, k1, psso, yf, sl 1, k2tog, psso, yf, k2tog, yf, k4.

Row 16: Purl.

Rep these 16 rows.

Zigzag eyelet panel

Worked over 11 sts on a background of st st.

Row 1 (RS): K6, yf, sl 1, k1, psso, k3.

Row 2 and every alt row: Purl.

Row 3: K7, yf, sl 1, k1, psso, k2.

Row 5: K3, k2tog, yf, k3, yf, sl 1, k1, psso, k1.

Row 7: K2, k2tog, yf, k5, yf, sl 1, k1, psso.

Row 9: K1, k2tog, yf, k8.

Row 11: K2tog, yf, k9.

Row 12: Purl.

Rep these 12 rows.

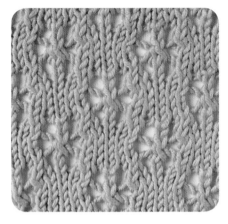

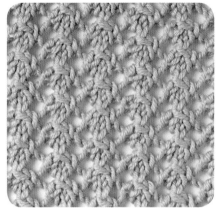

Snowflakes I

Multiple of 8 + 7.

Row 1 and every alt row (WS): Purl.

Row 2: K5, sl 1, k1, psso, yf, k1, yf, k2tog, *k3, sl 1, k1, psso, yf, k1, yf, k2tog; rep from * to last 5 sts, k5.

Row 4: K6, yf, sl 2, k1, p2sso, yf, *k5, yf, sl 2, k1, p2sso, yf; rep from * to last 6 sts, k6.

Row 6: As row 2.

Row 8: K1, sl 1, k1, psso, yf, k1, yf, k2tog, *k3, sl 1, k1, psso, yf, k1, yf, k2tog; rep from * to last st, k1.

Row 10: K2, yf, sl 2, k1, p2sso, yf, *k5, yf, sl 2, k1, p2sso, yf; rep from * to last 2 sts, k2.

Row 12: As row 8.

Rep these 12 rows.

Trellis lace

Multiple of 6 + 5.

Row 1 (RS): K4, *yf, sl 1, k2tog, psso, yf, k3; rep from * to last st, k1.

Row 2: Purl.

Row 3: K1, *yf, sl 1, k2tog, psso, yf, k3; rep from * to last 4 sts, yf, sl 1, k2tog, psso, yf, k1.

Row 4: Purl.

Rep these 4 rows.

Quatrefoil panel

Worked over 15 sts on a background of st st.

Note: Sts should not be counted after rows 6, 7, 8 or 9.

Row 1 (RS): K5, k2tog, yf, k1, yf, sl 1, k1, psso, k5.

Row 2: P4, p2tog tbl, yrn, p3, yrn, p2tog, p4.

Row 3: K3, k2tog, yf, k5, yf, sl 1, k1, psso, k3.

Row 4: P2, p2tog tbl, yrn, p1, yrn, p2tog, p1, p2tog tbl, yrn, p1, yrn, p2tog, p2.

Row 5: K1, k2tog, yf, k3, yf, k3tog, yf, k3, yf, sl 1, k1, psso, k1.

Row 6: P2, yrn, p5, yrn, p1, yrn, p5, yrn, p2.

Row 7: [K3, yf, sl 1, k1, psso, k1, k2tog, yf] twice, k3.

Row 8: P4, p3tog, yrn, p5, yrn, p3tog, p4.

Row 9: K6, yf, sl 1, k1, psso, k1, k2tog, yf, k6.

Row 10: P3, p2tog tbl, p2, yrn, p3tog, yrn, p2, p2tog, p3.

Rep these 10 rows.

Diamond and eyelet pattern

Multiple of 6 + 3.

Row 1 (WS): Knit.

Row 2: P1, *yrn, p2tog; rep from * to end.

Rows 3–4: Knit.

Row 5 and every WS row to 15: Purl.

Row 6: *K4, yf, sl 1, k1, psso; rep from * to last 3 sts, k3.

Row 8: K2, *k2tog, yf, k1, yf, sl 1, k1, psso, k1; rep from * to last st, k1.

Row 10: K1, k2tog, yf, *k3, yf, sl 1, k2tog, psso, yf; rep from * to last 6 sts, k3, yf, sl 1, k1, psso, k1.

Row 12: K3, *yf, sl 1, k2tog, psso, yf, k3; rep from * to end.

Row 14: As row 6.

Row 16: Knit.

Rep these 16 rows.

Snowflakes II

Multiple of 6 + 1.

Note: Sts should not be counted after rows 3, 4, 9, and 10.

Row 1 (RS): K1, *yf, sl 1, k1, psso, k1, k2tog, yf, k1; rep from * to end.

Row 2 and every alt row: Purl.

Row 3: K2, yf, *k3, yf; rep from * to last 2 sts, k2.

Row 5: K2tog, yf, sl 1, k1, psso, k1, k2tog, yf, *sl 1, k2tog, psso, yf, sl 1, k1, psso, k1, k2tog, yf; rep from * to last 2 sts, sl 1, k1, psso.

Row 7: K1, *k2tog, yf, k1, yf, sl 1, k1, psso, k1; rep from * to end.

Row 9: As row 3.

Row 11: K1, *k2tog, yf, sl 1, k2tog, psso, yf, sl 1, k1, psso, k1; rep from * to end.

Row 12: Purl.

Rep these 12 rows.

Lace chain panel

Worked over 10 sts on a background of st st.

Row 1 (RS): K2, k2tog, yf, k2tog but do not slip from needle, knit the first of these 2 sts again, then slip both sts from needle together, yf, sl 1, k1, psso, k2.

Row 2: Purl.

Row 3: K1, k2tog, yf, k4, yf, sl 1, k1, psso, k1.

Row 4: Purl.

Row 5: K2tog, yf, k1, k2tog, [yf] twice, sl 1, k1, psso, k1, yf, sl 1, k1, psso.

Row 6: P4, k1 into first yf, p1 into 2nd yf, p4.

Row 7: K2, yf, sl 1, k1, psso, k2, k2tog, yf, k2.

Row 8: Purl.

Row 9: K3, yf, sl 1, k1, psso, k2tog, yf, k3.

Row 10: Purl.

Rep these 10 rows.

Eyelet diamonds

Multiple of 16 + 11.

Row 1 (RS): K10, yf, sl 1, k1, psso, k3, k2tog, yf, *k9, yf, sl 1, k1, psso, k3, k2tog, yf; rep from * to last 10 sts, k10.

Row 2 and every alt row: Purl.

Row 3: K3, k2tog, yf, k1, yf, sl 1, k1, psso, *k3, yf, sl 1, k1, psso, k1, k2tog, yf, k3, k2tog, yf, k1, yf, sl 1, k1, psso; rep from * to last 3 sts, k3.

Row 5: K2, k2tog, yf, k3, yf, sl 1, k1, psso, *k3, yf, sl 1, k2tog, psso, yf, k3, k2tog, yf, k3, yf, sl 1, k1, psso; rep from * to last 2 sts, k2.

Row 7: K1, k2tog, yf, k5, yf, sl 1, k1, psso, *k7, k2tog, yf, k5, yf, sl 1, k1, psso; rep from * to last st, k1.

Row 9: K2, yf, sl 1, k1, psso, k3, k2tog, yf, *k9, yf, sl 1, k1, psso, k3, k2tog, yf; rep from * to last 2 sts, k2.

Row 11: K3, yf, sl 1, k1, psso, k1, k2tog, yf, k3, *k2tog, yf, k1, yf, sl 1, k1, psso, k3, yf, sl 1, k1, psso, k1, k2tog, yf, k3; rep from * to end.

Row 13: K4, yf, sl 1, k2tog, psso, yf, *k3, k2tog, yf, k3, yf, sl 1, k1, psso, k3, yf, sl 1, k2tog, psso, yf; rep from * to last 4 sts, k4.

Row 15: K9, k2tog, yf, k5, yf, sl 1, k1, psso, *k7, k2tog, yf, k5, yf, sl 1, k1, psso; rep from * to last 9 sts, k9.

Row 16: Purl.

Rep these 16 rows.

Ornamental tulip pattern

Multiple of 13.

Note: Sts should only be counted after rows 1, 2, 9 and 10 of this pattern.

Row 1 (RS): Purl.

Row 2: Knit.

Row 3: P6, [p1, k1] 3 times into next st, *p12, [p1, k1] 3 times into next st; rep from * to last 6 sts, p6.

Row 4: K6, p6, *k12, p6; rep from * to last 6 sts, k6.

Row 5: P6, k6, *p12, k6; rep from * to last 6 sts, p6.

Row 6: As row 4.

Row 7: [P2tog] twice, p2, [k2, yf] twice, k2, *p2, [p2tog] 4 times, p2, [k2, yf] twice, k2; rep from * to last 6 sts, p2, [p2tog] twice.

Row 8: K4, p8, *k8, p8; rep from * to last 4 sts, k4.

Row 9: [P2tog] twice, [k2tog, yf, k1, yf] twice, k2tog, *[p2tog] 4 times, [k2tog, yf, k1, yf] twice, k2tog; rep from * to last 4 sts, [p2tog] twice.

Row 10: K2, p9, *k4, p9; rep from * to last 2 sts, k2.

Rep these 10 rows.

Zigzag eyelets

Multiple of 9.

Row 1 (RS): K4, *yf, sl 1, k1, psso, k7; rep from * to last 5 sts, yf, sl 1, k1, psso, k3.

Row 2 and every alt row: Purl.

Row 3: K5, *yf, sl 1, k1, psso, k7; rep from * to last 4 sts, yf, sl 1, k1, psso, k2.

Row 5: K6, *yf, sl 1, k1, psso, k7; rep from * to last 3 sts, yf, sl 1, k1, psso, k1.

Row 7: *K7, yf, sl 1, k1, psso; rep from * to end.

Row 9: K3, *k2tog, yf, k7; rep from * to last 6 sts, k2tog, yf, k4.

Row 11: K2, *k2tog, yf, k7; rep from * to last 7 sts, k2tog, yf, k5.

Row 13: K1, *k2tog, yf, k7; rep from * to last 8 sts, k2tog, yf, k6.

Row 15: *K2tog, yf, k7; rep from * to end.

Row 16: Purl.

Rep these 16 rows.

Lacy checks

Multiple of 6 + 5.

Row 1 (RS): K1, *yf, sl 1, k2tog, psso, yf, k3; rep from * to last 4 sts, yf, sl 1, k2tog, psso, yf, k1.

Row 2 and every alt row: Purl.

Row 3: As row 1.

Row 5: Knit.

Row 7: K4, *yf, sl 1, k2tog, psso, yf, k3; rep from * to last st, k1.

Row 9: As row 7.

Row 11: Knit.

Row 12: Purl.

Rep these 12 rows.

Little and large diamonds

Multiple of 12 + 1.

Row 1 (RS): K1, *yf, sl 1, k1, psso, k7, k2tog, yf, k1; rep from * to end.

Row 2 and every alt row: Purl.

Row 3: K2, yf, sl 1, k1, psso, k5, *k2tog, yf, k3, yf, sl 1, k1, psso, k5; rep from * to last 4 sts, k2tog, yf, k2.

Row 5: K3, yf, sl 1, k1, psso, k3, *k2tog, yf, k5, yf, sl 1, k1, psso, k3; rep from * to last 5 sts, k2tog, yf, k3.

Row 7: *K1, k2tog, yf, k1, yf, sl 1, k1, psso; rep from * to last st, k1.

Row 9: K2tog, yf, k3, *yf, sl 1, k2tog, psso, yf, k3; rep from * to last 2 sts, yf, sl 1, k1, psso.

Row 11: K4, k2tog, yf, k1, yf, sl 1, k1, psso, *k7, k2tog, yf, k1, yf, sl 1, k1, psso; rep from * to last 4 sts, k4.

Row 13: K3, k2tog, yf, k3, yf, sl 1, k1, psso, *k5, k2tog, yf, k3, yf, sl 1, k1, psso; rep from * to last 3 sts, k3.

Row 15: K2, k2tog, yf, k5, yf, sl 1, k1, psso, *k3, k2tog, yf, k5, yf, sl 1, k1, psso; rep from * to last 2 sts, k2.

Row 17: As row 7.

Row 19: As row 9.

Row 20: Purl.

Rep these 20 rows.

Swinging triangles

Multiple of 12 + 1.

Row 1 and every alt row (WS): Purl.

Row 2: *K10, sl 1, k1, psso, yf; rep from * to last st, k1.

Row 4: K9, sl 1, k1, psso, yf, *k10, sl 1, k1, psso, yf; rep from * to last 2 sts, k2.

Row 6: *K8, [sl 1, k1, psso, yf] twice; rep from * to last st, k1.

Row 8: K7, [sl 1, k1, psso, yf] twice, *k8, [sl 1, k1, psso, yf] twice; rep from * to last 2 sts, k2.

Row 10: *K6, [sl 1, k1, psso, yf] 3 times; rep from * to last st, k1.

Row 12: K5, [sl 1, k1, psso, yf] 3 times, *k6, [sl 1, k1, psso, yf] 3 times; rep from * to last 2 sts, k2.

Row 14: *K4, [sl 1, k1, psso, yf] 4 times; rep from * to last st, k1.

Row 16: K1, *yf, k2tog, k10; rep from * to end.

Row 18: K2, yf, k2tog, *k10, yf, k2tog; rep from * to last 9 sts, k9.

Row 20: K1, *[yf, k2tog] twice, k8; rep from * to end.

Row 22: K2, [yf, k2tog] twice, *k8, [yf, k2tog] twice; rep from * to last 7 sts, k7.

Row 24: K1, *[yf, k2tog] 3 times, k6; rep from * to end.

Row 26: K2, [yf, k2tog] 3 times, *k6, [yf, k2tog] 3 times; rep from * to last 5 sts, k5.

Row 28: K1, *[yf, k2tog] 4 times, k4; rep from * to end.

Rep these 28 rows.

Snakes and ladders

Multiple of 8 + 2.

Row 1 (RS): K7, *k2tog, yf, k6; rep from * to last 3 sts, k2tog, yf, k1.

Row 2: K2, *yfrn, p2tog, k6; rep from * to end.

Row 3: K5, *k2tog, yf, k6; rep from * to last 5 sts, k2tog, yf, k3.

Row 4: K4, *yfrn, p2tog, k6; rep from * to last 6 sts, yfrn, p2tog, k4.

Row 5: K3, *k2tog, yf, k6; rep from * to last 7 sts, k2tog, yf, k5.

Row 6: *K6, yfrn, p2tog; rep from * to last 2 sts, k2.

Row 7: K1, *k2tog, yf, k6; rep from * to last st, k1.

Row 8: K7, *p2tog tbl, yon, k6; rep from * to last 3 sts, p2tog tbl, yon, k1.

Row 9: K2, *yf, k2tog tbl, k6; rep from * to end.

Row 10: K5, *p2tog tbl, yon, k6; rep from * to last 5 sts, p2tog tbl, yon, k3.

Row 11: K4, *yf, k2tog tbl, k6; rep from * to last 6 sts, yf, k2tog tbl, k4.

Row 12: K3, *p2tog tbl, yon, k6; rep from * to last 7 sts, p2tog tbl, yon, k5.

Row 13: *K6, yf, k2tog tbl; rep from * to last 2 sts, k2.

Row 14: K1, *p2tog tbl, yon, k6; rep from * to last st, k1.

Rep these 14 rows.

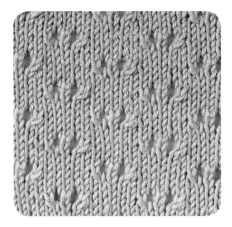

All-over eyelets

Multiple of 10 + 1.
Row 1 (RS): Knit.
Row 2 and every alt row: Purl.
Row 3: K3, *k2tog, yf, k1, yf, sl 1, k1, psso, k5; rep from * to last 8 sts, k2tog, yf, k1, yf, sl 1, k1, psso, k3.
Row 5: Knit.
Row 7: K1, *yf, sl 1, k1, psso, k5, k2tog, yf, k1; rep from * to end.
Row 8: Purl.
Rep these 8 rows.

Little lace panel

Worked over 5 sts on a background of st st.
Note: Sts should not be counted after rows 1 or 2 of this pattern.
Row 1 (RS): K1, yf, k3, yf, k1.
Row 2: Purl.
Row 3: K2, sl 1, k2tog, psso, k2.
Row 4: Purl.
Rep these 4 rows.

Eyelet lace

Multiple of 6 + 2.
Note: Sts should only be counted after rows 2 and 4.
Row 1 (RS): K1, yf, *k2tog tbl, k2, k2tog, yf; rep from * to last st, k1.
Row 2: K1, p5, *p into front and back of next st, p4; rep from * to last 2 sts, p1, k1.
Row 3: K2, *k2tog, yf, k2tog tbl, k2; rep from * to end.
Row 4: K1, p2, *p into front and back of next st, p4; rep from * to last 4 sts, p into front and back of next st, p2, k1.
Rep these 4 rows.

Tip

A yarnover ('yo' or 'yf') is the most common type of increase to be found in lace and eyelet stitch patterns. The increase is made by wrapping the yarn once around the right-hand needle, but without working any stitches on the left-hand needle. It is one of the easiest types of increases to make in knitting. The yarnover is nearly always paired with a decrease in order to keep the overall stitch count in a row consistent.

Trellis pattern

Multiple of 4 + 2.

Row 1 (RS): K1, yf, *sl 1, k1, psso, k2tog, [yfon] twice (2 sts made); rep from * to last 5 sts, sl 1, k1, psso, k2tog, yf, k1.

Row 2: K2, p2, *k into front of first loop of double yfon, then k into back of 2nd loop, p2; rep from * to last 2 sts, k2.

Row 3: K1, p1, *C2B, p2; rep from * to last 4 sts, C2B, p1, k1.

Row 4: K2, *p2, k2; rep from * to end.

Row 5: K1, k2tog, *[yfon] twice, sl 1, k1, psso, k2tog; rep from * to last 3 sts, [yfon] twice, sl 1, k1, psso, k1.

Row 6: K1, p1, k into front of first loop of double yfon, then k into back of 2nd loop, *p2, work into double yfon as before; rep from * to last 2 sts, p1, k1.

Row 7: K2, *p2, C2B; rep from * to last 4 sts, p2, k2.

Row 8: K1, p1, k2, *p2, k2; rep from * to last 2 sts, p1, k1.

Rep these 8 rows.

Rhombus lace

Multiple of 8 + 2.

Row 1 (RS): K1, [k2tog, yf] twice, *k4, [k2tog, yf] twice; rep from * to last 5 sts, k5.

Row 2 and every alt row: Purl.

Row 3: [K2tog, yf] twice, *k4, [k2tog, yf] twice; rep from * to last 6 sts, k6.

Row 5: K1, k2tog, yf, k4, *[k2tog, yf] twice, k4; rep from * to last 3 sts, k2tog, yf, k1.

Row 7: K3, [k2tog, yf] twice, *k4, [k2tog, yf] twice; rep from * to last 3 sts, k3.

Row 9: K2, *[k2tog, yf] twice, k4; rep from * to end.

Row 11: As Row 1.

Row 13: K5, [k2tog, yf] twice, *k4, [k2tog, yf] twice; rep from * to last st, k1.

Row 15: *K4, [k2tog, yf] twice; rep from * to last 2 sts, k2.

Row 17: As row 7.

Row 19: As row 5.

Row 21: K2tog, yf, k4, *[k2tog, yf] twice, k4; rep from * to last 4 sts, k2tog, yf, k2.

Row 23: As row 13.

Row 24: Purl.

Rep these 24 rows.

Fountains panel

Worked over 16 sts on a background of st st.

Row 1 (RS): K1, yf, k1, sl 1, k1, psso, p1, k2tog, k1, yfrn, p1, yb, sl 1, k1, psso, p1, k2tog, [yf, k1] twice.
Row 2: P5, k1, p1, k1, p3, k1, p4.
Row 3: K1, yf, k1, sl 1, k1, psso, p1, k2tog, k1, p1, yb, sl 1, k2tog, psso, yf, k3, yf, k1.
Row 4: P7, k1, p2, k1, p4.
Row 5: [K1, yf] twice, sl 1, k1, psso, p1, [k2tog] twice, yf, k5, yf, k1.
Row 6: P8, k1, p1, k1, p5.
Row 7: K1, yf, k3, yf, sl 1, k2tog, psso, p1, yon, k1, sl 1, k1, psso, p1, k2tog, k1, yf, k1.
Row 8: P4, k1, p3, k1, p7.
Row 9: K1, yf, k5, yf, sl 1, k1, psso, k1, sl 1, k1, psso, p1, k2tog, k1, yf, k1.
Row 10: P4, k1, p2, k1, p8.
Rep these 10 rows.

Shetland fern panel

Worked over 13 sts on a background of st st.

Row 1 (RS): K6, yf, sl 1, k1, psso, k5.
Row 2: Purl.
Row 3: K4, k2tog, yf, k1, yf, sl 1, k1, psso, k4.
Row 4: Purl.
Row 5: K3, k2tog, yf, k3, yf, sl 1, k1, psso, k3.
Row 6: Purl.
Row 7: K3, yf, sl 1, k1, psso, yf, sl 1, k2tog, psso, yf, k2tog, yf, k3.
Row 8: Purl.
Row 9: K1, k2tog, yf, k1, yf, sl 1, k1, psso, k1, k2tog, yf, k1, yf, sl 1, k1, psso, k1.
Row 10: Purl.
Row 11: K1, [yf, sl 1, k1, psso] twice, k3, [k2tog, yf] twice, k1.
Row 12: P2, [yrn, p2tog] twice, p1, [p2tog tbl, yrn] twice, p2.
Row 13: K3, yf, sl 1, k1, psso, yf, sl 1, k2tog, psso, yf, k2tog, yf, k3.
Row 14: P4, yrn, p2tog, p1, p2tog tbl, yrn, p4.
Row 15: K5, yf, sl 1, k2tog, psso, yf, k5.
Row 16: Purl.
Rep these 16 rows.

Eyelet boxes

Multiple of 14 + 11.

Row 1 (RS): K2, p7, *k3, yf, sl 1, k1, psso, k2, p7; rep from * to last 2 sts, k2.
Rows 2, 4, 6, 8 and 10: P2, k7, *p7, k7; rep from * to last 2 sts, p2.
Row 3: K2, p7, *k1, k2tog, yf, k1, yf, sl 1, k1, psso, k1, p7; rep from * to last 2 sts, k2.
Row 5: K2, p7, *k2tog, yf, k3, yf, sl 1, k1, psso, p7; rep from * to last 2 sts, k2.
Row 7: K2, p7, *k2, yf, sl 1, k2tog, psso, yf, k2, p7; rep from * to last 2 sts, k2.
Row 9: As row 1.
Row 11: P2, k3, yf, sl 1, k1, psso, k2, *p7, k3, yf, sl 1, k1, psso, k2; rep from * to last 2 sts, p2.
Rows 12, 14, 16 and 18: K2, p7, *k7, p7; rep from * to last 2 sts, k2.
Row 13: P2, k1, k2tog, yf, k1, yf, sl 1, k1, psso, k1, *p7, k1, k2tog, yf, k1, yf, sl 1, k1, psso, k1; rep from * to last 2 sts, p2.
Row 15: P2, k2tog, yf, k3, yf, sl 1, k1, psso, *p7, k2tog, yf, k3, yf, sl 1, k1, psso; rep from * to last 2 sts, p2.
Row 17: P2, k2, yf, sl 1, k2tog, psso, yf, k2, *p7, k2, yf, sl 1, k2tog, psso, yf, k2; rep from * to last 2 sts, p2.
Row 19: As row 11.
Row 20: K2, p7, *k7, p7; rep from * to last 2 sts, k2.
Rep these 20 rows.

Travelling vine

Multiple of 8 + 2.

Note: Sts should only be counted after WS rows.

Row 1 (RS): K1, *yf, KB1, yf, k2tog tbl, k5; rep from * to last st, k1.

Row 2: P5, *p2tog tbl, p7; rep from * to last 6 sts, p2tog tbl, p4.

Row 3: K1, *yf, KB1, yf, k2, k2tog tbl, k3; rep from * to last st, k1.

Row 4: P3, *p2tog tbl, p7; rep from * to last 8 sts, p2tog tbl, p6.

Row 5: K1, *KB1, yf, k4, k2tog tbl, k1, yf; rep from * to last st, k1.

Row 6: P2, *p2tog tbl, p7; rep from * to end.

Row 7: K6, *k2tog, yf, KB1, yf, k5; rep from * to last 4 sts, k2tog, yf, KB1, yf, k1.

Row 8: P4, *p2tog, p7; rep from * to last 7 sts, p2tog, p5.

Row 9: K4, *k2tog, k2, yf, KB1, yf, k3; rep from * to last 6 sts, k2tog, k2, yf, KB1, yf, k1.

Row 10: P6, *p2tog, p7; rep from * to last 5 sts, p2tog, p3.

Row 11: K1, *yf, k1, k2tog, k4, yf, KB1; rep from * to last st, k1.

Row 12: *P7, p2tog; rep from * to last 2 sts, p2.

Rep these 12 rows.

Shadow triangles

Multiple of 10 + 3.

Row 1 (RS): K2, yf, sl 1, k1, psso, k5, k2tog, yf, *k1, yf, sl 1, k1, psso, k5, k2tog, yf; rep from * to last 2 sts, k2.

Row 2: P4, k5, *p5, k5; rep from * to last 4 sts, p4.

Row 3: K3, *yf, sl 1, k1, psso, k3, k2tog, yf, k3; rep from * to end.

Row 4: P5, k3, *p7, k3; rep from * to last 5 sts, p5.

Row 5: K4, yf, sl 1, k1, psso, k1, k2tog, yf, *k5, yf, sl 1, k1, psso, k1, k2tog, yf; rep from * to last 4 sts, k4.

Row 6: P6, k1, *p9, k1; rep from * to last 6 sts, p6.

Row 7: K5, yf, sl 1, k2tog, psso, yf, *k7, yf, sl 1, k2tog, psso, yf; rep from * to last 5 sts, k5.

Row 8: Purl.

Row 9: K4, k2tog, yf, k1, yf, sl 1, k1, psso, *k5, k2tog, yf, k1, yf, sl 1, k1, psso; rep from * to last 4 sts, k4.

Row 10: K4, p5, *k5, p5; rep from * to last 4 sts, k4.

Row 11: K3, *k2tog, yf, k3, yf, sl 1, k1, psso, k3; rep from * to end.

Row 12: K3, *p7, k3; rep from * to end.

Row 13: K2, k2tog, yf, k5, yf, sl 1, k1, psso, *k1, k2tog, yf, k5, yf, sl 1, k1, psso; rep from * to last 2 sts, k2.

Row 14: P1, k1, *p9, k1; rep from * to last st, p1.

Row 15: K1, k2tog, yf, k7, *yf, sl 1, k2tog, psso, yf, k7; rep from * to last 3 sts, yf, sl 1, k1, psso, k1.

Row 16: Purl.

Rep these 16 rows.

Diagonal ridges

Multiple of 5 + 2.

Row 1 (RS): K2tog, yf, *k3, k2tog, yf; rep from * to last 5 sts, k5.

Row 2: P2, *k3, p2; rep from * to end.

Row 3: K4, k2tog, yf, *k3, k2tog, yf; rep from * to last st, k1.

Row 4: K1, *p2, k3; rep from * to last st, p1.

Row 5: *K3, k2tog, yf; rep from * to last 2 sts, k2.

Row 6: K2, *p2, k3; rep from * to end.

Row 7: K2, *k2tog, yf, k3; rep from * to end.

Row 8: *K3, p2; rep from * to last 2 sts, k2.

Row 9: K1, k2tog, yf, *k3, k2tog, yf; rep from * to last 4 sts, k4.

Row 10: P1, *k3, p2; rep from * to last st, k1.

Rep these 10 rows.

Checkerboard lace

Multiple of 12 + 8.

Row 1 (RS): K7, *[yf, k2tog] 3 times, k6; rep from * to last st, k1.

Row 2 and every alt row: Purl.

Row 3: K7, *[k2tog, yf] 3 times, k6; rep from * to last st, k1.

Row 5: As row 1.

Row 7: As row 3.

Row 9: K1, *[yf, k2tog] 3 times, k6; rep from * to last 7 sts, [yf, k2tog] 3 times, k1.

Row 11: K1, *[k2tog, yf] 3 times, k6; rep from * to last 7 sts, [k2tog, yf] 3 times, k1.

Row 13: As row 9.

Row 15: As row 11.

Row 16: Purl.

Rep these 16 rows.

Shetland eyelet panel

Worked over 9 sts on a background of st st.

Row 1 (RS): K2, k2tog, yf, k1, yf, sl 1, k1, psso, k2.

Row 2 and every alt row: Purl.

Row 3: K1, k2tog, yf, k3, yf, sl 1, k1, psso, k1.

Row 5: K1, yf, sl 1, k1, psso, yf, sl 2 knitwise, k1, p2sso, yf, k2tog, yf, k1.

Row 7: K3, yf, sl 2 knitwise, k1, p2sso, yf, k3.

Row 8: Purl.

Rep these 8 rows.

Tip

It is always advisable to block a piece of knitting that features lace or eyelet stitches. This helps to open up and set the lacework or eyelets and even out the pattern so the intricacy of the design becomes really clear. There are various ways to block knitted work, but the process basically involves wetting or dampening the piece, pinning it out to the desired shape and leaving it to dry.

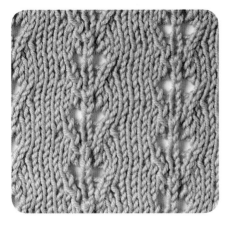  

Climbing leaf pattern

Multiple of 16 + 1.

Row 1 (RS): K1, *yf, k5, k2tog, k1, k2tog tbl, k5, yf, k1; rep from * to end.

Row 2 and every alt row: Purl.

Row 3: As row 1.

Row 5: K1, *k2tog tbl, k5, yf, k1, yf, k5, k2tog, k1; rep from * to end.

Row 7: As row 5.

Row 8: Purl.

Rep these 8 rows.

Twin leaf lace panel

Worked over 23 sts on a background of st st.

Row 1 (RS): K8, k2tog, yf, k1, p1, k1, yf, sl 1, k1, psso, k8.

Row 2: P7, p2tog tbl, p2, yon, k1, yfrn, p2, p2tog, p7.

Row 3: K6, k2tog, k1, yf, k2, p1, k2, yf, k1, sl 1, k1, psso, k6.

Row 4: P5, p2tog tbl, p3, yrn, p1, k1, p1, yrn, p3, p2tog, p5.

Row 5: K4, k2tog, k2, yf, k3, p1, k3, yf, k2, sl 1, k1, psso, k4.

Row 6: P3, p2tog tbl, p4, yrn, p2, k1, p2, yrn, p4, p2tog, p3.

Row 7: K2, k2tog, k3, yf, k4, p1, k4, yf, k3, sl 1, k1, psso, k2.

Row 8: P1, p2tog tbl, p5, yrn, p3, k1, p3, yrn, p5, p2tog, p1.

Row 9: K2tog, k4, yf, k5, p1, k5, yf, k4, sl 1, k1, psso.

Row 10: P11, k1, p11.

Row 11: K11, p1, k11.

Row 12: P11, k1, p11.

Rep these 12 rows.

Lacy diagonals

Multiple of 10 + 2

Row 1 (RS): K1, *k6, sl 1, k1, psso, yf, k2tog yf; rep from * to last st, k1.

Row 2 and every alt row: Purl.

Row 3: *K6, sl 1, k1, psso, yf, k2tog, yf; rep from * to last st, k2.

Row 5: K5, *sl 1, k1, psso, yf, k2tog, yf, k6; rep from *, k3.

Row 7: K4, *sl 1, k1, psso, yf, k2tog, yf, k6; rep from *, k4.

Row 9: K3, *sl 1, k1, psso, yf, k2tog, yf, k6; rep from *, k5.

Row 11: K2, *sl 1, k1, psso, yf, k2tog, yf, k6; rep from *.

Row 13: K1, *sl 1, k1, psso, yf, k2tog, yf, k6; rep from *, k1.

Row 15: *Sl 1, k1, psso, yf, k2tog, yf, k6; rep from *, k2.

Row 17: K1, k2tog, yf, *k6, sl 1, k1, psso, yf, k2tog, yf; rep from *, k6, sl 1, k1, psso, yf, k1.

Row 19: K2tog, yf, *k6, sl 1, k1, psso, yf, k2tog, yf; rep from *, k6, sl 1, k1, psso, yf, k2.

Row 20: Purl.

Rep these 20 rows.

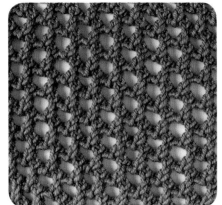

Diamond diagonal

Multiple of 8 + 2.

Row 1 (RS): K1, *yf, k2tog tbl, k6; rep from * to last st, k1.

Row 2: K1, *yfrn, p2tog, k3, p2tog tbl, yon, k1; rep from * to last st, k1.

Row 3: *K3, yf, k2tog tbl, k1, k2tog, yf; rep from * to last 2 sts, k2.

Row 4: K3, *yfrn, p3tog tbl, yon, k5; rep from * to last 7 sts, yfrn, p3tog tbl, yon, k4.

Row 5: K5, *yf, k2tog tbl, k6; rep from * to last 5 sts, yf, k2tog tbl, k3.

Row 6: K2, *p2tog tbl, yon, k1, yfrn, p2tog, k3; rep from * to end.

Row 7: K2, *k2tog, yf, k3, yf, k2tog tbl, k1; rep from * to end.

Row 8: P2tog tbl, *yon, k5, yfrn, p3tog tbl; rep from * to last 8 sts, yon, k5, yfrn, p2tog, k1.

Rep these 8 rows.

Fancy openwork

Multiple of 4.

Note: Sts should only be counted after rows 2 and 4.

Row 1 (RS): K2, *yf, k4; rep from * to last 2 sts, yf, k2.

Row 2: P2tog, *(k1, p1) into the yf of the previous row, [p2tog] twice; rep from * to last 3 sts, (k1, p1) into the yf, p2tog.

Row 3: K4, *yf, k4; rep from * to end.

Row 4: P2, p2tog, *(k1, p1) into the yf of previous row, [p2tog] twice; rep from * to last 5 sts, (k1, p1) into the yf, p2tog, p2.

Rep these 4 rows.

Florette pattern

Multiple of 12 + 7.

Row 1 (RS): K1, *p2tog, yon, k1, yfrn, p2tog, k7; rep from * to last 6 sts, p2tog, yon, k1, yfrn, p2tog, k1.

Row 2 and every alt row: Purl.

Row 3: K1, *yfrn, p2tog, k1, p2tog, yon, k7; rep from * to last 6 sts, yfrn, p2tog, k1, p2tog, yon, k1.

Row 5: As row 3.

Row 7: As row 1.

Row 9: K7, *p2tog, yon, k1, yfrn, p2tog, k7; rep from * to end.

Row 11: K7, *yfrn, p2tog, k1, p2tog, yon, k7; rep from * to end.

Row 13: As row 11.

Row 15: As row 9.

Row 16: Purl.

Rep these 16 rows.

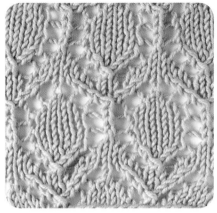

Cogwheel eyelets

Multiple of 8 + 1.

Row 1 (RS): K2, k2tog, yf, k1, yf, sl 1, k1, psso, *k3, k2tog, yf, k1, yf, sl 1, k1, psso; rep from * to last 2 sts, k2.

Row 2 and every alt row: Purl.

Row 3: K1, *k2tog, yf, k3, yf, sl 1, k1, psso, k1; rep from * to end.

Row 5: K2tog, yf, k5, *yf, sl 1, k2tog, psso, yf, k5; rep from * to last 2 sts, yf, sl 1, k1, psso.

Row 7: Sl 1, k1, psso, yf, k5, *yf, sl 2tog knitwise, k1, p2sso, yf, k5; rep from * to last 2 sts, yf, k2tog.

Row 9: As row 7.

Row 11: K2, yf, sl 1, k1, psso, k1, k2tog, yf, *k3, yf, sl 1, k1, psso, k1, k2tog, yf; rep from * to last 2 sts, k2.

Row 13: K3, yf, sl 1, k2tog, psso, yf, *k5, yf, sl 1, k2tog, psso, yf; rep from * to last 3 sts, k3.

Row 15: K1, *yf, sl 1, k1, psso, k3, k2tog, yf, k1; rep from * to end.

Row 17: As row 11.

Row 19: As row 13.

Row 21: K3, yf, sl 2tog knitwise, k1, p2sso, yf, *k5, yf, sl 2tog knitwise, k1, p2sso, yf; rep from * to last 3 sts, k3.

Row 23: As row 21.

Row 25: As row 3.

Row 27: As row 5.

Row 28: Purl.

Rep these 28 rows.

Bell lace

Multiple of 8 + 3.

Row 1 (RS): K1, p1, k1, *p1, yon, sl 1, k2tog, psso, yfrn, [p1, k1] twice; rep from * to end.

Row 2: P1, k1, p1, *k1, p3, [k1, p1] twice; rep from * to end.

Rep last 2 rows twice more.

Row 7: K1, k2tog, *yfrn, [p1, k1] twice, p1, yon, sl 1, k2tog, psso; rep from * to last 8 sts, yfrn, [p1, k1] twice, p1, yon, sl 1, k1, psso, k1.

Row 8: P3, *[k1, p1] twice, k1, p3; rep from * to end.

Rep the last 2 rows twice more.

Rep these 12 rows.

Inverted hearts

Multiple of 14 + 1.

Row 1 (RS): P2tog, yon, k11, *yfrn, p3tog, yon, k11; rep from * to last 2 sts, yfrn, p2tog.

Row 2: K1, *p13, k1; rep from * to end.

Row 3: P2, yon, sl 1, k1, psso, k7, *k2tog, yfrn, p3, yon, sl 1, k1, psso, k7; rep from * to last 4 sts, k2tog, yfrn, p2.

Row 4: K2, p11, *k3, p11; rep from * to last 2 sts, k2.

Row 5: P3, yon, sl 1, k1, psso, k5, k2tog, yfrn, *p5, yon, sl 1, k1, psso, k5, k2tog, yfrn; rep from * to last 3 sts, p3.

Row 6: K3, p9, *k5, p9; rep from * to last 3 sts, k3.

Row 7: P4, yon, sl 1, k1, psso, k3, k2tog, yfrn, *p7, yon, sl 1, k1, psso, k3, k2tog, yfrn; rep from * to last 4 sts, p4.

Row 8: K4, p7, *k7, p7; rep from * to last 4 sts, k4.

Row 9: P2, p2tog, yon, k1, yf, sl 1, k1, psso, k1, k2tog, yf, k1, yfrn, p2tog, *p3, p2tog, yon, k1, yf, sl 1, k1, psso, k1, k2tog, yf, k1, yfrn, p2tog; rep from * to last 2 sts, p2.

Row 10: As row 6.

Row 11: P1, *p2tog, yon, k3, yf, sl 1, k2tog, psso, yf, k3, yfrn, p2tog, p1; rep from * to end.

Row 12: As row 4.

Rep these 12 rows.

Ears of corn

Multiple of 12 + 2.

Row 1 (RS): Knit.

Row 2: Purl.

Row 3: K4, k2tog, k1, yf, *k9, k2tog, k1, yf; rep from * to last 7 sts, k7.

Row 4: P8, yrn, p1, p2tog, *p9, yrn, p1, p2tog; rep from * to last 3 sts, p3.

Row 5: K2, *k2tog, k1, yf, k9; rep from * to end.

Row 6: P10, yrn, p1, p2tog, *p9, yrn, p1, p2tog; rep from * to last st, p1.

Work 2 rows in st st, starting with knit.

Row 9: K7, yf, k1, sl 1, k1, psso, *k9, yf, k1, sl 1, k1, psso; rep from * to last 4 sts, k4.

Row 10: P3, p2tog tbl, p1, yrn, *p9, p2tog tbl, p1, yrn; rep from * to last 8 sts, p8.

Row 11: *K9, yf, k1, sl 1, k1, psso; rep from * to last 2 sts, k2.

Row 12: P1, p2tog tbl, p1, yrn, *p9, p2tog tbl, p1, yrn; rep from * to last 10 sts, p10.

Rep these 12 rows.

Creeping vines

Multiple of 22 + 3.

Row 1 (RS): K4, k2tog, k3, [yf, k2tog] twice, *yf, k13, k2tog, k3, [yf, k2tog] twice; rep from * to last 12 sts, yf, k12.

Row 2 and every alt row: Purl.

Row 3: K3, *k2tog, k3, yf, k1, yf, [sl 1, k1, psso, yf] twice, k3, sl 1, k1, psso, k7; rep from * to end.

Row 5: K2, k2tog, [k3, yf] twice, [sl 1, k1, psso, yf] twice, k3, sl 1, k1, psso, *k5, k2tog, [k3, yf] twice, [sl 1, k1, psso, yf] twice, k3, sl 1, k1, psso; rep from * to last 6 sts, k6.

Row 7: K1, k2tog, k3, yf, k5, yf, [sl 1, k1, psso, yf] twice, k3, sl 1, k1, psso, *k3, k2tog, k3, yf, k5, yf, [sl 1, k1, psso, yf] twice, k3, sl 1, k1, psso; rep from * to last 5 sts, k5.

Row 9: K12, yf, [sl 1, k1, psso, yf] twice, k3, sl 1, k1, psso, *k13, yf, [sl 1, k1, psso, yf] twice, k3, sl 1, k1, psso; rep from * to last 4 sts, k4.

Row 11: *K7, k2tog, k3, [yf, k2tog] twice, yf, k1, yf, k3, sl 1, k1, psso; rep from * to last 3 sts, k3.

Row 13: K6, k2tog, k3, [yf, k2tog] twice, [yf, k3] twice, sl 1, k1, psso, *k5, k2tog, k3, [yf, k2tog] twice, [yf, k3] twice, sl 1, k1, psso; rep from * to last 2 sts, k2.

Row 15: K5, k2tog, k3, [yf, k2tog] twice, yf, k5, yf, k3, sl 1, k1, psso, *k3, k2tog, k3, [yf, k2tog] twice, yf, k5, yf, k3, sl 1, k1, psso; rep from * to last st, k1.

Row 16: Purl.

Rep these 16 rows.

Snow shoe pattern

Multiple of 8 + 4.

Note: Sts should only be counted after rows 8, 9, 10, 18, 19 or 20.

Row 1 (RS): K2, M1, *k1, p2, k2, p2, k1, M1; rep from * to last 2 sts, k2.

Row 2: P4, k2, p2, k2, *p3, k2, p2, k2; rep from * to last 4 sts, p4.

Row 3: K4, p2, k2, p2, *k3, p2, k2, p2; rep from * to last 4 sts, k4.

Rep the last 2 rows twice more.

Row 8: P2, drop next st down 7 rows, *p1, k2, p2, k2, p1, drop next st down 7 rows; rep from * to last 2 sts, p2.

Row 9: K3, p2, *k2, p2; rep from * to last 3 sts, k3.

Row 10: P3, k2, *p2, k2; rep from * to last 3 sts, p3.

Row 11: K3, p2, k1, M1, k1, p2, *k2, p2, k1, M1, k1, p2; rep from * to last 3 sts, k3.

Row 12: P3, k2, p3, k2, *p2, k2, p3, k2; rep from * to last 3 sts, p3.

Row 13: K3, p2, k3, p2, *k2, p2, k3, p2; rep from * to last 3 sts, k3.

Rep the last 2 rows twice more.

Row 18: P3, k2, p1, drop next st down 7 rows, p1, k2, *p2, k2, p1, drop next st down 7 rows, p1, k2; rep from * to last 3 sts, p3.

Row 19: K3, p2, *k2, p2; rep from * to last 3 sts, k3.

Row 20: P3, k2, *p2, k2; rep from * to last 3 sts, p3.

Rep these 20 rows.

Chalice cup panel

Worked over 13 sts on a background of st st.

Note: Sts should not be counted after rows 7, 8, 15 or 16 of this pattern.

Row 1 (RS): P1, k3, k2tog, yf, k1, yf, sl 1, k1, psso, k3, p1.

Row 2: K1, p11, k1.

Row 3: P1, k2, k2tog, yf, k3, yf, sl 1, k1, psso, k2, p1.

Row 4: As row 2.

Row 5: P1, k1, k2tog, yf, k1, yf, sl 1, k2tog, psso, yf, k1, yf, sl 1, k1, psso, k1, p1.

Row 6: As row 2.

Row 7: P1, k2tog, yf, k3, yf, k1, yf, k3, yf, sl 1, k1, psso, p1.

Row 8: K1, p13, k1.

Row 9: P1, k2tog, yf, sl 1, k1, psso, k5, k2tog, yf, sl 1, k1, psso, p1.

Row 10: As row 2.

Row 11: P1, k2tog, yf, k1, yf, sl 1, k1, psso, k1, k2tog, yf, k1, yf, sl 1, k1, psso, p1.

Row 12: As row 2.

Rep the last 2 rows once more.

Row 15: P1, k1, yf, k3, yf, sl 1, k2tog, psso, yf, k3, yf, k1, p1.

Row 16: As row 8.

Row 17: P1, k3, k2tog, yf, sl 1, k2tog, psso, yf, sl 1, k1, psso, k3, p1.

Row 18: As row 2.

Rep these 18 rows.

Pyramid lace panel

Worked over 25 sts on a background of st st.

Row 1 (RS): (RS): Purl.

Row 2: Knit.

Row 3: K3, yf, k8, sl 1, k2tog, psso, k8, yf, k3.

Row 4 and every following alt row to 18: Purl.

Row 5: K4, yf, k7, sl 1, k2tog, psso, k7, yf, k4.

Row 7: K2, k2tog, yf, k1, yf, k6, sl 1, k2tog, psso, k6, yf, k1, yf, sl 1, k1, psso, k2.

Row 9: K6, yf, k5, sl 1, k2tog, psso, k5, yf, k6.

Row 11: K3, yf, sl 1, k2tog, psso, yf, k1, yf, k4, sl 1, k2tog, psso, k4, yf, k1, yf, sl 1, k2tog, psso, yf, k3.

Row 13: K8, yf, k3, sl 1, k2tog, psso, k3, yf, k8.

Row 15: K2, k2tog, yf, k1, yf, sl 1, k2tog, psso, yf, k1, yf, k2, sl 1, k2tog, psso, k2, yf, k1, yf, sl 1, k2tog, psso, yf, k1, yf, sl 1, k1, psso, k2.

Row 17: K10, yf, k1, sl 1, k2tog, psso, k1, yf, k10.

Row 19: K3, [yf, sl 1, k2tog, psso, yf, k1] 4 times, yf, sl 1, k2tog, psso, yf, k3.

Row 20: Knit.

Rep these 20 rows.

Staggered fern lace panel

Worked over 20 sts on a background of st st.

Row 1 (RS): P2, k9, yf, k1, yf, k3, sl 1, k2tog, psso, p2.

Row 2 and every alt row: Purl.

Row 3: P2, k10, yf, k1, yf, k2, sl 1, k2tog, psso, p2.

Row 5: P2, k3tog, k4, yf, k1, yf, k3, [yf, k1] twice, sl 1, k2tog, psso, p2.

Row 7: P2, k3tog, k3, yf, k1, yf, k9, p2.

Row 9: P2, k3tog, k2, yf, k1, yf, k10, p2.

Row 11: P2, k3tog, [k1, yf] twice, k3, yf, k1, yf, k4, sl 1, k2tog, psso, p2.

Row 12: Purl.

Rep these 12 rows.

Embossed rosebud panel

Worked over 9 sts on a background of rev st st.

Row 1 (WS): K3, p3, k3.

Row 2: P3, slip next st onto cable needle and hold at front of work, k1, [k1, yf, k1, yf, k1] into next st on left-hand needle, then knit st from cable needle, p3.

Row 3: K3, p1, [KB1] 5 times, p1, k3.

Row 4: P3, [k1, yf] 6 times, k1, p3.

Row 5: K3, p13, k3.

Row 6: P3, k13, p3.

Row 7: K3, p2tog, p9, p2tog tbl, k3.

Row 8: P3, yb, sl 1, k1, psso, k7, k2tog, p3.

Row 9: K3, p2tog, p5, p2tog tbl, k3.

Row 10: P3, yb, sl 1, k1, psso, k3, k2tog, p3.

Row 11: K3, p2tog, p1, p2tog tbl, k3.

Row 12: P3, k3, p3.

Rep these 12 rows.

Fish scale lace panel

Worked over 17 sts on a background of st st.

Row 1 (RS): K1, yf, k3, sl 1, k1, psso, p5, k2tog, k3, yf, k1.

Row 2: P6, k5, p6.

Row 3: K2, yf, k3, sl 1, k1, psso, p3, k2tog, k3, yf, k2.

Row 4: P7, k3, p7.

Row 5: K3, yf, k3, sl 1, k1, psso, p1, k2tog, k3, yf, k3.

Row 6: P8, k1, p8.

Row 7: K4, yf, k3, sl 1, k2tog, psso, k3, yf, k4.

Row 8: Purl.

Rep these 8 rows.

Cascading leaves

Worked over 16 sts on a background of rev st st.

Row 1 (RS): P1, k3, k2tog, k1, yfrn, p2, yon, k1, sl 1, k1, psso, k3, p1.

Row 2 and every alt row: K1, p6, k2, p6, k1.

Row 3: P1, k2, k2tog, k1, yf, k1, p2, k1, yf, k1, sl 1, k1, psso, k2, p1.

Row 5: P1, k1, k2tog, k1, yf, k2, p2, k2, yf, k1, sl 1, k1, psso, k1, p1.

Row 7: P1, k2tog, k1, yf, k3, p2, k3, yf, k1, sl 1, k1, psso, p1.

Row 8: K1, p6, k2, p6, k1.

Rep these 8 rows.

Flower buds

Multiple of 8 + 5.

Row 1 (RS): K3, *yf, k2, p3tog, k2, yf, k1; rep from * to last 2 sts, k2.

Row 2: Purl.

Rep the last 2 rows twice more.

Row 7: K2, p2tog, *k2, yf, k1, yf, k2, p3tog; rep from * to last 9 sts, k2, yf, k1, yf, k2, p2tog, k2.

Row 8: Purl.

Rep the last 2 rows twice more.

Rep these 12 rows.

Puff stitch check

Multiple of 10 + 7.

Special abbreviation:

K5W = knit next 5 sts wrapping yarn twice around needle for each st.

Row 1 (RS): P6, k5W, *p5, k5W; rep from * to last 6 sts, p6.

Row 2: K6, p5 dropping extra loops, *k5, p5 dropping extra loops; rep from * to last 6 sts, k6.

Rep the last 2 rows 3 times more.

Row 9: P1, k5W, *p5, k5W; rep from * to last st, p1.

Row 10: K1, p5 dropping extra loops, *k5, p5 dropping extra loops; rep from * to last st, k1.

Rep the last 2 rows 3 times more.

Rep these 16 rows.

Tip

If you are working a lace or eyelet design set against a plain knitted fabric (a lace panel on the front of an otherwise plain sweater, for example), then you will find stitch markers a useful aid. Count the stitches on your needles within each section of the pattern when you reach each marker to check that you are on track and haven't made any accidental extra yarnovers or decreases.

Lacy diamonds

Multiple of 6 + 1.

Row 1 (RS): *K1, k2tog, yf, k1, yf, k2tog tbl; rep from * to last st, k1.

Row 2 and every alt row: Purl.

Row 3: K2tog, *yf, k3, yf, [sl 1] twice, k1, p2sso; rep from * to last 5 sts, yf, k3, yf, k2tog tbl.

Row 5: *K1, yf, k2tog tbl, k1, k2tog, yf; rep from * to last st, k1.

Row 7: K2, *yf, [sl 1] twice, k1, p2sso, yf, k3; rep from * to last 5 sts, yf, [sl 1] twice, k1, p2sso, yf, k2.

Row 8: Purl.

Rep these 8 rows.

Eyelet ribs

Multiple of 11 + 4.

Row 1 (RS): K1, yfrn, p2tog, k1, *p1, k2, yf, sl 1, k1, psso, k1, p1, k1, yfrn, p2tog, k1; rep from * to end.

Row 2 and every alt row: K1, yfrn, p2tog, *k2, p5, k2, yfrn, p2tog; rep from * to last st, k1.

Row 3: K1, yfrn, p2tog, k1, *p1, k1, yf, sl 1, k2tog, psso, yf, k1, p1, k1, yfrn, p2tog, k1; rep from * to end.

Row 5: As row 1.

Row 7: K1, yfrn, p2tog, k1, *p1, k5, p1, k1, yfrn, p2tog, k1; rep from * to end.

Row 8: As row 2.

Rep these 8 rows.

Zigzag lace

Multiple of 4 + 3.

Row 1 (RS): K4, *k2tog, yf, k2; rep from * to last 3 sts, k2tog, yf, k1.

Row 2: *P2, yrn, p2tog; rep from * to last 3 sts, p3.

Row 3: *K2, k2tog, yf; rep from * to last 3 sts, k3.

Row 4: P4, *yrn, p2tog, p2; rep from * to last 3 sts, yrn, p2tog, p1.

Row 5: K1, *yf, sl 1, k1, psso, k2; rep from * to last 2 sts, k2.

Row 6: P3, *p2tog tbl, yrn, p2; rep from * to end.

Row 7: K3, *yf, sl 1, k1, psso, k2; rep from * to end.

Row 8: P1, *p2tog tbl, yrn, p2; rep from * to last 2 sts, p2.

Rep these 8 rows.

Little shell insertion

Worked over 7 sts on a background
of st st.
Row 1 (RS): Knit.
Row 2: Purl.
Row 3: K1, yfrn, p1, p3tog, p1, yon, k1.
Row 4: Purl.
Rep these 4 rows.

Feather and fan

Multiple of 18 + 2.
Row 1 (RS): Knit.
Row 2: Purl.
Row 3: K1, *[k2tog] 3 times, [yf, k1] 6
times, [k2tog] 3 times; rep from * to last
st, k1.
Row 4: Knit.
Rep these 4 rows.

Eyelet lattice insertion

Worked over 8 sts on a background of
st st.
Row 1 (RS): K1, [k2tog, yf] 3 times, k1.
Row 2: Purl.
Row 3: K2, [k2tog, yf] twice, k2.
Row 4: Purl.
Rep these 4 rows.

Lacy openwork

Multiple of 4 + 1.
Row 1: K1, *yfrn, p3tog, yon, k1; rep from
* to end.
Row 2: P2tog, yon, k1, yfrn, *p3tog, yon,
k1, yfrn; rep from * to last 2 sts, p2tog.
Rep these 2 rows.

Double lace rib

Multiple of 6 + 2.
Row 1 (RS): K2, *p1, yon, k2tog tb1, p1,
k2; rep from * to end.
Row 2: P2, *k1, p2; rep from * to end.
Row 3: K2, *p1, k2tog, yfrn, p1, k2; rep
from * to end.
Row 4: As row 2.
Rep these 4 rows.

Gate and ladder pattern

Multiple of 9 + 3.
Foundation row (WS): Purl.
Row 1: K1, k2tog, k3, [yf] twice, k3,
*k3tog, k3, [yf] twice, k3; rep from * to last
3 sts, k2tog, k1.
Row 2: P6, k1, *p8, k1; rep from * to last
5 sts, p5.
Rep the last 2 rows.

Diamond and bobble panel

Worked over 11 sts on a background of rev st st.

Row 1 (RS): P1, yon, sl 1, k1, psso, p5, k2tog, yfrn, p1.

Row 2: K2, p1, k5, p1, k2.

Row 3: P2, yon, sl 1, k1, psso, p3, k2tog, yfrn, p2.

Row 4: K3, [p1, k3] twice.

Row 5: P3, yon, sl 1, k1, psso, p1, k2tog, yfrn, p3.

Row 6: K4, p1, k1, p1, k4.

Row 7: P4, yon, sl 1, k2tog, psso, yfrn, p4.

Row 8: K5, p1, k5.

Row 9: P3, k2tog, yfrn, p1, yon, sl 1, k1, psso, p3.

Row 10: As row 4.

Row 11: P2, k2tog, yfrn, p3, yon, sl 1, k1, psso, p2.

Row 12: As row 2.

Row 13: P1, k2tog, yfrn, p5, yon, sl 1, k1, psso, p1.

Row 14: K1, p1, k7, p1, k1.

Row 15: K2tog, yfrn, p3, make bobble as follows: into next st work [k1, yf, k1, yf, k1] turn, p5, turn, k5, turn, p2tog, p1, p2tog tbl, turn, sl 1, k2tog, psso, p3, yon, sl 1, k1, psso.

Row 16: K1, p1, k3, KB1, k3, p1, k1.

Rep these 16 rows.

Twist cable and ladder lace

Multiple of 7 + 6.

Row 1 (RS): K1, *k2tog, [yf] twice, sl 1, k1, psso, k3; rep from * to last 5 sts, k2tog, [yf] twice, sl 1, k1, psso, k1.

Row 2: K2, *[KB1, k1] into double yf of previous row, k1, p3, k1; rep from * to last 4 sts, [KB1, k1] into double yf of previous row, k2.

Row 3: K1, *k2tog, [yf] twice, sl 1, k1, psso, knit into 3rd st on left-hand needle, then knit into 2nd st, then knit into 1st st, slipping all 3 sts onto right-hand needle tog; rep from * to last 5 sts, k2tog, [yf] twice, sl 1, k1, psso, k1.

Row 4: As row 2.

Rep these 4 rows.

Eyelet twigs

Worked over 14 sts on a background of st st.

Row 1 (RS): K1, yf, k3tog, yf, k3, yf, sl 1, k2tog, psso, yf, k4.

Row 2 and every alt row: Purl.

Row 3: Yf, k3tog, yf, k5, yf, sl 1, k2tog, psso, yf, k3.

Row 5: K5, yf, k3tog, yf, k1, yf, sl 1, k2tog, psso, yf, k2.

Row 7: K4, yf, k3tog, yf, k3, yf, sl 1, k2tog, psso, yf, k1.

Row 9: K3, yf, k3tog, yf, k5, yf, sl 1, k2tog, psso, yf.

Row 11: K2, yf, k3tog, yf, k1, yf, sl 1, k2tog, psso, yf, k5.

Row 12: Purl.

Rep these 12 rows.

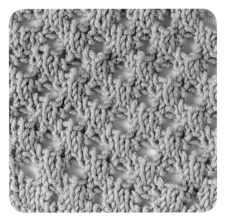

Large lattice lace

Multiple of 6 + 2.

Row 1 (RS): K1, p1, *yon, k2tog tbl, k2tog, yfrn, p2; rep from * to last 6 sts, yon, k2tog tbl, k2tog, yfrn, p1, k1.

Row 2: K2, *p4, k2; rep from * to end.

Row 3: K1, p1, *k2tog, [yf] twice, k2tog tbl, p2; rep from * to last 6 sts, k2tog, [yf] twice, k2tog tbl, p1, k1.

Row 4: K2, *p1, [k1, p1] into double yf of previous row, p1, k2; rep from * to end.

Row 5: K1, *k2tog, yfrn, p2, yon, k2tog tbl; rep from * to last st, k1.

Row 6: K1, p2, *k2, p4; rep from * to last 5 sts, k2, p2, k1.

Row 7: K1, yf, *k2tog tbl, p2, k2tog, [yf] twice; rep from * to last 7 sts, k2tog tbl, p2, k2tog, yf, k1.

Row 8: K1, p2, k2, p1, *[k1, p1] into double yf of previous row, p1, k2, p1; rep from * to last 2 sts, p1, k1.

Rep these 8 rows.

Waterfall pattern

Multiple of 6 + 3.

Row 1 (RS): P3, *k3, yo, p3; rep from * to end.

Row 2: K3, *p4, k3; rep from * to end.

Row 3: P3, *k1, k2tog, yo, k1, p3; rep from * to end.

Row 4: K3, *p2, p2tog, k3; rep from * to end.

Row 5: P3, *k1, yo, k2tog, p3; rep from * to end.

Row 6: K3, *p3, k3; rep from * to end.

Rep these 6 rows.

Eyelet twigs and bobbles

Worked over 16 sts on a background of st st.

Row 1 (RS): K2, yf, k3tog, yf, k3, yf, sl 1, k2tog, psso, yf, k5.

Row 2 and every alt row: Purl.

Row 3: K1, yf, k3tog, yf, k5, yf, sl 1, k2tog, psso, yf, k4.

Row 5: MB, k5, yf, k3tog, yf, k1, yf, sl 1, k2tog, psso, yf, k3.

Row 7: K5, yf, k3tog, yf, k3, yf, sl 1, k2tog, psso, yf, k2.

Row 9: K4, yf, k3tog, yf, k5, yf, sl 1, k2tog, psso, yf, MB.

Row 11: K3, yf, k3tog, yf, k1, yf, sl 1, k2tog, psso, yf, k6.

Row 12: Purl.

Rep these 12 rows.

Diamond lace II

Multiple of 6 + 3.
Row 1 (RS): *K4, yf, sl 1, k1, psso; rep from * to last 3 sts, k3.
Row 2 and every alt row: Purl.
Row 3: K2, *k2tog, yf, k1, yf, sl 1, k1, psso, k1; rep from * to last st, k1.
Row 5: K1, k2tog, yf, *k3, yf, sl 1, k2tog, psso, yf; rep from * to last 6 sts, k3, yf, sl 1, k1, psso, k1.
Row 7: K3, *yf, sl 1, k2tog, psso, yf, k3; rep from * to end.
Row 9: As row 1.
Row 11: K1, *yf, sl 1, k1, psso, k4; rep from * to last 2 sts, yf, sl 1, k1, psso.
Row 13: K2, *yf, sl 1, k1, psso, k1, k2tog, yf, k1; rep from * to last st, k1.
Row 15: As row 7.
Row 17: As row 5.
Row 19: As row 11.
Row 20: Purl.
Rep these 20 rows.

Lacy chain

Worked over 16 sts on a background of st st.
Row 1 (RS): K5, yf, sl 1, k1, psso, k2, yf, sl 1, k1, psso, k5.
Row 2 and every alt row: Purl.
Row 3: K3, k2tog, yf, k1, yf, sl 1, k1, psso, k2, yf, sl 1, k1, psso, k4.
Row 5: K2, k2tog, yf, k3, yf, sl 1, k1, psso, k2, yf, sl 1, k1, psso, k3.
Row 7: K1, k2tog, yf, k2, k2tog, yf, k1, yf, sl 1, k1, psso, k2, yf, sl 1, k1, psso, k2.
Row 9: K2tog, yf, k2, k2tog, yf, k3, yf, sl 1, k1, psso, k2, yf, sl 1, k1, psso, k1.
Row 11: K2, yf, sl 1, k1, psso, k2, yf, sl 1, k1, psso, yf, k2tog, yf, k2, k2tog, yf, k2tog.
Row 13: K3, yf, sl 1, k1, psso, k2, yf, sl 1, k2tog, psso, yf, k2, k2tog, yf, k2.
Row 15: K4, yf, sl 1, k1, psso, k2, yf, sl 1, k1, psso, k1, k2tog, yf, k3.
Row 16: Purl.
Rep these 16 rows.

Horseshoe print

Multiple of 10 + 1.
Row 1 (WS): Purl.
Row 2: K1, *yf, k3, sl 1, k2tog, psso, k3, yf, k1; rep from * to end.
Row 3: Purl.
Row 4: P1, *k1, yf, k2, sl 1, k2tog, psso, k2, yf, k1, p1; rep from * to end.
Row 5: K1, *p9, k1; rep from * to end.
Row 6: P1, *k2, yf, k1, sl 1, k2tog, psso, k1, yf, k2, p1; rep from * to end.
Row 7: As row 5.
Row 8: P1, *k3, yf, sl 1, k2tog, psso, yf, k3, p1; rep from * to end.
Rep these 8 rows.

Little dots (single)

Rep 2 sts x 1 row

Little dots (double)

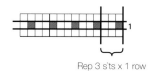

Rep 3 sts x 1 row

Short dash

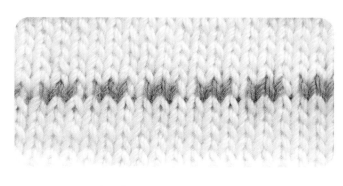

Rep 3 sts x 1 row

Dash

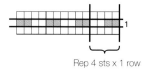

Rep 4 sts x 1 row

Dot and dash

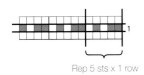

Rep 5 sts x 1 row

Long dash

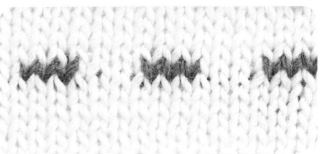

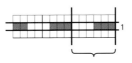

Rep 6 sts x 1 row

Dot and long dash

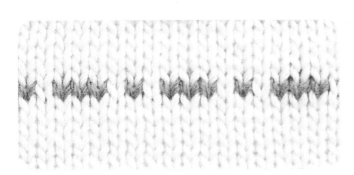

Rep 6 sts x 1 row

Small zigzag

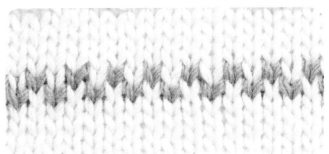

Rep 2 sts x 2 rows

Small wave

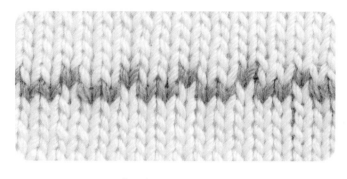

Rep 3 sts x 2 rows

Back stroke

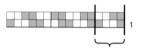

Rep 4 sts x 2 rows

Two-wave

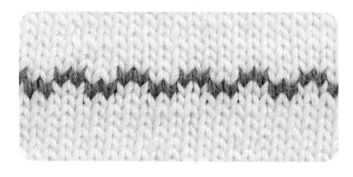

Rep 4 sts x 2 rows

Three-wave

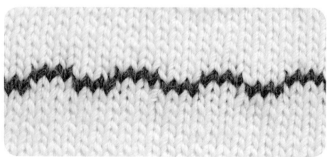

Rep 6 sts x 2 rows

Small arch

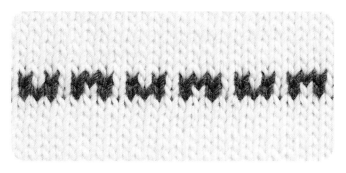

Rep 8 sts x 2 rows

Triangle wave I

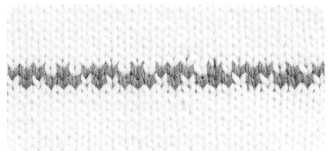

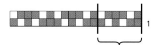

Rep 6 sts x 2 rows

Triangle and square I

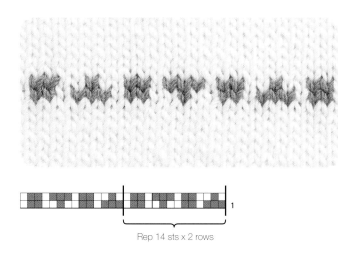

Rep 14 sts x 2 rows

Threaded squares

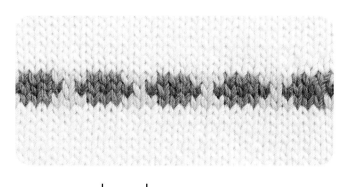

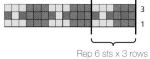

Rep 6 sts x 3 rows

Seeded vertical stripe

Rep 6 sts x 2 rows

Triangle and square II

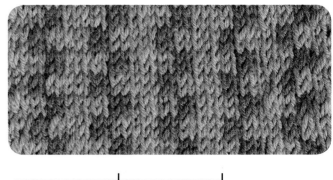

3
1

Rep 14 sts x 4 rows

Tall blocks

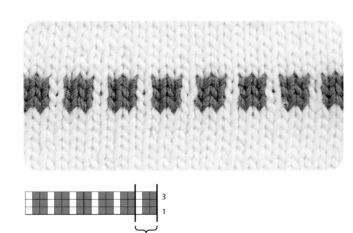

3
1

Rep 3 sts x 3 rows

Post and hook

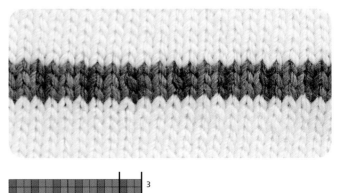

3
1

Rep 3 sts x 3 rows

Broken fence

Rep 4 sts x 3 rows

Single fence

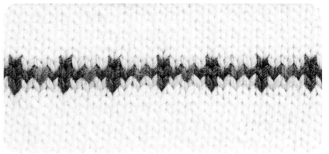

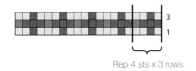

Rep 4 sts x 3 rows

Broken rows I

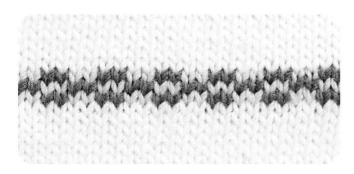

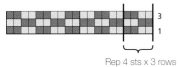

Rep 4 sts x 3 rows

Broken rows II

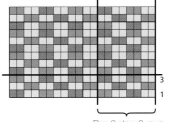

Rep 8 sts x 3 rows

Small arrowhead

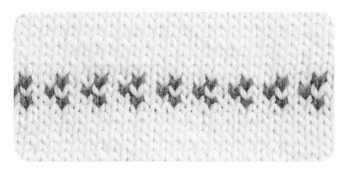

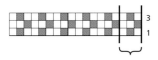

Rep 3 sts x 3 rows

Speckled fence

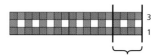

Rep 4 sts x 3 rows

High tide

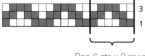

Rep 6 sts x 3 rows

Kirkwall border

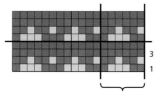

Rep 6 sts x 4 rows

Dancing bears

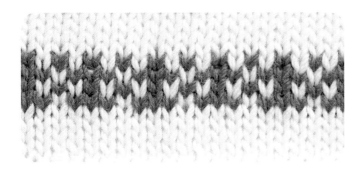

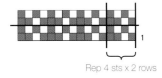

Rep 4 sts x 2 rows

Triangle stacks

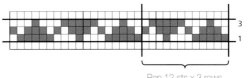

3
1

Rep 12 sts x 3 rows

Flotsam

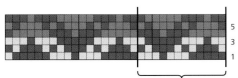

5
3
1

Rep 12 sts x 6 rows

Battlements (3-count)

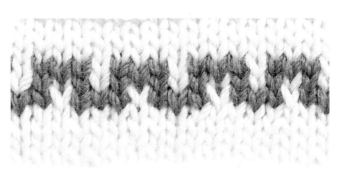

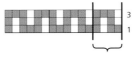

3
1

Rep 4 sts x 3 rows

Breakers

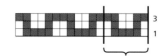

Rep 5 sts x 3 rows

Battlements (4-count) I

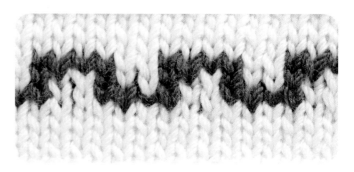

Rep 6 sts x 3 rows

Battlements (4-count) II

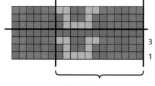

Rep 12 sts x 4 rows

Heather peerie

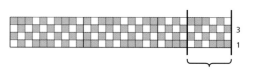

Rep 6 sts x 4 rows

Triangle and dot

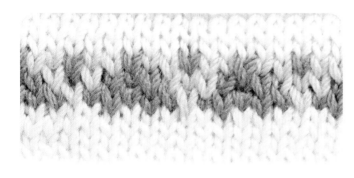

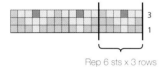

Rep 6 sts x 3 rows

Shoots and seeds

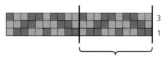

Rep 10 sts x 3 rows

Triangle wave II

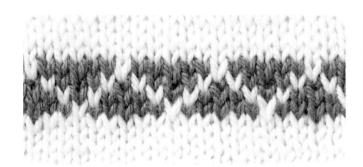

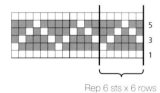

Rep 6 sts x 6 rows

Outline triangle

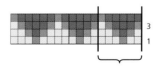

Rep 6 sts x 4 rows

Five and one

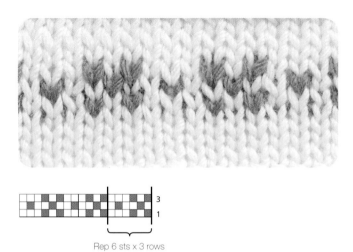

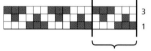

3
1

Rep 6 sts x 3 rows

Triangle wave III

3
1

Rep 6 sts x 3 rows

Triangle wave border

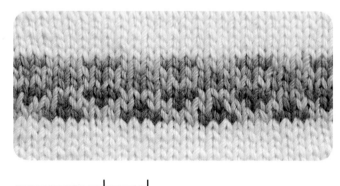

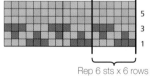

5
3
1

Rep 6 sts x 6 rows

H-border

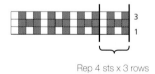

3
1

Rep 4 sts x 3 rows

Harvest furrows

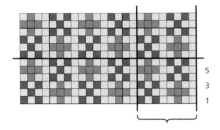

5
3
1

Rep 8 sts x 6 rows

Ploughed furrows

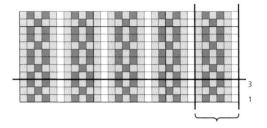

3
1

Rep 6 sts x 3 rows

Heraldic border

11
9
7
5
3
1

Rep 14 sts x 11 rows

Minerva

11
9
7
5
3
1

Rep 20 sts x 11 rows

Tree of life

Diagonal lattice

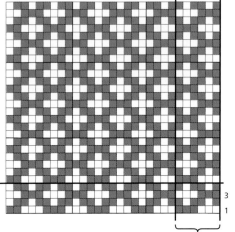

Rep 16 sts x 3 rows

3
1

Rep 6 sts x 4 rows

3
1

Triangles and strokes

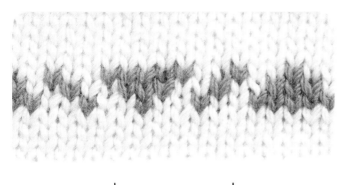

Rep 16 sts x 3 rows

Seeded back stroke

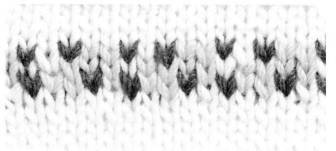

Rep 5 sts x 3 rows

Box and dot

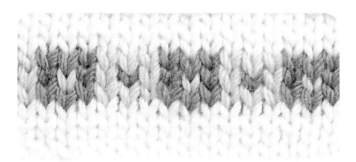

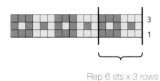

Rep 6 sts x 3 rows

Checkered dot border

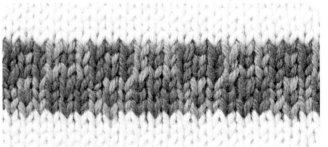

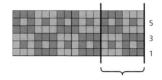

Rep 6 sts x 6 rows

Gull wings

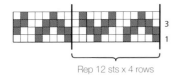

Rep 12 sts x 4 rows

Twinkling diamonds

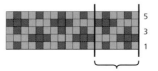

Rep 6 sts x 5 rows

Broken crests

Rep 10 sts x 4 rows

Broken zigzags

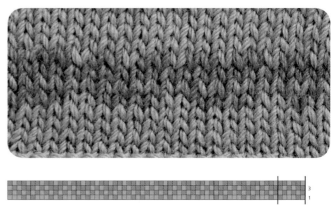

Rep 6 sts x 4 rows

Battlements (5-count)

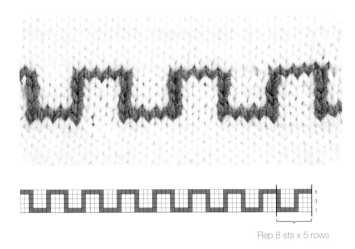

Rep 8 sts x 5 rows

Stormy sea

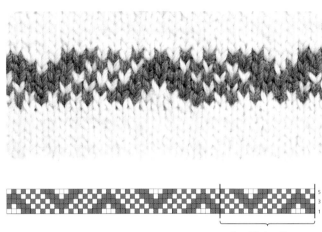

Rep 20 sts x 5 rows

Tulip wave

Rep 14 sts x 4 rows

Wave crest I

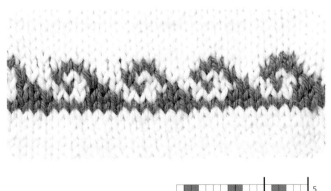

Rep 6 sts x 5 rows

Rocky shore

Arrowhead tweed border

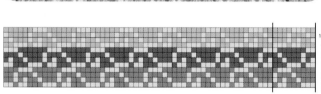

Rep 9 sts x 12 rows

Rep 20 sts x 10 rows

Tip

If you are new to Fair Isle designs, tackling a simple banded pattern such as Pretty maids or Crossed battlements might be a good starting point. Try adapting a plain hat pattern and incorporating the colourwork to introduce one striking design element.

Flight

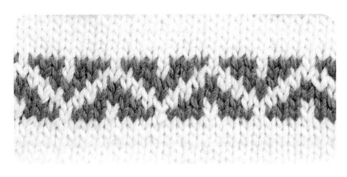

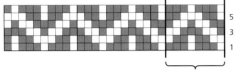

5
3
1

Rep 8 sts x 6 rows

Triangle zigzag

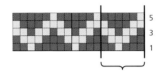

5
3
1

Rep 6 sts x 5 rows

Pretty maids

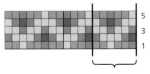

5
3
1

Rep 6 sts x 5 rows

Crossed battlements

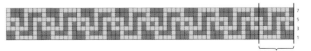

7
5
3
1

Rep 8 sts x 7 rows

Bannock trellis pattern

Wave crest II

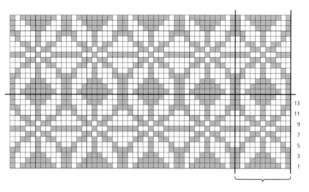

13
11
9
7
5
3
1

Rep 11 sts x 19 rows

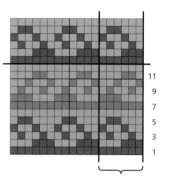

11
9
7
5
3
1

Rep 6 sts x 12 rows

Phlox

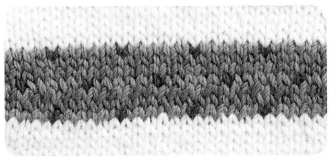

Rep 6 sts x 7 rows

Double-row diamond

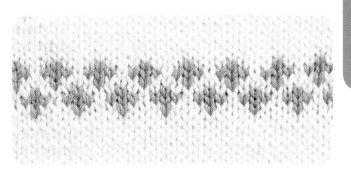

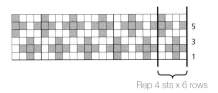

Rep 4 sts x 6 rows

Diamond footpath

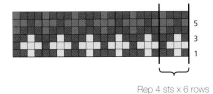

Rep 4 sts x 6 rows

Rose and thistle

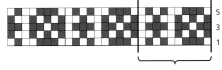

Rep 10 sts x 5 rows

Wave and diamond border

Lattice window I

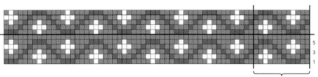

5
3
1

Rep 12 sts x 6 rows

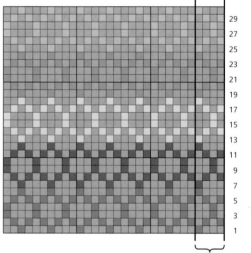

29
27
25
23
21
19
17
15
13
11
9
7
5
3
1

Rep 4 sts x 30 rows

Diamond tweed pattern

Celtic rose

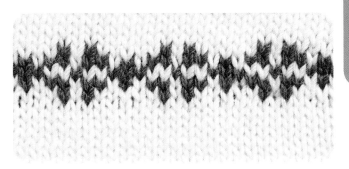

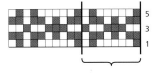

Rep 8 sts x 7 rows

Rep 8 sts x 5 rows

Diamond link and dot

Captive diamond border

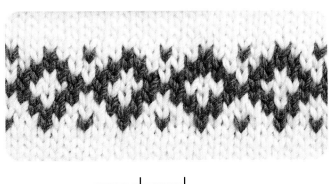

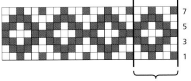

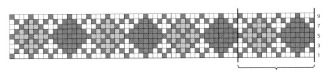

Rep 6 sts x 7 rows

Rep 16 sts x 18 rows

Zigzag fence

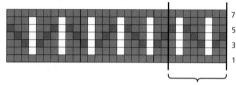

7
5
3
1

Rep 8 sts x 7 rows

Diamond filigree

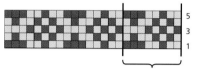

5
3
1

Rep 8 sts x 5 rows

Cabbages

5
3
1

Rep 8 sts x 5 rows

Wandering zigzag

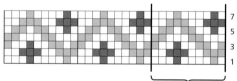

7
5
3
1

Rep 10 sts x 7 rows

Chain link I

Berwick

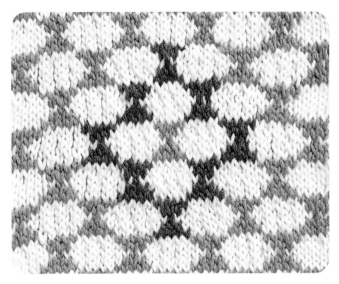

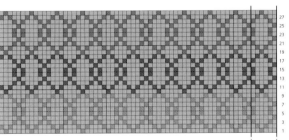

Rep 6 sts x 28 rows

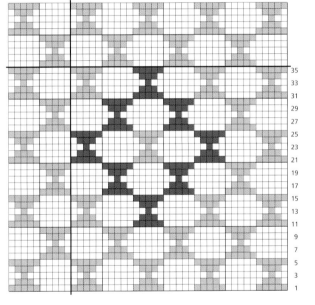

Rep 35 sts x 35 rows

Speckled trellis

Diamond box border

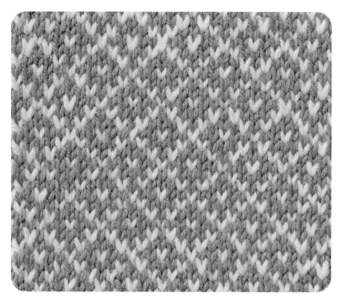

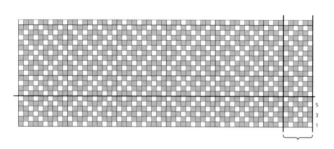

Rep 6 sts x 6 rows

Rep 12 sts x 17 rows

Diamond and cross windowpane I

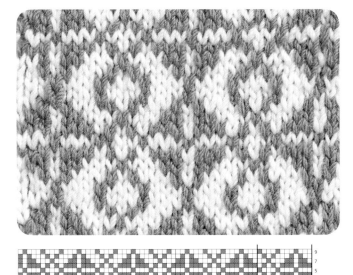

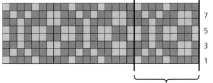

Rep 12 sts x 9 rows

Flower and chalice

Rep 9 sts x 8 rows

Wall-walk

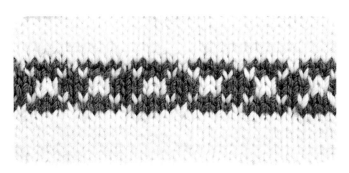

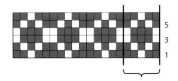

Rep 5 sts x 6 rows

Diamond and cross

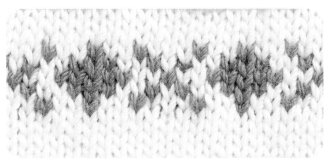

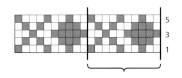

Rep 10 sts x 5 rows

Lattice window II

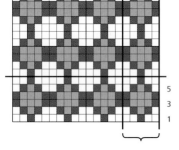

5
3
1

Rep 5 sts x 6 rows

Trellis with blocks

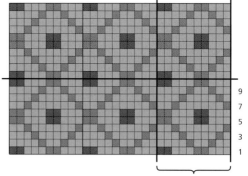

9
7
5
3
1

Rep 10 sts x 10 rows

Speckled zigzag

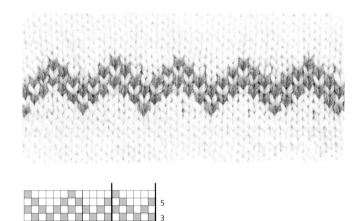

Rep 6 sts x 6 rows

Arrowhead zigzag

Rep 16 sts x 9 rows

Ripples border

Rep 5 sts x 9 rows

Flora

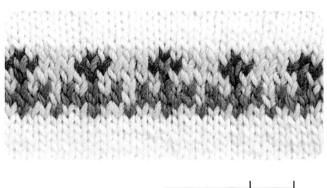

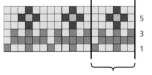

Rep 6 sts x 6 rows

Zigzag tweed

Vertical basketweave lattice

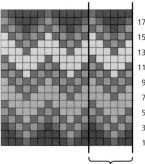

Rep 6 sts x 18 rows

Rep 30 sts x 8 rows

Aubrieta

Cosmea

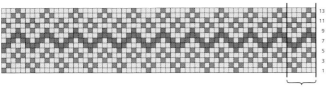

Rep 6 sts x 13 rows

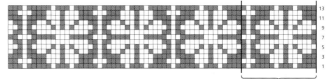

Rep 16 sts x 13 rows

Tip

Colourwork is nearly always worked in stocking stitch fabric to provide a clean and simple canvas for the design. Otherwise complex and colourful patterns such as Aubrieta or Zigzag tweed could look overworked and fussy and lose their impact.

Diamond and cross windowpane II

Mosaic path

Rep 12 sts x 11 rows

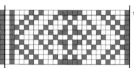

Rep 26 sts x 11 rows

Tip

Fair Isle patterns often include a vertical motif, as in the Castle window variations shown here. This means it is easy to adapt the design to fit all the way around a length of knitting, whether it forms the decorative element on a sweater or the brim of a hat.

Castle window I

Castle window II

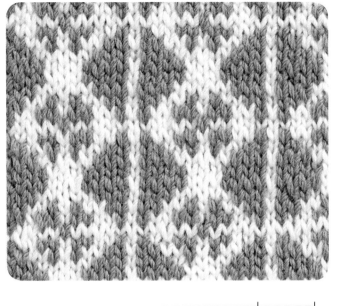

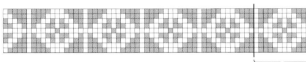

Rep 12 sts x 9 rows

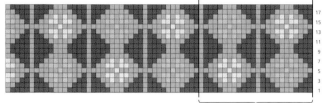

Rep 24 sts x 18 rows

Vertical stripes I

Rep 2 sts x 1 row

Line and dot

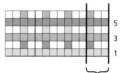

Rep 2 sts x 6 rows

Diamond links

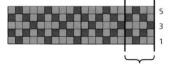

Rep 4 sts x 5 rows

Vertical stripes II

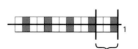

Rep 3 sts x 1 row

Country lanes

Chain link II

Rep 12 sts x 11 rows

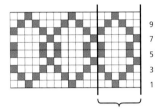

Rep 6 sts x 10 rows

Crossroads

Parterre

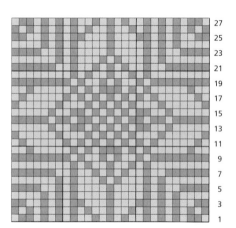

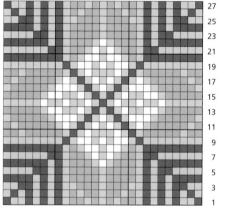

				27
				25
				23
				21
				19
				17
				15
				13
				11
				9
				7
				5
				3
				1

Rep 27 sts x 27 rows

Rep 27 sts x 27 rows

Melissa

Diamonds in the snow

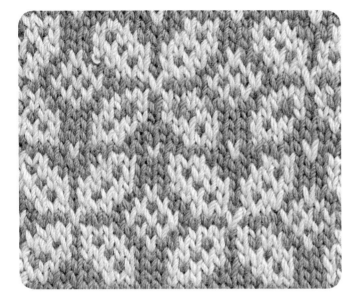

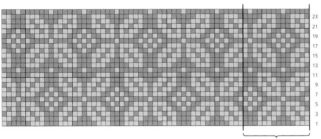

23
21
19
17
15
13
11
9
7
5
3
1

Rep 14 sts x 24 rows

11
9
7
5
3
1

Rep 6 sts x 12 rows

Kirkwall

Argyll check

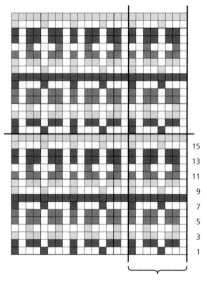

15
13
11
9
7
5
3
1

Rep 8 sts x 16 rows

56
50
40
30
27
25
23
21
19
17
15
13
11
9
7
5
3
1

Rep 32 sts x 28 rows

Diamond zigzag bands

Banded lattice and cross

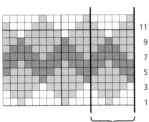

11
9
7
5
3
1

Rep 6 sts x 12 rows

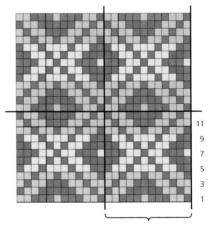

11
9
7
5
3
1

Rep 12 sts x 12 rows

Diamond flower border I

Whirligig

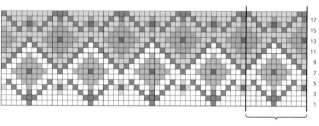

Rep 12 sts x 18 rows

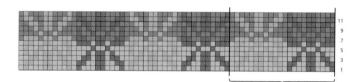

Rep 22 sts x 12 rows

Diamond and snowflake paths

Diamond flower border II

Rep 32 sts x 15 rows

Rep 12 sts x 18 rows

Rose crest

Winter rose medallion

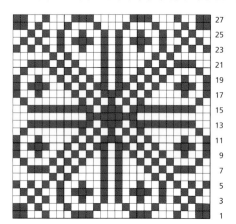

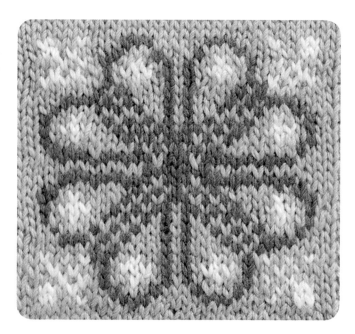

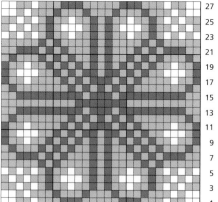

Rep 27 sts x 27 rows

Rep 27 sts x 27 rows

Quatrefoil

Rep 27 sts x 27 rows

Argyll diamond motif

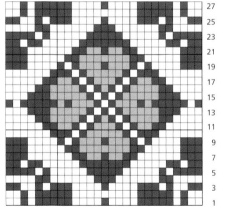

Rep 27 sts x 27 rows

Diamond and lozenge
tweed border

Diamond and lozenge
banded border

Rep 10 sts x 27 rows

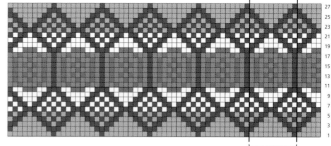

Rep 10 sts x 27 rows

Scottish thistles I

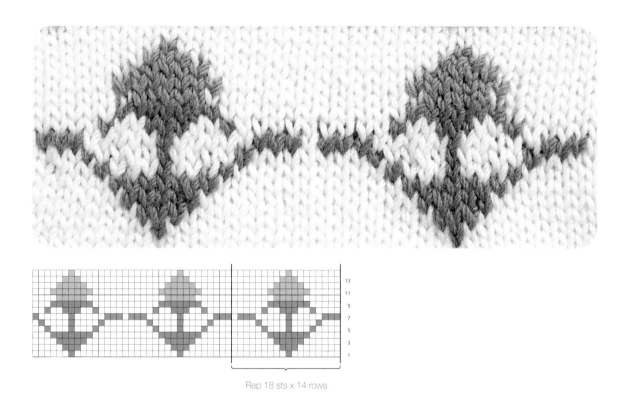

Rep 18 sts x 14 rows

Scottish thistles II

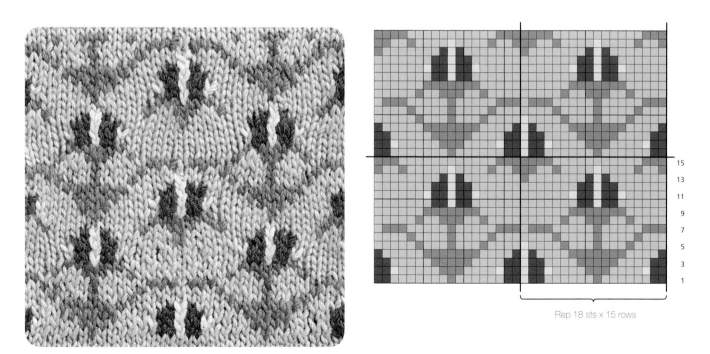

Rep 18 sts x 15 rows

Dancing diamonds

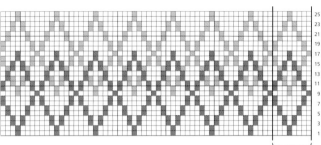

Rep 8 sts x 25 rows

Hellenic wave

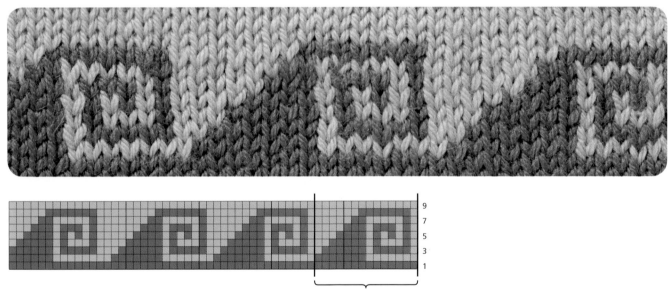

Rep 14 sts x 9 rows

Cairn

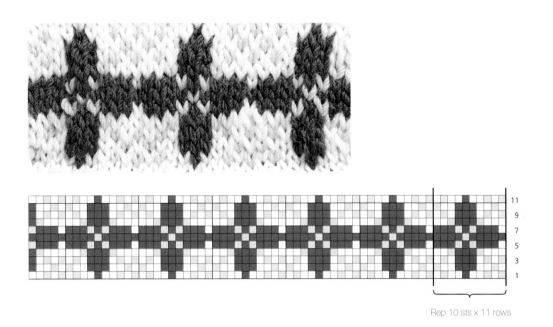

Rep 10 sts x 11 rows

Shield and cross

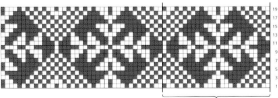

Rep 26 sts x 19 rows

Dianthus and pannier border

Rep 18 sts x 11 rows

Campion and pannier border

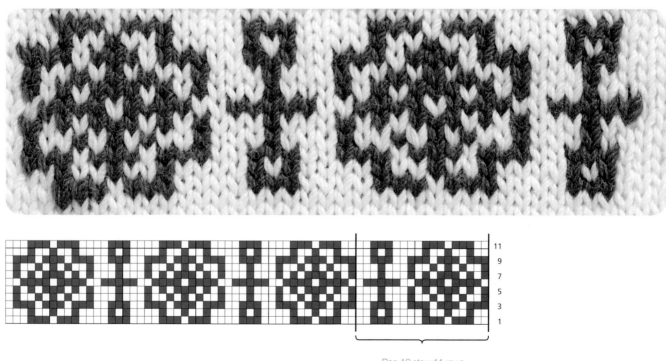

Rep 18 sts x 11 rows

Herbaceous border

Michaelmas

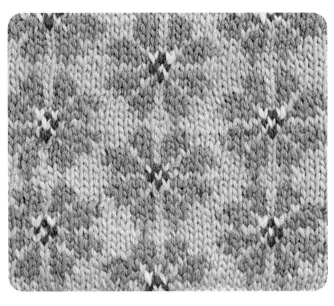

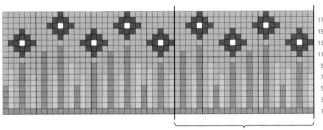

Rep 25 sts x 18 rows

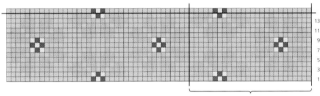

Rep 26 sts x 14 rows

Lads and lasses I

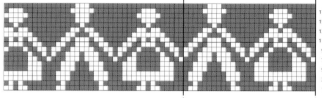

Rep 28 sts x 18 rows

Lads and lasses II

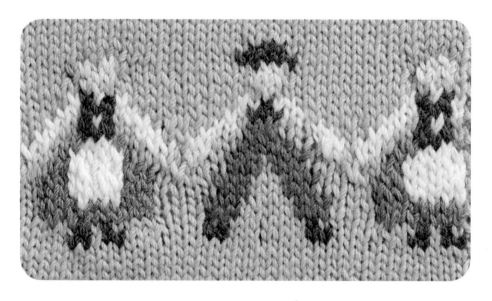

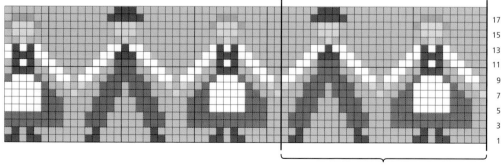

Rep 28 sts x 18 rows

Acrobats

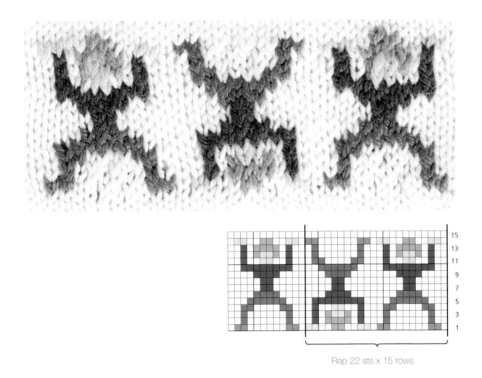

Rep 22 sts x 15 rows

Dancing ballerinas

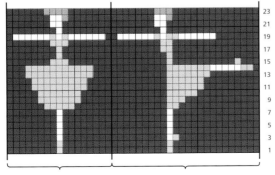

Rep 17 sts + 24 sts x 23 rows

Framed heart motif

Belladonna

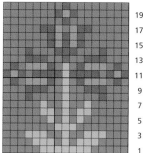

Rep 17 sts x 18 rows

Rep 17 sts x 20 rows

Campion

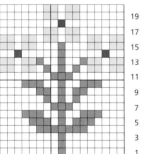

Rep 17sts x 20 rows

Floret

Rep 33 sts x 35 rows

Leaf edging

Beaded thumb cast-on

Worked lengthways over 8 sts.

Note: increases are worked purlwise.

Row 1 (RS): K5, yo, k1, yo, k2. (10 sts)

Row 2: P6, inc, k3. (11 sts)

Row 3: K4, p1, k2, yo, k1, yo, k3. (13 sts)

Row 4: P8, inc, k4. (14 sts)

Row 5: K4, p2, k3, yo, k1, yo, k4. (16 sts)

Row 6: P10, inc, k5. (17 sts)

Row 7: K4, p3, k4, yo, k1, yo, k5. (19 sts)

Row 8: P12, inc, k6. (20 sts)

Row 9: K4, p4, yb, skpo, k7, k2tog, k1. (18 sts)

Row 10: P10, inc, k7. (19 sts)

Row 11: K4, p5, yb, skpo, k5, k2tog, k1. (17 sts)

Row 12: P8, inc, k2, p1, k5. (18 sts)

Row 13: K4, p1, k1, p4, yb, skpo, k3, k2tog, k1. (16 sts)

Row 14: P6, inc, k3, p1, k5. (17 sts)

Row 15: K4, p1, k1, p5, yb, skpo, k1, k2tog, k1. (15 sts)

Row 16: P4, inc, k4, p1, k5. (16 sts)

Row 17: K4, p1, k1, p6, yb, sk2po, k1. (14 sts)

Row 18: P2tog, cast off 5 sts purlwise using p2tog as first of these sts, k1, p1, k5. (8 sts)

Rep these 18 rows.

Worked from bottom edge upwards.

Starts and ends with multiple of 2 sts + 1 st.

Note: Thread beads onto knitting yarn before casting on, 1 bead for each alt st, less 2, to give a selvedge st at each end. Leaving a tail of yarn long enough for the required number of sts to be cast on, make a slip knot in the yarn above the threaded beads and place this on the needle.

Cast on 1 st.

*Slide 1 bead up against the needle before looping the yarn around the thumb to cast on next st.

Cast on 1 st.

Rep from * until 1 less than required number of sts are on left-hand needle.

Cast on 1 st.

This forms the edging.

Cont as required. Usually row 1 will be a WS row to show the beads to best effect.

Layered rib

Box pleats

Worked from bottom edge upwards.

Starts and ends with multiple of 2 sts + 1 st.

Note: two colours of yarn are used, A and B. Cast on same number of sts for each layer using the thumb method and A.

Bottom layer

Row 1 (RS): K1, *p1, k1; rep from * to end.

Row 2: P1, *k1, p1; rep from * to end.

Rep row 1 once more.

Change to B.

Rep rows 2 and 1, 4 more times.

Place sts on spare needle.

Top layer

Row 1 (RS): K1, *p1, k1; rep from * to end.

Change to B.

Row 2: P1, *k1, p1; rep from * to end.

Using B, rep rows 1–2 once more, then rep row 1 once more. WS facing, hold top layer in front of bottom layer. Using 3rd needle, work 1 st from each needle tog across row, working p1 *k1, p1; rep from * to end.

Rep rows 1–2 once more.

These rows form the edging.

Cast off or cont as required.

Worked from bottom edge upwards.

Starts with multiple of 24 sts.

Ends with multiple of 8 sts.

Note: Cast on using the cable method. Slip all sts purlwise. Slipping the st wyif (with yarn in front) makes a back fold: slipping the st wyib (with yarn at back) makes a front fold.

Row 1 (RS): K4, *sl 1 wyif, k3, sl 1 wyib, k6, sl 1 wyib, k3, sl 1 wyif, k8; rep from *, ending k4.

Row 2: Purl.

Rep rows 1–2, 5 more times.

Row 13 (join pleats): *[Slip next 4 sts onto a double-pointed needle] twice, fold fabric on columns of slip sts so that left-hand needle and double-pointed needles are parallel and fold is at the back and k 1 st from each needle tog 4 times; rep from *, folding into box pleats.

Rows 14–15: Knit.

These 15 rows form the edging.

Cast off or cont as required.

Cast-off fringe

Worked lengthways over 3 sts.
Note: cast on using the cable method.
Rows 1–3: Sl 1, k2.
Row 4 (WS): Cast on 6 sts, cast off 6 sts, k2. (3 sts)
Rep these 4 rows, ending with row 3.

Twist edge

Worked from bottom edge upwards.
Starts and ends with a multiple of 6 sts.
Note: cast on using the thumb method.
Starting with a k row, work 6 rows in st st.
Row 7 (RS): *K6, take the tip of the left-hand needle under the cast-on edge to the back of the work and around to the working position again; rep from *, ending k6.
These 7 rows form the edging.
Cont as required.

Moss stitch cord

Worked lengthways over 5 sts on double-pointed needles.
Row 1: K1, *p1, k1; rep from * to end, do not turn, slide sts to other end of needle.
Row 2: P1, *k1, p1; rep from * to end, do not turn, slide sts to other end of needle.
Rep these 2 rows.

Ridged eyelet edge

Worked from bottom edge upwards.
Starts and ends with multiple of 2 sts + 1 st.
Note: cast on using the thumb method.
Work 3 rows in garter st.
Row 4 (WS): *P2tog, yo; rep from * to last st, p1.
Work 3 rows in garter st.
These 7 rows form the edging.
Cast off or cont as required.

Picot braid

Worked lengthways over 5 sts.
Foundation row: Knit.
Row 1 (RS): Cast on 2 sts, cast off 2 sts, k4.
Rep this 1 row.

Trefoil bunting

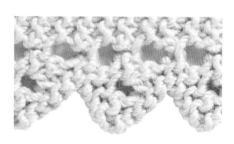

Worked lengthways over 5 sts.
Row 1 (RS): K3, yo2, k2. (7 sts)
Row 2: K3, p1, k3.
Work 2 rows in garter st.
Row 5: K3, yo2, k2tog, yo2, k2. (10 sts)
Row 6: K3, p1, k2, p1, k3.
Row 7: Knit.
Row 8: Cast off 5 sts, k4. (5 sts)
Rep these 8 rows.

Ladder braid

Worked lengthways over 11 sts.
Row 1 (RS): Sl 1, k10.
Row 2: Sl 1, k1, p7, k2.
Rep rows 1–2 once more.
Row 5: Sl 1, k1, p7, k2.
Row 6: As row 2.
Row 7: As row 1.
Rep rows 6–7 once more.
Row 10: Sl 1, k10.
Rep these 10 rows.

Butterfly edging

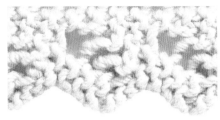

Worked lengthways over 8 sts.
Row 1 (RS): Sl 1, k2, yo, k2tog yo2, k2tog, k1. (9 sts)
Row 2: K3, p1, k2, yo, k2tog, k1.
Row 3: Sl 1, k2, yo, k2tog, k1, yo2, k2tog, k1. (10 sts)
Row 4: K3, p1, k3, yo, k2tog, k1.
Row 5: Sl 1, k2, yo, k2tog, k2, yo2, k2tog, k1. (11 sts)
Row 6: K3, p1, k4, yo, k2tog, k1.
Row 7: Sl 1, k2, yo, k2tog, k6.
Row 8: Cast off 3 sts, k4, yo, k2tog, k1. (8 sts)
Rep these 8 rows.

Wavy border

Worked lengthways over 13 sts.
Row 1 and every alt row (WS): K2, p to last 2 sts, k2.
Row 2: K4, yo, k5, yo, k2tog, yo, k2. (15 sts)
Row 4: K5, sk2po, k2, [yo, k2tog] twice, k1. (13 sts)
Row 6: K4, skpo, k2, [yo, k2tog] twice, k1. (12 sts)
Row 8: K3, skpo, k2, [yo, k2tog] twice, k1. (11 sts)
Row 10: K2, skpo, k2, [yo, k2tog] twice, k1. (10 sts)
Row 12: K1, skpo, k2, yo, k1, yo, k2tog, yo, k2. (11 sts)
Row 14: K4, yo, k3, yo, k2tog, yo, k2. (13 sts)
Rep these 14 rows.

Arrow braid

Moss and faggot

Worked lengthways over 9 sts.

Triangles
Put a slip knot on the needle.
Row 1 (RS): Inc. (2 sts)
Row 2: Inc, k1. (3 sts)
Row 3: Inc, k2. (4 sts)
Row 4: Inc, k3. (5 sts)
Row 5: Inc, k4. (6 sts)
Row 6: Inc, k5. (7 sts)
Row 7: Inc, k6. (8 sts)
Row 8: Inc, k7. (9 sts)
Cut yarn and leave sts on spare needle. Rep these 8 rows to make as many triangles as required.

Band
Cast on 9 sts.
Rows 1–6: Sl 1, k8.
Row 7 (RS): Slip 9 sts of one triangle onto cable needle and, RS facing, hold in front of needle with band and k 1 st from each needle tog across the row.
Row 8: Sl 1, k8.
Rep these 8 rows, ending with row 6.

Worked lengthways over 17 sts.
Row 1 (RS): K2, yo, k3, yo, k2tog, [p1, k1] 5 times. (18 sts)
Row 2: [K1, p1] 4 times, k1, k2tog, yo, k5, yo, k2. (19 sts)
Row 3: K2, yo, k1, k2tog, yo, k1, yo, k2tog, k1, yo, k2tog, [p1, k1] 4 times. (20 sts)
Row 4: [K1, p1] 3 times, k1, [k2tog, yo, k1] twice, k2, yo, k2tog, k1, yo, k2. (21 sts)
Row 5: K2, yo, k1, k2tog, yo, k5, yo, k2tog, k1, yo, k2tog, [p1, k1] 3 times. (22 sts)
Row 6: [K1, p1] twice, k1, [k2tog, yo, k1] twice, k6, yo, k2tog, k1, yo, k2. (23 sts)
Row 7: [K2tog, k1, yo] twice, k2tog, k3, [k2tog, yo, k1] twice, [p1, k1] 3 times. (22 sts)
Row 8: [K1, p1] 4 times, yo, k2tog, k1, yo, k2tog, [k1, k2tog, yo] twice, k1, k2tog. (21 sts)
Row 9: [K2tog, k1, yo] twice, k3tog, yo, k1, k2tog, yo, [k1, p1] 4 times, k1. (20 sts)
Row 10: [K1, p1] 5 times, yo, k2tog, k3, k2tog, yo, k1, k2tog. (19 sts)
Row 11: K2tog, k1, yo, k2tog, k1, k2tog, yo, [k1, p1] 5 times, k1. (18 sts)
Row 12: [K1, p1] 6 times, yo, k3tog, yo, k1, k2tog. (17 sts)
Rep these 12 rows.

Lace and bobble

Worked from bottom edge upwards.

Starts and ends with multiple of 10 sts + 1 st.

Note: cast on using the thumb method.

Special abbreviation:

MB (make bobble): (p1, k1, p1) in next st, turn, k1, p1, k1, turn, p1, k1, p1, pass 2nd and 3rd sts over 1st st.

Row 1 (WS): *P5, MB, p4; rep from *, ending last rep p5.

Row 2: K1, *yo, k3, sk2po, k3, yo, k1; rep from * to end.

Row 3: Purl.

Row 4: P1, *k1, yo, k2, sk2po, k2, yo, k1, p1; rep from * to end.

Row 5: *K1, p9; rep from *, ending last rep k1.

Row 6: P1, *k2, yo, k1, sk2po, k1, yo, k2, p1; rep from * to end.

Row 7: As row 5.

Row 8: P1, *k3, yo, sk2po, yo, k3, p1; rep from * to end.

Row 9: Purl.

Row 10: K1, *k3, yo, sk2po, yo, k4; rep from * to end.

Row 11: Purl.

Rep rows 10–11 once more.

These 13 rows form the edging.

Cast off or cont as required.

Snail shell lace

Worked lengthways over 19 sts.

Foundation row: Knit.

Row 1 (WS): K5, p1, yo, p2tog, k8, yo, k2tog, k1.

Row 2: K3, yo, k2tog, k5, k2tog, yo, k1, yo, ssk, k2, yo2, k2. (21 sts)

Row 3: K3, p1, k1, p2tog tbl, yo, p3, yo, p2tog, k6, yo, k2tog, k1.

Row 4: K3, yo, k2tog, k3, k2tog, yo, k2, k2tog, yo, k1, yo, ssk, k2, yo2, k2. (23 sts)

Row 5: K3, p1, k1, p2tog tbl, yo, p3, yo, p2tog, p2, yo, p2tog, k4, yo, k2tog, k1.

Row 6: K3, yo, k2tog, k1, [k2tog, yo, k2] twice, yo, ssk, k1, yo, ssk, k2, yo2, k2. (25 sts)

Row 7: K3, p1, k1, [p2tog tbl, yo, p1] twice, yo, p2tog, p1, yo, p2tog, p2, yo, p2tog, k2, yo, k2tog, k1.

Row 8: K3, yo, k3tog, yo, k2, k2tog, yo, k1, k2tog, yo, k3, yo, ssk, k1, yo, ssk, k2tog, yo2, k2tog.

Row 9: K2, p1, k1, p2, yo, p2tog, p1, yo, p3tog, yo, p1, p2tog tbl, yo, p2, p2tog tbl, yo, k3, yo, k2tog, k1.

Row 10: K3, yo, k2tog, [k2, yo, ssk] twice, k3, k2tog, yo, k2, sk2po, yo2, k2tog. (24 sts)

Row 11: K2, p5, yo, p2tog, p1, p2tog tbl, yo, p2, p2tog tbl, yo, k5, yo, k2tog, k1.

Row 12: K3, yo, k2tog, k4, yo, ssk, k2, yo, k3tog, yo, k2, k3tog, yo, k2tog, k1. (22 sts)

Row 13: K3, p1, k3, yo, p2tog, p1, p2tog tbl, yo, k7, yo, k2tog, k1.

Row 14: K3, yo, k2tog, k6, yo, k3tog, yo, k2, k3tog, yo, k3tog. (19 sts)

Rep rows 1–14.

Fern lace edging

Accordion pleat

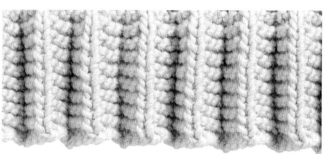

Worked lengthways over 14 sts.

Row 1 (RS): Sl 1, k2, [yo, k2tog] twice, k1, yo2, [k2tog] twice, yo, k2. (15 sts)

Row 2: K5, [k1, p1] twice in yo2, k8. (17 sts)

Row 3: Sl 1, k3, [yo, k2tog] twice, k5, k2tog, yo, k2.

Row 4 and every alt row: Knit.

Row 5: Sl 1, k4, [yo, k2tog] twice, k4, k2tog, yo, k2.

Row 7: Sl 1, k5, [yo, k2tog] twice, k3, k2tog, yo, k2.

Row 9: Sl 1, k6, [yo, k2tog] twice, k2, k2tog, yo, k2.

Row 11: Sl 1, k7, [yo, k2tog] twice, k1, k2tog, yo, k2.

Row 13: Sl 1, k8, [yo, k2tog] twice, k2tog, yo, k2.

Row 15: Sl 1, k9, [yo, k2tog] twice, k1, yo, k2. (18 sts)

Row 17: Sl 1, k10, yo, [k2tog] twice, sl last st back onto left-hand needle, 1 at a time, lift next 3 sts over it then replace st on right-hand needle. (14 sts)

Row 18: Knit.

Rep these 18 rows, ending with row 17.

Worked from bottom edge upwards.

Starts with twice the number of sts needed that is a multiple of 8 sts.

Ends with multiple of 8 sts.

Note: cast on using the thumb method.

Row 1 (RS): *K7, p1; rep from * to end.

Row 2: K4, *p1, k7; rep from * to last 4 sts, p1, k3.

Rep rows 1–2 as required, ending with row 2.

Next row: [K2tog] to end.

These rows form the edging.

Cast off or cont as required.

Thick and thin rib

Scallop lace edging

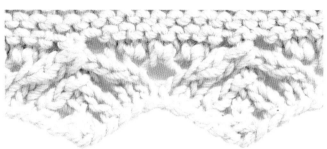

Worked from bottom edge upwards.

Starts and ends with multiple of 8 sts + 6 sts.

Note: cast on using the thumb method.

Row 1 (RS): K6, *p2, k6; rep from * to end.

Row 2: P6, *k2, p6; rep from * to end.

Rep rows 1–2 twice more.

Row 7: K2, *p2, k2; rep from * to end.

Row 8: P2, *k2, p2; rep from * to end.

Rep rows 7–8 twice more.

Row 13: K2, p2, *k6, p2; rep from * to last 2 sts, k2.

Row 14: P2, k2, *p6, k2; rep from * to last 2 sts, p2.

Rep rows 13–14 twice more.

These 18 rows form the edging.

Cast off or cont as required.

Worked from bottom edge upwards.

Starts with multiple of 13 sts + 2 sts.

Ends with multiple of 10 sts + 3 sts.

Note: cast on using the thumb method.

Row 1 (RS): K3, *skpo, sl 2, k3tog, p2sso, k2tog, k4; rep from * to last 12 sts, skpo, sl 2, k3tog, p2sso, k2tog, k3.

Row 2: P4, *yo, p1, yo, p6; rep from * to last 5 sts, yo, p1, yo, p4.

Row 3: K1, yo, *k2, skpo, k1, k2tog, k2, yo; rep from * to last st, k1.

Row 4: P2, *yo, p2, yo, p3, yo, p2, yo, p1; rep from * to last st, p1.

Row 5: K2, yo, k1, *yo, skpo, k1, sk2po, k1, k2tog, [yo, k1] 3 times; rep from * to last 12 sts, yo, skpo, k1, sk2po, k1, k2tog, yo, k1, yo, k2.

Row 6: Purl.

Row 7: K5, *yo, sl 2, k3tog, p2sso, yo, k7; rep from * to last 10 sts, yo, sl 2, k3tog, p2sso, yo, k5.

Work 4 rows in garter st.

These 11 rows form the edging.

Cast off or cont as required.

Loop flower appliqué

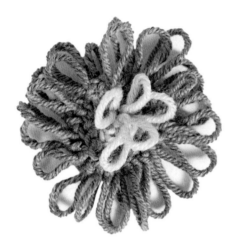

Note: two colours of yarn are used, A and B.

With A, cast on 27 sts.

Row 1 (RS): ML in every st.

Row 2: K2tog to last st, k1. (14 sts)
Change to B.

Row 3: ML in first five sts, k2tog to last st, k1. (10 sts)

Row 4: [K2tog] twice, *pass 1st st over 2nd st, k2tog; rep from * twice more, pass 1st st over 2nd st, fasten off.
Coil up with B loops in centre, loops facing inwards.
Sew coil together around base.

Perforated rib

Worked from bottom edge upwards.
Starts and ends with multiple of 4 sts + 1 st.

Note: cast on using the thumb method.

Row 1 (RS): K1, *p3, k1; rep from * to end.

Row 2: P1, *k3, p1; rep from * to end.
Rep rows 1–2 once more.

Row 5: K1, *p2tog, yo, p1, k1; rep from * to end.

Row 6: As row 2.
Rep rows 1–6 once more then rows 1–4 once more.
These 16 rows form the edging.
Cast off or cont as required.

Horizontal rib

Worked from bottom edge upwards.
Worked over any odd number of sts for required depth of rib.

Note: 1 st can be picked up from each row end of the rib band for a fuller fabric. If a flatter fabric is required, skip every row 4 end when picking up. Stitch counts will need to be calculated accordingly.

Row 1 (RS): K1, *p1, k1; rep from * to end.

Row 2: P1, *k1, p1; rep from * to end.
Rep these 2 rows until rib band is required length and cast off.
Pick up sts (see note above) along one side edge and cont as required.

Leaf and fringe

Worked lengthways over 13 sts.

Foundation row: [K5, p1] twice, k1.

Row 1 (RS): P1, k1 tbl, p2, ([k1, k1 tbl, yo] twice, k1, k1 tbl) in same st, p2, k1 tbl, k5. (20 sts)

Row 2: K5, p1 tbl, k2, p8, k2, p1 tbl, k1.

Row 3: P1, k1 tbl, p2, k6, k2tog, p2, k1 tbl, k5. (19 sts)

Row 4: K5, p1 tbl, k2, p7, k2, p1 tbl, k1.

Row 5: P1, k1 tbl, p2, k5, k2tog, p2, k1 tbl, k5. (18 sts)

Row 6: K5, p1 tbl, k2, p6, k2, p1 tbl, k1.

Row 7: P1, k1 tbl, p2, k4, k2tog, p2, k1 tbl, k5. (17 sts)

Row 8: K5, p1 tbl, k2, p5, k2, p1 tbl, k1.

Row 9: P1, k1 tbl, p2, k3, k2tog, p2, k1 tbl, k5. (16 sts)

Row 10: K5, p1 tbl, k2, p4, k2, p1 tbl, k1.

Row 11: P1, k1 tbl, p2, k2, k2tog, p2, k1 tbl, k5. (15 sts)

Row 12: K5, p1 tbl, k2, p3, k2, p1 tbl, k1.

Row 13: P1, k1 tbl, p2, k1, k2tog, p2, k1 tbl, k5. (14 sts)

Row 14: K5, p1 tbl, k2, p2, k2, p1 tbl, k1.

Row 15: P1, k1 tbl, p2, k2tog, p2, k1 tbl, k5. (13 sts)

Row 16: K5, p1 tbl, k2, p1, k2, p1 tbl, k1.

Rep rows 1–16 as required, ending with row 16.

Next row: K5, cast off rem sts.

Slip 5 sts off needle and unravel across knitted fabric to create fringe. Loops can be cut to make strands.

Leafy trim

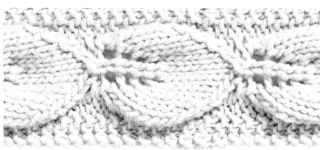

Worked lengthways over 13 sts.

Row 1 (RS): Sl 1, k2, p2, [k1, yo] twice, k1, p2, k3. (15 sts)

Row 2: Sl 1, k4, p5, k5.

Row 3: Sl 1, k2, p2, k2, yo, k1, yo, k2, p2, k3. (17 sts)

Row 4: Sl 1, k4, p7, k5.

Row 5: Sl 1, k2, p2, k3, yo, k1, yo, k3, p2, k3. (19 sts)

Row 6: Sl 1, k4, p9, k5.

Row 7: Sl 1, k2, p2, k4, yo, k1, yo, k4, p2, k3. (21 sts)

Row 8: Sl 1, k4, p11, k5.

Row 9: Sl 1, k2, p2, k11, p2, k3.

Row 10: As row 8.

Row 11: Sl 1, k2, p2, skpo, k7, k2tog, p2, k3. (19 sts)

Row 12: As row 6.

Row 13: Sl 1, k2, p2, skpo, k5, k2tog, p2, k3. (17 sts)

Row 14: As row 4.

Row 15: Sl 1, k2, p2, skpo, k3, k2tog, p2, k3. (15 sts)

Row 16: As row 2.

Row 17: Sl 1, k2, p2, skpo, k1, k2tog, p2, k3. (13 sts)

Row 18: Sl 1, k4, p3, k5.

Row 19: Sl 1, k2, p2, M1p, sk2po, M1p, p2, k3.

Row 20: Sl 1, k5, p1, k6.

Rep these 20 rows.

Willow edging

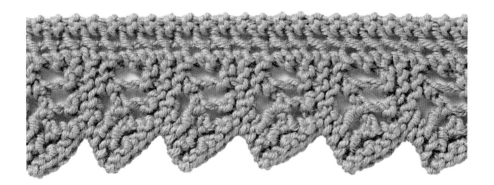

Worked lengthways over 10 sts.

Row 1 (RS): Sl 1, k2, yo, k2tog, *yo2, k2tog; rep from * once more, k1. (12 sts)

Row 2: K3, [p1, k2] twice, yo, k2tog, k1.

Row 3: Sl 1, k2, yo, k2tog, k2, *yo2, k2tog; rep from * once more, k1. (14 sts)

Row 4: K3, p1, k2, p1, k4, yo, k2tog, k1.

Row 5: Sl 1, k2, yo, k2tog, k4, *yo2, k2tog; rep from * once more, k1. (16 sts)

Row 6: K3, p1, k2, p1, k6, yo, k2tog, k1.

Row 7: Sl 1, k2, yo, k2tog, k11.

Row 8: Cast off 6 sts, k6, yo, k2tog, k1. (10 sts)

Rep these 8 rows.

Scalloped ruffle

Worked from bottom edge upwards.

Starts with multiple of 11 sts + 2 sts.

Ends with multiple of 2 sts.

Note: cast on using the thumb method.

Row 1 (WS): Purl.

Row 2: K2, *k1, sl st back onto left-hand needle, with right-hand needle, 1 at a time, lift next 8 sts over this st and off needle, yo2, k first st again, k2; rep from * to end.

Row 3: K1, *p2tog, drop first loop of yo2, [k1, p1] twice in second loop, p1; rep from *, ending k1.

Row 4: *K4, yo, k2tog; rep from * to last 2 sts, k2.

Row 5: Purl.

Rep rows 4–5 twice more.

Row 10: K2, *k2tog, k1; rep from * to end.

Work 3 rows in garter st.

These 13 rows form the edging.

Cast off or cont as required.

Buttoned tags

Lace cable

Worked from bottom edge upwards.

Starts and ends with multiple of 7 sts.

Note: cast on using the thumb method. Each tag is worked separately and then joined on one row. Tags can be same length or, as here, different lengths.

Cast on 7 sts.

Row 1 (RS): K1, [p1, k1] three times.

Rep row 1, 6 more times.

Row 8: K1, p1, k1, yo, k2tog, p1, k1.

Rep row 1 as required, ending with a WS row. These rows form one tag. Cut yarn and leave finished tag on needle. On the same needle, cast on 7 sts and work 2nd tag.

Cont in this way until there are as many tags as required.

Join tags

Do not cut yarn after completing the last tag.

Next row (RS): K1, [p1, k1] three times, *cast on 3 sts, k1, [p1, k1] three times across next tag; rep from * until all tags are joined.

Next row: K1, *p1, k1; rep from * to end.

Rep last row 5 more times.

These rows form the edging.

Cast off or cont as required.

Sew buttons to fabric above tags and slip eyelets over buttons.

Worked from bottom edge upwards.

Starts and ends with multiple of 11 sts + 7 sts.

Note: cast on using the thumb method.

Row 1 and every alt row: Purl.

Row 2 (RS): K1, *yo, ssk, k1, k2tog, yo, k6; rep from *, ending last rep with k1.

Row 4: K2, *yo, sk2po, yo, k1, C6B, k1; rep from *, ending yo, sk2po, yo, k2.

Row 6: As row 2.

Row 8: K2, *yo, sk2po, yo, k8; rep from *, ending last last rep with k2.

Rep rows 1–8 once more.

Row 17: Purl.

These 17 rows form the edging.

Cast off or cont as required.

Smocked rib

Double diamond edging

Hunter's rib

Worked from bottom edge upwards. Starts and ends with multiple of 6 sts + 3 sts.

Special abbreviation:

S3 (smock 3): Yb, sl next 3 sts purlwise, yf, sl same 3 sts back onto left-hand needle, yb, sl same 3 sts back to right-hand needle.

Note: cast on using the thumb method.

Rows 1 and 3 (RS): P3, *k3, p3; rep from * to end.

Row 2 and every alt row: K3, *p3, k3; rep from * to end.

Row 5: P3, *S3, p3; rep from * to end.

Row 6: K3, *p3, k3; rep from * to end.

Rep rows 1–6 once more.

These 12 rows form the edging.

Cast off or cont as required.

Worked lengthways over 9 sts.

Row 1 and every alt row (RS): Knit.

Row 2: K3, k2tog, yo, k2tog, [yo, k1] twice. (10 sts)

Row 4: K2, [k2tog, yo] twice, k3, yo, k1. (11 sts)

Row 6: K1, [k2tog, yo] twice, k5, yo, k1. (12 sts)

Row 8: K3, [yo, k2tog] twice, k1, k2tog, yo, k2tog. (11 sts)

Row 10: K4, yo, k2tog, yo, k3tog, yo, k2tog. (10 sts)

Row 12: K5, yo, k3tog, yo, k2tog. (9 sts)

Rep these 12 rows.

Worked from bottom edge upwards. Starts and ends with multiple of 11 sts + 4 sts.

Note: cast on using the thumb method.

Row 1 (RS): P4, *[k1 tbl, p1] 3 times, k1 tbl, p4; rep from * to end.

Row 2: K4, *p1, [k1 tbl, p1] 3 times, k4; rep from * to end.

Rep rows 1–2, 4 more times.

These 10 rows form the edging.

Cast off or cont as required.

Tip

You can use a knitted edging or trim as a means to experiment with colour in a design. Bear in mind that your edging does not need to be the same colour as the main knitted piece: you could use a contrasting or a complementary colour. Other decorative elements such as beads and tassels can also be added in either contrast or complementary colours. Also remember that knitted trims can be added to other types of fabric such as woven material; attach the knitted trim with a sharp sewing needle and matching sewing thread.

Points and bobbles

Tassel fringe

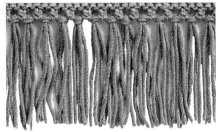

Scalloped eyelet edging

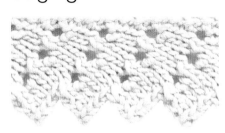

Points and bobbles

Worked lengthways over 6 sts.

Special abbreviation:

MB (make bobble): (K1, p1, k1, p1, k1) in next st, [turn, sl 1, k4] 4 times, turn, 1 at a time, lift 2nd, 3rd, 4th and 5th st over 1st st.

Row 1 (RS): K3, yo, k3. (7 sts)

Row 2 and every alt row: Knit.

Row 3: K3, yo, k4. (8 sts)

Row 5: K3, yo, k5. (9 sts)

Row 7: K3, yo, k6. (10 sts)

Row 9: K3, yo, k7. (11 sts)

Row 11: K3, yo, k7, MB. (12 sts)

Row 12: Cast off 6 sts, k to end. (6 sts)

Rep these 12 rows.

Tassel fringe

Worked lengthways over any odd number of sts.

Row 1 (RS): *K2tog, yo; rep from * to last st, k1.

Work 2 rows in garter st.

Cast off or cont as required.

Tassels

Cut two 10cm (4in) lengths of yarn for each eyelet. Fold two strands in half together. WS facing, put a crochet hook through an eyelet and pull the folded loop of the strands through. Slip the cut ends through the loop and pull taut. When all the tassels have been added, trim the ends of the strands.

Scalloped eyelet edging

Worked lengthways over 11 sts.

Row 1 (RS): Sl 1, k2, yo, p2tog, yo, skpo, [yo, skpo] twice.

Row 2: Yo, *p1, (k1, p1) in next st; rep from * twice more, p2, yo, p2tog, k1 tbl. (15 sts)

Row 3: Sl 1, k2, yo, p2tog, k10.

Row 4: Sl 1, p11, yo, p2tog, k1 tbl.

Row 5: Sl 1, k2, yo, p2tog, k10.

Row 6: Cast off 4 sts purlwise, p7, yo, p2tog, k1 tbl. (11 sts)

Rep these 6 rows.

Diagonal rib and scallop

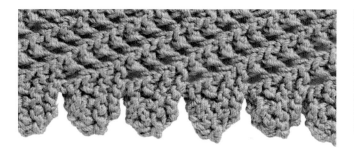

Ribbed tags

Worked lengthways over 8 sts.

Foundation row 1 (RS): K6, inc, yf, sl 1 purlwise. (9 sts)

Foundation row 2: K1 tbl, k1, [yo, skpo, k1] twice, yf, sl 1 purlwise. (9 sts)

Row 1: K1 tbl, k to last st, inc, turn and cast on 2 sts. (12 sts)

Row 2: K1, inc, k2, [yo, skpo, k1] twice, yo, k1, yf, sl 1 purlwise. (14 sts)

Row 3: K1 tbl, k to last 2 sts, inc, yf, sl 1 purlwise. (15 sts)

Row 4: K1 tbl, inc, k2, [yo, skpo, k1] 3 times, k1, yf, sl 1 purlwise. (16 sts)

Row 5: K1 tbl, k to last 2 sts, k2tog. (15 sts)

Row 6: Sl 1 purlwise, k1, psso, skpo, k4, [yo, skpo, k1] twice, yf, sl 1 purlwise. (13 sts)

Row 7: K1 tbl, k to last 2 sts, k2tog. (12 sts)

Row 8: Cast off 3 sts, k2, yo, skpo, k1, yo, skpo, yf, sl 1 purlwise. (9 sts)

Rep these 8 rows.

Worked from bottom edge upwards.

Starts and ends with multiple of 9 sts.

Note: cast on using the thumb method. Each tag is worked separately and then joined on one row.

Cast on 9 sts.

Row 1 (RS): Knit.

Row 2: K1, p to last st, k1.

Rows 3–4: As row 2.

Rows 5–6: As row 1.

Rep rows 1–5 once more.

Rows 1–11 form one tag. Cut yarn and leave finished tag on needle. On the free needle, cast on 9 sts and work 2nd tag. Cont in this way until there are as many tags as required.

Join tags

Do not cut yarn after completing the last tag, but turn and knit across all tags on needle.

Rep rows 1–6 once more.

These 18 rows form the edging.

Cast off or cont as required.

Lace ruffle

Worked from bottom edge upwards.

Starts with twice the number of sts needed that is a multiple of 4 sts + 2 sts.

Ends with multiple of 2 sts + 1 st.

Note: cast on using the thumb method.

Row 1 (WS): Knit.

Row 2: K1, *skpo, yo2, k2tog; rep from *, ending k1.

Row 3: P1, *p1, (p1, k1) in yo2, p1; rep from *, ending p1.

Rep rows 2–3, 6 more times.

Row 10: [K2tog] to end.

Row 11: Purl.

Row 12: K1, *yo, k2tog; rep from * to end.

Work 3 rows in st st.

These 15 rows form the edging.

Cast off or cont as required.

Big lace check

Worked from bottom edge upwards.

Starts and ends with multiple of 18 sts + 9 sts.

Note: cast on using the thumb method.

Row 1 and foll alt row (WS): Purl.

Row 2: K1, *[yo, k2tog] 4 times, k10; rep from * to last 8 sts, [yo, k2tog] 4 times.

Row 4: *[Skpo, yo] 4 times, k10; rep from * to last 9 sts, [skpo, yo] 4 times, k1.

Rep rows 1–4 twice more.

Row 13 and foll alt row: Purl.

Row 14: *K10, [yo, k2tog] 4 times; rep from * to last 9 sts, k9.

Row 16: K9 *[skpo, yo] 4 times, k10; rep from * to end.

Rep rows 13–16 twice more.

These 24 rows form the edging.

Cast off or cont as required.

Heart appliqué

Cast on 2 sts.
Row 1 (RS): Inc, k1. (3 sts)
Row 2 and every alt row: Purl.
Row 3: K1, [M1, k1] twice. (5 sts)
Row 5: K2, M1, k1, M1, k2. (7 sts)
Row 7: K3, M1, k1, M1, k3. (9 sts)
Row 9: K4, M1, k1, M1, k4. (11 sts)
Row 11: K5, M1, k1, M1, k5. (13 sts)
Row 13: K 6, k in back loop of st below
next st then k in next st, k6. (14 sts)
Row 15: Ssk, k3, k2tog, turn.
Cont on these 5 sts only and leave rem sts
on a stitch holder.
Row 17: Ssk, k1, k2tog. (3 sts)
Row 18: P3tog tbl.
Fasten off.
Next row (RS): Rejoin yarn to inner end of
rem sts, ssk, k3, k2tog. (5 sts)
Next RS row: Ssk, k1, k2tog. (3 sts)
Next row: P3tog.
Fasten off.

Eyelet rib

Worked from bottom edge upwards.
Starts and ends with multiple of 8 sts
+ 2 sts.
Note: cast on using the thumb method.
Row 1: *P2, k2; rep from *, ending p2.
Row 2: K2, p2, *yo, k2tog, p2; rep from *,
ending k2.
Rep rows 1–2, 3 more times.
Row 9: P2, *k6, p2; rep from * to end.
Row 10: K2, p6, *yo, k2tog, p6; rep
from *, ending k2.
Rep rows 9–10 once more, then row
9 once more.
These 13 rows form the edging.
Cast off or cont as required.

Tiny bobble braid

Worked lengthways over 5 sts.
Special abbreviation:
MB (make bobble): (K1, p1, k1, p1, k1)
in next st, 1 at a time, lift 2nd, 3rd, 4th and
5th sts over 1st st.
Rows 1–2: Sl 1, k4.
Row 3 (RS): Sl 1, k1, MB, k2.
Row 4: Sl 1, k4.
Rep these 4 rows, ending with row 2.

Casing and drawstring

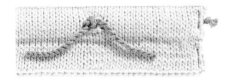

Double pintuck

Noughts and crosses trim

Casing and drawstring

Worked from bottom edge upwards or top edge downwards.

Starts and ends with multiple of 2 sts + 1 st.

Starting with a k row, work 7 rows in st st.

Row 8 (WS): Knit.

Starting with a k row, work 3 rows in st st.

Row 12 (drawstring opening): P to centre 3 sts, cast off 3 sts, p to end.

Row 13: K to cast off sts, cast on 3 sts, k to end.

Starting with a p row, work 3 rows in st st.

Fold hem over at ridge row.

Row 17: *Slip horizontal strand from 1st cast-on st onto left-hand needle, then k this strand tog with 1st st on needle; rep from * to end.

Cont as required.

Cord

Make a twisted cord, a plaited cord or a 3-st I-cord of required length.

Thread cord through casing.

Double pintuck

Worked from bottom edge upwards.

Starts and ends with multiple of 2 sts + 1 st.

Note: two colours of yarn, A and B, are used here, but the pintuck can be worked in one colour if preferred.

Starting with a knit row and A, work 12 rows in st st.

Row 13 (RS): *Lift horizontal strand from cast-on edge below st on needle and place on left-hand needle, then k this strand tog with st on needle; rep from * to end.

Work 7 rows in st st.

Change to B and work 12 rows in st st.

Row 33 (RS): * Lift stitch loop from 12 rows below st on needle and place on left-hand needle, then k this loop tog with st on needle; rep from * to end.

These 33 rows form the edging.

Cast off or cont as required.

Noughts and crosses trim

Worked over lengthways over 16 sts.

Row 1 (RS): Sl 1, k15.

Row 2: Sl 1, k1, p12, k2.

Rep rows 1–2 once more.

Row 5: Sl 1, k1, C6B, C6F, k2.

Row 6: Sl 1, k1, p12, k2.

Rep rows 1–6 once more.

Row 13: Sl 1, k15.

Row 14: Sl 1, k1, p12, k2.

Rep rows 13–14 once more.

Row 17: Sl 1, k1, C6F, C6B, k2.

Row 18: Sl 1, k1, p12, k2.

Rep rows 13–18 once more.

Rep these 24 rows.

Lace picot

Worked from bottom edge upwards.

Starts and ends with multiple of 8 sts + 1 st.

Note: cast on using the thumb method.

Starting with a k row, work 3 rows in st st.

Row 4 (WS): P1, *yo, p2tog; rep from * to end.

Work 4 rows in st st.

Row 9: K2 *yo, k2tog; rep from *, ending k1.

Work 3 rows in st st.

Row 13: K1, *yo, ssk, k3, k2tog, yo, k1; rep from * to end.

Row 14: P2, yo, p2tog, k1, p2tog tbl, yo, *p3, yo, p2tog, p1, p2tog tbl, yo; rep from *, ending p2.

Row 15: K2, *k1, yo, k3tog, yo, k4; rep from *, ending last rep k3.

Row 16: P2, p2tog tbl, yo, p1, yo, p2tog, *p3, p2tog tbl, yo, p1, yo, p2tog; rep from *, ending p2.

Row 17: K1, k2tog, *yo, k3, yo, ssk, k1, k2tog; rep from *, ending last rep yo, k3, yo, ssk, k1.

Row 18: P2tog tbl, yo, p5, *yo, p3tog, yo, p5; rep from *, ending yo, p2tog.

Work 2 rows in st st.

Row 21: As row 9.

Work 3 rows in st st.

Fold hem to back along row 4 and slip stitch in place.

These 24 rows form the edging.

Cast off or cont as required.

Fern and bobble edging

Worked lengthways over 21 sts.

Special abbreviation:

MB (make bobble): (K1, k1 tbl, k1) in next st, turn, k3, turn, p3, turn, k3, sk2po.

Row 1 (RS): K2, k2tog, yo2, [k2tog] twice, yo2, k2tog, k2, yo2, k2tog k7. (22 sts)

Row 2: K9, p1, k4, [p1, k3] twice.

Row 3: K2, k2tog, yo2, [k2tog] twice, yo2, k2tog, k1, MB, k2, yo2, k2tog, k6. (23 sts)

Row 4: K8, p1, k6, [p1, k3] twice.

Row 5: K2, k2tog, yo2, [k2tog] twice, yo2, k2tog, k3, MB, k2, yo2, k2tog, k5. (24 sts)

Row 6: K7, p1, k8, [p1, k3] twice.

Row 7: K2, k2tog, yo2, [k2tog] twice, yo2, k2tog, k5, MB, k2, yo2, k2tog, k4. (25 sts)

Row 8: K6, p1, k10, [p1, k3] twice.

Row 9: K2, k2tog, yo2, [k2tog] twice, yo2, k2tog, k7, MB, k2, yo2, k2tog, k3. (26 sts)

Row 10: K5, p1, k12, [p1, k3] twice.

Row 11: K2, k2tog, yo2, [k2tog] twice, yo2, k2tog, k9, MB, k2, yo2, k2tog, k2. (27 sts)

Row 12: K4, p1, k14, [p1, k3] twice.

Row 13: K2, k2tog, yo2, [k2tog] twice, yo2, k2tog, k11, MB, k2, yo2, k2tog, k1. (28 sts)

Row 14: K3, p1, k16, [p1, k3] twice.

Row 15: K2, k2tog, yo2, [k2tog] twice, yo2, k2tog, k18. (28 sts)

Row 16: Cast off 7 sts, knit until there are 13 sts on right-hand needle, [p1, k3] twice. (21 sts)

Rep these 16 rows.

Garter stitch points

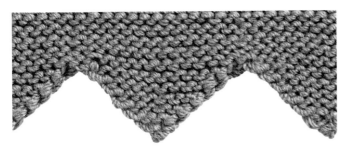

Moss diamonds edging

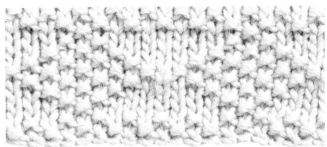

Worked from bottom edge upwards.

Ends with multiple of 13 sts.

Note: Each point is worked separately and then joined on one row.

Cast on 2 sts.

Row 1: K2.

Row 2: Yo, k2. (3 sts)

Row 3: Yo, k3. (4 sts)

Row 4: Yo, k4. (5 sts)

Row 5: Yo, k5. (6 sts)

Row 6: Yo, k6. (7 sts)

Row 7: Yo, k7. (8 sts)

Row 8: Yo, k8. (9 sts)

Row 9: Yo, k9. (10 sts)

Row 10: Yo, k10. (11 sts)

Row 11: Yo, k11. (12 sts)

Row 12: Yo, k12. (13 sts)

Rows 1–12 form one point.

Cut yarn and leave finished point on needle.

On the same needle, cast on 2 sts and work 2nd point.

Cont in this way until there are as many points as required.

Do not cut yarn after completing the last point, but turn and knit across all points on needle.

Work 9 rows in garter st.

These 21 rows form the edging.

Cast off or cont as required.

Worked from bottom edge upwards.

Starts and ends with multiple of 10 sts + 9 sts.

Note: cast on using the thumb method.

Row 1 (RS): P1, *k1, p1; rep from * to end.

Row 2: As row 1.

Row 3: K4, *p1, k9; rep from * to last 5 sts, p1, k4.

Row 4: P3, *k1, p1, k1, p7; rep from * to last 6 sts, k1, p1, k1, p3.

Row 5: K2, *[p1, k1] twice, p1, k5; rep from * to last 7 sts, [p1, k1] twice, p1, k2.

Row 6: [P1, k1] 4 times, *p3, [k1, p1] 3 times, k1; rep from * to last st, p1.

Row 7: P1, *k1, p1; rep from * to end.

Row 8: As row 6.

Row 9: As row 5.

Row 10: As row 4.

Row 11: As row 3.

Row 12: As row 2.

Row 13: As row 1.

These 13 rows form the edging.

Cast off or cont as required.

Leaf appliqué

Cast on 3 sts.
Row 1 (RS): K1 tbl, yo, k1, yo, k1 tbl. (5 sts)
Row 2 and foll 2 alt rows: P1 tbl, p to last st, p1 tbl.
Row 3: K1 tbl, k1, [yo, k1] twice, k1 tbl. (7 sts)
Row 5: K1 tbl, k2, yo, k1, yo, k2, k1 tbl. (9 sts)
Row 7: K1 tbl, k3, yo, k1, yo, k3, k1 tbl. (11 sts)
Row 8 and rem alt rows: Purl.
Row 9: Ssk, k7, k2tog. (9 sts)
Row 11: Ssk, k5, k2tog. (7 sts)
Row 13: Ssk, k3, k2tog. (5 sts)
Row 15: Ssk, k1, k2tog. (3 sts)
Row 17: Sk2po. (1 st)
Fasten off.

Daisy appliqué

Cast on 6 sts.
Row 1 (RS): Knit.
Row 2: (K1, p1, k1, p1, k1) in first st, turn, k5, turn, p5, turn, k5, turn, [p2tog] twice, p1, yb, 1 at a time, lift 2nd and 3rd sts over 1st st, yf *p3, turn, sl 1, k3.
Row 3: Purl.
Rep rows 1–3 6 more times, then rep row 1 once more and row 2 to *.
Cast off purlwise.
Join cast on and cast off edges.
Press.
Sew button to centre of flower.

Cable rib

Worked from bottom edge upwards. Starts and ends with multiple of 10 sts + 6 sts.
Note: cast on using the thumb method.
Row 1 (RS): *P2, k2, p2, k4; rep from *, ending p2, k2, p2.
Row 2: *K2, p2, k2, p4; rep from *, ending k2, p2, k2.
Rep rows 1–2 once more.
Row 5: *P2, k2, p2, C4B; rep from *, ending p2, k2, p2.
Row 6: As row 2.
Rep these 6 rows once more.
These 12 rows form the edging.
Cast off or cont as required.

Zigzag moss edging

Worked from bottom edge upwards.
Starts and ends with multiple of 6 sts
+ 1 st.

Note: cast on using the thumb method.

Row 1 (RS): K1, *p1, k1; rep from
* to end.

Row 2: As row 1.

Row 3: Knit.

Row 4: Purl.

Row 5: P1, *k5, p1; rep from * to end.

Row 6: P1, *k1, p3, k1, p1; rep from
* to end.

Row 7: P1, *k1, p1; rep from * to end.

Row 8: As row 7.

Row 9: K2, p1, k1, p1, *k3, p1, k1, p1;
rep from * to last 2 sts, k2.

Row 10: P3, k1, *p5, k1; rep from * to last
3 sts, p3.

Row 11: Knit.

Row 12: Purl.

These 12 rows form the edging.

Cast off or cont as required.

Daisy braid

Worked lengthways over 12 sts.

Row 1 (RS): Sl 1, k11.

Rows 2 and 4: Sl 1, k1, p8, k2.

Row 3: Sl 1, k11.

Row 5: Sl 1, k3, k2tog, yo2, skpo, k4.

Row 6: Sl 1, k1, p3, k1, p4, k2.

Row 7: Sl 1, k1, [k2tog, yo2, skpo]
twice, k2.

Row 8: Sl 1, k1, p1, k1, p3, k1, p2, k2.

Row 9: As row 5.

Row 10: As row 6.

Row 11: As row 7.

Row 12: As row 8.

Row 13: As row 5.

Row 14: As row 6.

Rep these 14 rows, ending with row 3.

Castle edging

Worked lengthways over 7 sts.

Note: cast on using the cable method.

Work 3 rows in garter st.

Row 4 (WS): Cast on 3 sts, knit all sts.
(10 sts)

Work 3 rows in garter st.

Row 8: Cast on 3 sts, knit all sts. (13 sts)

Row 9: K1, *p1, k1; rep from * to end.

Row 10: P1, *k1, p1; rep from * to end.

Rep rows 9–10 twice more then row 9
once more.

Row 16: Cast off 3 sts knitwise, k to end.
(10 sts)

Work 3 rows in garter st.

Row 20: Cast off 3 sts knitwise, k to end.
(7 sts)

Rep these 20 rows.

Lace bunting

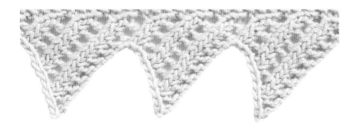

Fir cone and twig lace

Worked lengthways over 4 sts.

Foundation row: K1, yo, k1, p1, k1.

(5 sts)

Row 1 and every alt row (WS): K2, p
to end.

Row 2: K1, yo, k2, p1, k1. (6 sts)

Row 4: K1, yo, k1, k2tog, yo, p1, k1.
(7 sts)

Row 6: K1, yo, k1, k2tog, yo, k1, p1, k1. (8 sts)

Row 8: K1, yo, k1, k2tog, yo, k2, p1, k1. (9 sts)

Row 10: K1, yo, [k1, k2tog, yo] twice, p1, k1. (10 sts)

Row 12: K1, yo, [k1, k2tog, yo] twice, k1, p1, k1. (11 sts)

Row 14: K1, yo, [k1, k2tog, yo] twice, k2, p1, k1. (12 sts)

Row 16: K1, yo, [k1, k2tog, yo] 3 times, p1, k1. (13 sts)

Row 18: Loosely cast off 9 sts, yo, k1, p1, k1. (5 sts)

Rep rows 1–18.

Worked from bottom edge upwards.

Starts and ends with multiple of 10 sts
+ 1 st.

Note: cast on using the thumb method.

Row 1 (WS): Purl.

Row 2: K1, *yo, k3, sk2po, k3, yo, k1; rep from * to end.

Rep rows 1–2, 3 more times.

Row 9: Purl.

Row 10: K2tog, *k3, yo, k1, yo, k3, sk2po; rep from * to last
9 sts, k3, yo, k1, yo, k3, skpo.

Rep rows 9–10, 3 more times.

These 16 rows form the edging.

Cast off or cont as required.

Bell edging I

Arches lace

Worked from bottom edge upwards.

Starts with multiple of 12 sts + 3 sts.

Ends with multiple of 4 sts + 3 sts.

Note: cast on using the cable method.

Row 1 (RS): P3, *k9, p3; rep from* to end.

Row 2: K3, *p9, k3; rep from * to end.

Row 3: P3, *yb, skpo, k5, k2tog, p3; rep from * to end.

Row 4: K3, *p7, k3; rep from * to end.

Row 5: P3, *yb, skpo, k3, k2tog, p3; rep from * to end.

Row 6: K3, *p5, k3; rep from * to end.

Row 7: P3, *yb, skpo, k1, k2tog, p3; rep from * to end.

Row 8: K3, *p3, k3; rep from * to end.

Row 9: P3, *yb, sk2po, p3; rep from *
to end.

Row 10: K3, *p1, k3; rep from * to end.

Row 11: P3, *k1, p3; rep from * to end.

Row 12: As row 10.

These 12 rows form the edging.

Cast off or cont as required.

Worked from bottom edge upwards.

Starts and ends with multiple of 11 sts.

Note: cast on using the thumb method.

Row 1 (RS): *Ssk, k3 tbl, yo, k1, yo, k3 tbl, k2tog; rep from
* to end.

Row 2 and foll 3 alt rows: Purl.

Row 3: *Ssk, k2 tbl, yo, k1, yo, ssk, yo, k2 tbl, k2tog; rep from
* to end.

Row 5: *Ssk, k1 tbl, yo, k1, [yo, ssk] twice, yo, k1 tbl, k2tog; rep
from * to end.

Row 7: *Ssk, yo, k1, [yo, ssk] 3 times, yo, k2tog; rep from
* to end.

Row 9: *K1, p1, k7, p1, k1; rep from *
to end.

Row 10: *P1, k1, p7, k1, p1; rep from * to end.

Rep rows 9–10 once more.

These 12 rows form the edging.

Cast off or cont as required.

Oyster shells lace

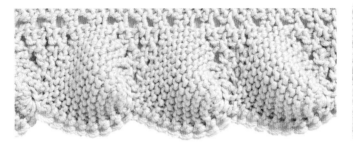

Hearts braid

Worked lengthways over 16 sts.

Row 1 (RS): Sl 1, k2, yo2, k13. (18 sts)

Row 2: Yo, k2tog, k12, p1, k3.

Row 3: Sl 1, k to end.

Row 4: Yo, k2tog, k16.

Row 5: Sl 1, k2, yo2, k2tog, yo2, k13. (21 sts)

Row 6: Yo, k2tog, k12, p1, k2, p1, k3.

Row 7: As row 3.

Row 8: Yo, k2tog, k19.

Row 9: Sl 1, k2, [yo2, k2tog] 3 times, k12. (24 sts)

Row 10: Yo, k2tog, k12, p1, [k2, p1] twice, k3.

Row 11: As row 3.

Row 12: Yo, k2tog, k22.

Row 13: Sl 1, k2, [yo2, k2tog] 4 times, k13. (28 sts)

Row 14: Yo, k2tog, k13, p1, [k2, p1] 3 times, k3.

Row 15: As row 3.

Row 16: Yo, k2tog, k26.

Row 17: Sl 1, k13, sl 1, then, 1 at a time, lift 10 sts over first 2 sts on left-hand needle, k these 2 sts tog, pass slipped st over, k1. (16 sts)

Row 18: Yo, k2tog, k14.

Rep these 18 rows, ending with row 17.

Worked from bottom edge upwards.

Starts and ends with multiple of 12 sts + 9 sts.

Note: cast on using the thumb method.

Work 2 rows in garter st.

Row 3 (RS): P4, k1, *p11, k1; rep from *, ending p4.

Row 4: K3, p3, *k9, p3; rep from *, ending k3.

Row 5: P3, k3, *p9, k3; rep from *, ending p3.

Row 6: K2, p5, *k7, p5; rep from *, ending k2.

Row 7: P1, k7, *p5, k7; rep from *, ending p1.

Row 8: P9, *k3, p9; rep from * to end.

Row 9: K9, *p3, k9; rep from * to end.

Row 10: As row 8.

Row 11: K4, p1, *k4, p3, k4, p1; rep from *, ending k4.

Row 12: K1, p2, k3, p2, *k5, p2, k3, p2; rep from *, ending k1.

Row 13: Purl.

Work 2 rows in garter st.

Row 16: Purl.

These 16 rows form the edging.

Cast off or cont as required.

Loop trim

Scallops trim

Worked from bottom edge upwards.

Ends with multiple of 12 sts for an odd number of sts and 12 sts + 6 sts for an even number of strips.

Note: Each strip is worked separately and then joined to make loops on one row. Loops can be longer if required.

Cast on 6 sts.

Row 1 (RS): Sl 1, k5.

Row 2: Sl 1, p5.

Rep rows 1–2, 12 more times.

Rows 1–26 form one strip. Cut yarn and leave strip on needle.

On the same needle, cast on 6 sts and work second strip.

Cont in this way until there are as many strips as required.

Join strips and make loops.

Do not cut yarn after completing last strip.

*K6 of first strip, RS facing, position cast-on edge of first strip behind second strip, *slip horizontal strand from 1st cast-on st onto left-hand needle, then k this strand tog with 1st st of second strip; rep from * for each st.

Cont in this way across strips, ending with k6 from cast-on edge of last strip.

Purl 1 row.

These rows form the edging.

Cast off or cont as required.

Worked from bottom edge upwards.

Starts with multiple of 12 sts.

Ends with multiple of 8 sts.

Note: cast on using the thumb method.

Row 1 (RS): Knit.

Row 2: Purl.

Row 3: *[K2tog] twice, [M1, k1] 4 times, [skpo] twice; rep from * to end.

Row 4: Purl.

Row 5: *[K2tog] twice, k4, [skpo] twice; rep from * to end.

Work 2 rows in garter st.

These 7 rows form the edging.

Cast off or cont as required.

Striped slip stitch edging

Worked from bottom edge upwards.
Starts and ends with multiple of 2 sts
+ 1 st.

Note: use three colours of yarn, A, B and C, and strand colours not in use up side of work. Cast on using the cable method and A.

Row 1 (RS): With A, knit.

Row 2: With A, purl.

Row 3: With B, k1, *sl 1 purlwise, k1; rep from * to end.

Row 4: With B, k1, *yf, sl 1 purlwise, yb, k1; rep from * to end.

Row 5: With C, knit.

Row 6: With C, purl.

Row 7: With A, k1, *sl 1 purlwise, k1; rep from * to end.

Row 8: With A, k1, * yf, sl 1 purlwise, yb, k1; rep from * to end.

Row 9: With B, knit.

Row 10: With B, purl.

Row 11: With C, k1, *sl 1 purlwise, k1; rep from * to end.

Row 12: With C, k1, * yf, sl 1 purlwise, yb, k1; rep from * to end.

Row 13: With A, knit.

Row 14: With A, purl.

These 14 rows form the edging.

Cast off or cont as required.

Lace stripes

Worked lengthways over 15 sts.

Note: to prevent holes forming when turning, wrap the yarn around the next stitch in this way: turn, leaving the yarn at the front, slip the first st from the right-hand needle to the left-hand needle, take the yarn to the back, slip the st back onto the right-hand needle, then cont.

Row 1 (WS): Knit.

Row 2: K12, turn, k to end.

Row 3: Knit.

Row 4: K4, [yo, k2tog] 4 times, yo2, k2tog, k1. (16 sts)

Row 5: K3, p1, k12.

Row 6: K5, [yo, k2tog] 4 times, yo2, k2tog, k1. (17 sts)

Row 7: K3, p1, k13.

Row 8: K6, [yo, k2tog] 4 times, yo2, k2tog, k1. (18 sts)

Row 9: K3, p1, k14.

Row 10: Knit.

Row 11: K15, turn, k to end.

Row 12: Cast off 3 sts, k14. (15 sts)

Rep these 12 rows.

Star braid

Worked lengthways over 17 sts.

Row 1 (WS): Sl 1, k1, p13, k2.

Row 2: Sl 1, k16.

Row 3: Sl 1, k1, p6, k1, p6, k2.

Row 4: Sl 1, k16.

Row 5: Sl 1, k2, [p5, k1] twice, k2.

Row 6: Sl 1, k2, p1, k9, p1, k3.

Row 7: Sl 1, k1, p2, [k1, p3] twice, k1, p2, k2.

Row 8: Sl 1, k4, p1, k5, p1, k5.

Row 9: Sl 1, k1, p4, [k1, p1] twice, k1, p4, k2.

Row 10: Sl 1, k6, p1, k1, p1, k7.

Rep row 10 twice more.

Row 13: Sl 1, k1, p4, [k1, p1] twice, k1, p4, k2.

Row 14: Sl 1, k4, p1, k5, p1, k5.

Row 15: Sl 1, k1, p2, [k1, p3] twice, k1, p2, k2.

Row 16: Sl 1, k2, p1, k9, p1, k3.

Row 17: Sl 1, k2, [p5, k1] twice, k2.

Row 18: Sl 1, k16.

Row 19: Sl 1, k1, p6, k1, p6, k2.

Row 20: Sl 1, k16.

Rep rows 3–20.

Openwork points

Long loop fur

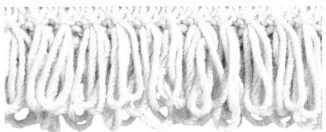

Worked lengthways over 7 sts.

Row 1 (RS): K3, yo, skpo, yo, k2. (8 sts)

Row 2 and foll 6 alt rows: Sl 1, p to last 2 sts, k2.

Row 3: K4, yo, skpo, yo, k2. (9 sts)

Row 5: K5, yo skpo, yo, k2. (10 sts)

Row 7: K6, yo, skpo, yo, k2. (11 sts)

Row 9: K7, yo, skpo, yo, k2. (12 sts)

Row 11: K8, yo, skpo, yo, k2. (13 sts)

Row 13: K9, yo, skpo, yo, k2. (14 sts)

Row 15: K10, yo, skpo, yo, k2. (15 sts)

Row 16: Cast off 8 sts knitwise, p4, k2. (7 sts)

Rep these 16 rows.

Worked from bottom edge upwards.

Starts and ends with multiple of 2 sts + 1 st.

Special abbreviation:

ML2 (make double loop): Insert right-hand needle knitwise into next st, wind yarn over right-hand needle and around first and second fingers of left hand twice, then over right-hand needle point once more, draw all 3 loops through st and sl onto left-hand needle, insert right-hand needle through back of these 3 loops and original st and k them tog tbl.

Note: Cast on using the cable method. Loops appear on RS rows but are made on WS rows.

Work 3 rows in garter st.

Row 4 (WS): K1, * ML2, k1; rep from * to end.

Work 3 rows in garter st.

Row 8: K1, *k1, ML2; rep from * to last 2 sts, k2.

Rep these 8 rows.

Unravelled fringe

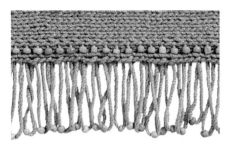

Worked lengthways over any number of sts.

Note: Thread beads onto knitting yarn before casting on, 2 beads for each alt row. First bead is not knitted in.

Row 1 (RS): K2, slide bead up to back of work, k2, PB, k to end.

Row 2: Purl.

Rep rows 1–2 as required, ending with row 2.

Next row: K3, cast off rem sts.

Slip 3 sts off needle and unravel across knitted fabric to create fringe. Slide 1 bead down to sit at the bottom of each loop.

Antique edging

Worked lengthways over 13 sts.

Note: cast off knitwise throughout.

Row 1 (RS): K2, yo, skpo, yo, k1, yo, sk2po, yo, k3, yo, k2. (15 sts)

Row 2: K4, [k1, p1] 3 times into next st, p2, k1, p3, k4. (20 sts)

Row 3: K2, yo, skpo, [k1, p1] 3 times into next st, yb, skpo, p1, k2tog, cast off next 5 sts, k to last 2 sts, yo, k2. (19 sts)

Row 4: K5, yo, [k1, p1] twice, cast off next 5 sts, k to end. (15 sts)

Row 5: K2, yo, skpo, yo, k1, yo, sk2po, yo, k3, yo, k2tog, yo, k2. (17 sts)

Row 6: K6, [k1, p1] 3 times into next st, p2, k1, p3, k4. (22 sts)

Row 7: K2, yo, skpo, [k1, p1] 3 times into next st, yb, skpo, p1, k2tog, cast off next 5 sts, k to last 4 sts, yo, k2tog, yo, k2. (21 sts)

Row 8: Cast off 4 sts, k2, yo, p2, k1, p1, cast off next 5 sts, k to end. (13 sts)

Rep these 8 rows.

Bell edging II

Worked from upper edge downwards. Starts with multiple of 8 sts + 7 sts. Ends with multiple of 20 sts + 7 sts.

Row 1 (RS): P7, *k1, p7; rep from * to end.

Row 2: K7, *p1, k7; rep from * to end.

Row 3: P7, *yo, k1, yo, p7; rep from * to end.

Row 4: K7, *p1 tbl, p1, p1 tbl, k7; rep from * to end.

Row 5: P7, *yo, k3, yo, p7; rep from * to end.

Row 6: K7, * p1 tbl, p3, p1 tbl, k7; rep from * to end.

Row 7: P7, *yo, k5, yo, p7; rep from * to end.

Row 8: K7, * p1 tbl, p5, p1 tbl, k7; rep from * to end.

Row 9: P7, *yo, k7, yo, p7; rep from * to end.

Row 10: K7, * p1 tbl, p7, p1 tbl, k7; rep from * to end.

Row 11: P7, *yo, k9, yo, p7; rep from * to end.

Row 12: K7, * p1 tbl, p9, p1 tbl, k7; rep from * to end.

Row 13: P7, *yo, k11, yo, p7; rep from * to end.

Row 14: K7, * p1 tbl, p11, p1 tbl, k7; rep from * to end.

Cast off.

These 14 rows form the edging.

Beaded frill

Worked from bottom edge upwards.
Starts with twice the number of sts
required + 1 st.
Note: Thread beads onto knitting yarn
before casting on, 1 bead for each alt st.
Cast on using Beaded thumb cast-on
(see page 234), omitting the selvedge sts.
Row 1 (WS): Purl.
Row 2: [K2tog] to last st, k1.
These 2 rows form the edging.
Cont as required.

Maypole lace

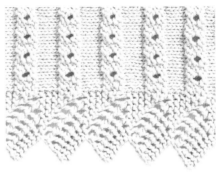

Worked lengthways over 26 sts.
Foundation row: Knit.
Row 1: Sl 1, k19, [yo, k2tog] twice, yo,
k2. (27 sts)
Row 2: K8, p14, k5.
Row 3: Sl 1, k6, [yo, k2tog, k1] 4 times,
k2, [yo, k2tog] twice, yo, k2. (28 sts)
Row 4: K9, p14, k5.
Row 5: Sl 1, k21, [yo, k2tog] twice, yo,
k2. (29 sts)
Row 6: Knit.
Row 7: Sl 1, k4, p14, k4, [yo, k2tog]
twice, yo, k2. (30 sts)
Row 8: Knit.
Row 9: Sl 1, k4, p14, k5, [yo, k2tog]
twice, yo, k2. (31 sts)
Row 10: Knit.
Row 11: Sl 1, k4, p14, k6, [yo, k2tog]
twice, yo, k2. (32 sts)
Row 12: Cast off 6 sts, k25. (26 sts)
Rep rows 1–12.

Spiral rib edging

Worked from bottom edge upwards.
Starts and ends with multiple of 7 sts.
Note: cast on using the thumb method.
Row 1 (RS): P2, k4, *p3, k4; rep from * to
last st, p1.
Row 2: K1, p3, * k4, p3; rep from * to last
3 sts, k3.
Row 3: P1, k1, p2, *k2, p2, k1, p2; rep
from * to last 3 sts, k2, p1.
Row 4: K1, p1, k2, p2, *k2, p1, k2, p2;
rep from * to last st, k1.
Row 5: P1, k3, *p4, k3; rep from * to last
3 sts, p3.
Row 6: K2, p4, *k3, p4; rep from * to last
st, k1.
Row 7: P1, k5, *p2, k5; rep from * to last
st, p1.
Row 8: K1, p5, *k2, p5; rep from * to last
st, k1.
Rep rows 1–8 once more.
These 16 rows form the edging.
Cast off or cont as required.

Bobble rib edging

Worked from bottom edge upwards. Starts and ends with multiple of 4 sts + 3 sts.

Special abbreviation:

MB (make bobble): (K1, k1 tbl, k1, k1 tbl) in next st, turn, p4, turn, k4, turn, p4, turn, ssk, k2tog, slip 2nd st over 1st st.

Note: cast on using the thumb method.

Row 1 (RS): P1, *k1, p1; rep from * to end.

Row 2 and every alt row: K1, *p1, k1; rep from * to end.

Row 3: P1, k1, p1, *MB, p1, k1, p1; rep from * to end.

Row 5: As row 1.

These 5 rows form the edging.

Cast off or cont as required.

Beaded cast-off

Note: before casting off, measure out a length of yarn 4 times the width of the knitted fabric. Cut yarn. Thread on beads, 1 bead for every alt st.

Cast off 1 st.

*Slide a bead up to sit behind the st, insert right-hand needle knitwise into next st and knit, drawing bead through on stitch loop. Lift 1st loop on right-hand needle over 2nd loop.

Cast off 1 st.

Rep from *, fastening off last st.

Ruched edging

Worked from bottom edge upwards. Starts and ends with multiple of 3 sts.

Note: cast on using the thumb method.

Row 1 (RS): K2, *sl 1 purlwise, k2; rep from * to last st, k1.

Row 2: P3, *sl 1 purlwise, p2; rep from * to end.

Row 3: K2, *C3F; rep from * to last st, k1.

Row 4 and foll alt row: Purl.

Row 5: K2, *yo, k2tog, k1; rep from * to last st, k1.

Row 7: K4, *sl 1 purlwise, k2; rep from * to last 2 sts, sl 1 purlwise, k1.

Row 8: P1, *sl 1 purlwise, p2; rep from * to last 2 sts, p2.

Row 9: K2, *C3B; rep from * to last st, k1.

These 9 rows form the edging.

Cast off or cont as required.

Scallop shell lace

Worked from bottom edge upwards.
Starts with multiple of 5 sts + 2 sts.
Ends with multiple of 4 sts + 5 sts.
Note: Cast on using thumb method.
Row 1 (RS): K1, yo, *k5, 1 at a time, lift the 2nd, 3rd, 4th and 5th sts just worked over the 1st st and off needle, yo; rep from * to last st, k1.
Row 2: P1, *(p1, yo, k1 tbl) into next st, p1; rep from * to end.
Row 3: K2, k1 tbl, *k3, k1 tbl; rep from * to last 2 sts, k2.
Work 3 rows in garter st.
These 6 rows form the edging.
Cast off or cont as required.

Short loop fur

Worked from bottom edge upwards.
Starts and ends with multiple of 2 sts + 1 st.
Note: cast on using the cable method.
Loops are made and appear on RS rows.
Row 1 (RS): Knit.
Row 2 and every alt row: Purl.
Row 3: *K1, ML; rep from * to last st, k1.
Row 5: Knit.
Row 7: K1, *k1 ML; rep from * to last 2 sts, k2.
Row 8: Purl.
Rep these 8 rows.

Parasol lace

Worked lengthways over 23 sts.
Row 1: Sl 1, k2, yo, k1, [p3, k1] 4 times, yo, k3. (25 sts)
Row 2 and every alt row: Sl 1, k1, p to last 2 sts, k2.
Row 3: Sl 1, k3, yo, k1, [p3, k1] 4 times, yo, k4. (27 sts)
Row 5: Sl 1, k4, yo, k1, [p3, k1] 4 times, yo, k5. (29 sts)
Row 7: Sl 1, k5, yo, k1, [p2tog, p1, k1] 4 times, yo, k6. (27 sts)
Row 9: Sl 1, k6, yo, k1, [p2tog, k1] 4 times, yo, k7. (25 sts)
Row 11: Sl 1, k7, yo, k1, [k3tog, k1] twice, yo, k8. (23 sts)
Row 12: Sl 1, k1, p to last 2 sts, k2.
Rep these 12 rows.

Lace bells

Laburnum edging

Worked from bottom edge upwards.

Starts with multiple of 14 sts + 3 sts.

Ends with multiple of 4 sts + 3 sts.

Note: Cast on using the thumb method.

Work 2 rows in garter st.

Row 3 (RS): P3, *k11, p3; rep from * to end.

Row 4: K3, *p11, k3; rep from * to end.

Row 5: P3, *yb, skpo, k2, yo, sk2po, yo, k2, k2tog, p3; rep from * to end.

Row 6: K3, *p9, k3; rep from * to end.

Row 7: P3, *yb, skpo, k1, yo, sk2po, yo, k1, k2tog, p3; rep from * to end.

Row 8: K3, *p7, k3; rep from * to end.

Row 9: P3, *yb, skpo, yo, sk2po, yo, k2tog, p3; rep from * to end.

Row 10: K3, *p5, k3; rep from * to end.

Row 11: P3, *yb, skpo, k1, k2tog, p3; rep from * to end.

Row 12: K3, *p3, k3; rep from * to end.

Row 13: P3, *yb, sk2po, p3; rep from * to end.

Row 14: K3, *p1, k3; rep from * to end.

Row 15: P3, *k1, p3; rep from * to end.

Row 16: As row 14.

These 16 rows form the edging.

Cast off or cont as required.

Worked lengthways over 13 sts.

Row 1 (RS): K2, yo, p2tog, k1, [yo, skpo] 3 times, yo2, k2tog. (14 sts)

Row 2: P1, k1, p9, yo, p2tog, k1.

Row 3: K2, yo, p2tog, k2, [yo, skpo] 3 times, yo2, k2tog. (15 sts)

Row 4: P1, k1, p10, yo, p2tog, k1.

Row 5: K2, yo, p2tog, k3, [yo, skpo] 3 times, yo2, k2tog. (16 sts)

Row 6: P1, k1, p11, yo, p2tog, k1.

Row 7: K2, yo, p2tog, k4, [yo, skpo] 3 times, yo2, k2tog. (17 sts)

Row 8: P1, k1, p12, yo, p2tog, k1.

Row 9: K2, yo, p2tog, k5, [yo, skpo] 3 times, yo2, k2tog. (18 sts)

Row 10: P1, k1, p13, yo, p2tog, k1.

Row 11: K2, yo, p2tog, k6, [yo, skpo] 3 times, yo2, k2tog. (19 sts)

Row 12: P1, k1, p14, yo, p2tog, k1.

Row 13: K2, yo, p2tog, k7, [yo, skpo] 3 times, yo2, k2tog. (20 sts)

Row 14: P1, k1, p15, yo, p2tog, k1.

Row 15: K2, yo, p2tog, k8, yo, k1, slip last st worked back onto left-hand needle, then, 1 at a time, lift next 7 sts over this st and off needle, then slip st back onto right-hand needle. (14 sts)

Row 16: P2tog, p9, yo, p2tog, k1. (13 sts)

Rep these 16 rows.

Layered tags

Lace diamonds

Worked from bottom edge upwards.

Starts and ends with multiple of 10 sts.

Note: cast on using the thumb method. Each tag is worked separately and then joined on one row.

Bottom layer

Cast on 10 sts.

Rows 1–10: Sl 1, k9.

Rows 1–10 form one tag. Cut yarn and leave finished tag on needle. On the same needle, cast on 10 sts and work 2nd tag. Cont in this way until there are as many tags as required.

Join tags

Do not cut yarn after completing the last tag, but turn and knit across all tags on needle.

Work 7 rows in garter st.

Leave sts on spare needle.

Top layer

Cast on 5 sts to make a half-width tag.

Rows 1–10: Sl1, k4.

Cut yarn and leave sts on needle.

Make full-width tags as for bottom layer, making one less tag, and end with another half-width tag.

Join layers

RS facing, hold top layer in front of bottom layer. Using 3rd needle, k tog 1 st from each needle across row.

These rows form the edging.

Cast off or cont as required.

Worked from bottom edge upwards.

Starts and ends with multiple of 8 sts.

Note: cast on using the thumb method.

Row 1 and every alt row (WS): Purl.

Row 2: *K1, yo, k3, pass 3rd st on right-hand needle over first 2 sts; rep from * to end.

Row 4: Knit.

Row 6: K3, *yo, skpo, k6; rep from * to last 5 sts, yo, skpo, k3.

Row 8: K2, *[yo, skpo] twice, k4; rep from * to last 6 sts, [yo, skpo] twice, k2.

Row 10: K1, *[yo, skpo] 3 times, k2; rep from * to last 7 sts, [yo, skpo] 3 times, k1.

Row 12: As row 8.

Row 14: As row 6.

Row 16: Knit.

Row 18: As row 2.

Row 19: Purl.

These 19 rows form the edging.

Cast off or cont as required.

Two-colour fringe

Little lace

Sugar scallops

Worked lengthways over 12 sts using 1 strand each of A and B held together.

Row 1: K2, yo, k2tog, k1, yo, k2tog, k5.

Row 2: P4, k2, [yo, k2tog, k1] twice.

Rep rows 1–2 as required, ending with row 2.

Next row: Cast off 8 sts and fasten off 9th st.

Slip rem 3 sts off needle and unravel across knitted fabric to make fringe. Loops can be cut to make single strands.

Worked from bottom edge upwards.

Starts and ends with multiple of 9 sts + 4 sts.

Note: cast on using the thumb method.

Rows 1 and 3 (WS): Purl.

Row 2: K3, *yo, k2, ssk, k2tog, k2, yo, k1; rep from *, ending last rep k2.

Row 4: K2, *yo, k2, ssk, k2tog, k2, yo, k1; rep from *, ending last rep k3.

Rep rows 1–4 once more.

Row 9: Knit.

These 9 rows form the edging.

Cast off or cont as required.

Worked from bottom edge upwards.

Start with multiple of 11 sts + 2 sts.

Ends with multiple of 6 sts + 2 sts.

Note: cast on using the thumb method.

Row 1 (RS): Purl.

Row 2: K2, *k1, slip this st back onto left-hand needle, 1 at a time, lift the next 8 sts on left-hand needle over this st and off needle, yo2, knit the first st again, k2; rep from * to end.

Row 3: K1, *p2tog, drop 1 loop of double yo made in previous row: and [k1, p1] twice into rem loop, p1; rep from * to last st, k1.

Work 5 rows in garter st.

These 8 rows form the edging.

Cast off or cont as required.

Holly leaf appliqué

Cast on 3 sts.

Row 1 (RS): K1 tbl, yo, k1, yo, k1 tbl. (5 sts)

Row 2 and foll 3 alt rows: P1 tbl, p to last st, p1 tbl.

Row 3: K1 tbl, M1, k1, [yo, k1] twice, M1, k1 tbl. (9 sts)

Row 5: K1 tbl, k3, yo, k1, yo, k3, k1 tbl. (11 sts)

Row 7: K1 tbl, k4, yo, k1, yo, k4, k1 tbl. (13 sts)

Row 9: Cast off 3 sts, k2, yo, k1, yo, k5, k1 tbl. (12 sts)

Row 10: Cast off 3 sts, p7, p1 tbl. (9 sts)

Row 11: As row 5. (11 sts)

Row 12 and foll alt row: P1 tbl, p to last st, p1 tbl.

Row 13: As row 7. (13 sts)

Row 15: Cast off 3 sts, k8, k1 tbl. (10 sts)

Row 16: Cast off 3 sts, p5, p1 tbl. (7 sts)

Row 17: Ssk, k3, k2tog. (5 sts)

Row 18 and foll alt row: P1 tbl, p to last st, p1 tbl.

Row 19: Ssk, k1, k2tog. (3 sts)

Row 21: Sk2po. (1 st)

Fasten off.

Darn in loose ends.

Knots or bobbles can be worked for berries.

Star lace

Worked lengthways over 15 sts.

Foundation row: Knit.

Row 1 (RS): K3, yo, k3tog, yo, k3, yo, k2tog, [yo2, k2tog] twice. (17 sts)

Row 2: Yo, [k2, p1] twice, k2, yo, k2tog, k7. (18 sts)

Row 3: K3, [yo, k2tog] twice, p1, k2tog, yo, k8.

Row 4: K1, cast off 3 sts, k3, p6, k1, yo, k2tog, k1. (15 sts)

Row 5: K3, yo, k2tog, k1, yo, k3tog, yo, k2, [yo2, k2tog] twice. (17 sts)

Row 6: Yo, [k2, p1] twice, k1, p6, k1, yo, k2tog, k1. (18 sts)

Row 7: K3, yo, [k2tog] twice, yo, k1, yo, k2tog, k8.

Row 8: K1, cast off 3 sts, k3, p6, k1, yo, k2tog, k1. (15 sts)

Rep rows 1–8.

Cable and eyelet rib

Worked from bottom edge upwards.

Starts and ends with multiple of 7 sts + 3 sts.

Note: cast on using the thumb method.

Row 1 (RS): P3, *k4, p3; rep from * to end.

Row 2: K1, yo, k2tog, *p4, k1, yo, k2tog; rep from * to end.

Row 3: P3, *C4B, p3; rep from * to end.

Row 4: As row 2.

Row 5: As row 1.

Row 6: As row 2.

Rep rows 1–6 once more.

These 12 rows form the edging.

Cast off or cont as required.

Double knot edge

Worked lengthways over 8 sts.

Row 1 (RS): Sl 1, k1, *yo, p2tog, (k1, p1, k1) in next st; rep from * once more. (12 sts)

Row 2: [K3, yo, p2tog] twice, k2.

Row 3: Sl 1, k1, [yo, p2tog, k3] twice.

Row 4: Cast off 2 sts knitwise, yo, p2tog, cast off next 2 sts knitwise (4 sts on right-hand needle), yo, p2tog, k2. (8 sts)

Rep these 4 rows.

Cable rope

Worked lengthways over 10 sts.

Row 1 (WS): K2, p6, k2.

Row 2: P2, k6, p2.

Row 3: As row 1.

Row 4: P2, C6B, p2.

Row 5: As row 1.

Row 6: P1, T4BR, T4FL, p1.

Row 7: K1, p3, k2, p3, k1.

Row 8: P1, k3, p2, k3, p1.

Rep rows 7–8, 5 more times, then rep row 7 once more.

Row 20: P1, T4FL, T4BR, p1.

Rep rows 1–4 once more, then rep rows 1–2 once more.

Rep these 26 rows.

Layered picots

Worked from bottom edge upwards.

Multiple of 3 sts.

Note: two colours of yarn are used, A and B. Use cable cast-on throughout. Cast on same number of sts for each layer.

Bottom layer

*Using A, cast on 6 sts, cast off 3 sts, slip st on right-hand needle onto left-hand needle, rep from * until required number of stitches are on the left-hand needle.

Row 1 (RS): Knit.

Row 2: Purl.

Rep rows 1–2 once more.

Put sts on spare needle.

Top layer

*Using B, cast on 6 sts, cast off 3 sts, slip st on right-hand needle onto left-hand needle, rep from * until required number of stitches are on the left-hand needle.

Row 1 (WS): Purl.

RS facing, hold top layer in front of bottom layer. Using 3rd needle, knit together 1 st from each needle across row.

These rows form the edging.

Cast off or cont as required.

Beaded fringe

Worked lengthways over 5 sts.

Note: Thread beads onto knitting yarn before casting on, 1 bead for each loop.

Special abbreviation:

MBL (make bead loop): K1 but do not slip st off left-hand needle, bring yarn between needles to the front, slide bead up to sit below needles, wind yarn under and over your left thumb, take yarn back between needles to the WS, knit st on left-hand needle again ensuring bead remains on loop, then slip second st on right-hand needle over first st.

Row 1 (RS): Sl 1, k1, MBL, k2.

Row 2: Sl 1, k4.

Rows 3–4: As row 2.

Rep these 4 rows.

Layered ruffle

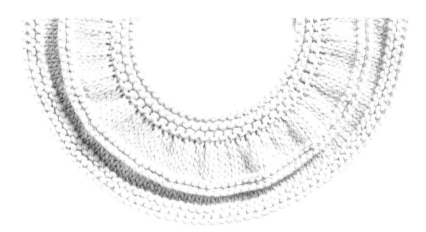

Worked from bottom edge upwards.

Starts with twice the number of sts needed that is an even number. Cast on same number of sts for each layer.

Note: cast on using the thumb method.

Bottom layer

Work 5 rows in garter st.

Beg with p row, work 9 rows in st st.

Row 15 (RS): [K2tog] to end.

Row 16: Purl.

Row 17: Knit.

Place sts on spare needle.

Top layer

Work 3 rows in garter st.

Beg with p row, work 5 rows in st st.

Row 9 (RS): [K2tog] to end.

Join layers

RS facing, hold top layer in front of bottom layer. Using 3rd needle, knit together 1 st from each needle across the row.

Work 4 rows in garter st.

These rows form the edging.

Cast off or cont as required.

Layered leaves braid

Worked lengthways over 18 sts.

Row 1 (RS): K3, k2tog, yo, k5, yo, k3, skpo, k3.

Row 2 and every alt row: K3, p12, k3.

Row 3: K3, k2tog, k5, yo, k1, yo, k2, skpo, k3.

Row 5: K3, k2tog, k4, yo, k3, yo, k1, skpo, k3.

Row 7: K3, k2tog, k3, yo, k5, yo,
skpo, k3.

Row 9: K3, k2tog, k2, yo, k1, yo, k5, skpo, k3.

Row 11: K3, k2tog, k1, yo, k3, yo, k4, skpo, k3.

Row 12: As row 2.

Rep these 12 rows.

Cockleshells trim

Worked lengthways over 23 sts.

Work 2 rows in garter st.

Row 3 (RS): K3, yo2, p2tog tbl, k13, p2tog, yo2, k3. (25 sts)

Row 4: K4, p1, k15, p1, k4.

Work 2 rows in garter st.

Row 7: K3, yo2, p2tog tbl, yo2, p2tog tbl, k11, p2tog, yo2, p2tog, yo2, k3. (29 sts)

Row 8: K4, p1, k2, p1, k13, p1, k2, p1, k4.

Row 9: Knit.

Row 10: K7, k15 wrapping yarn 3 times around needle for each st, k7.

Row 11: K3, yo2, p2tog tbl, yo2, p2tog tbl, yo2, pass next 15 sts to right-hand needle dropping extra loops, pass same 15 sts back to left-hand needle and p all 15 sts tog, yo2, p2tog, yo2, p2tog, yo2, k3. (23 sts)

Row 12: K3, p1, [k2, p1] twice, k3, [p1, k2] twice, p1, k3.

Rep these 12 rows.

Ric-rac

Worked from bottom edge upwards.
Starts with multiple of 10 sts + 1 st.
Ends with multiple of 8 sts + 1 st before casting off.
Note: cast on using the thumb method.
Row 1 (RS): K4, *sk2po, k7; rep from *, ending sk2po, k4.
Row 2 and foll alt row: Knit.
Row 3: K1, *M1, k2, sk2po, k2, M1, k1; rep from * to end.
Row 5: As row 3.
Row 6: Knit.
Cast off, working k1, *M1, k7, M1, k1; rep from * across row.
These 6 rows form the edging.

Scallop edging

Worked from top edge downwards.
Starts and ends with multiple of 13 sts + 2 sts.
Note: cast on using the thumb method.
Row 1 (RS): K1, *skpo, k9, k2tog; rep from * to last st, k1.
Row 2 and foll alt row: Purl.
Row 3: K1, *skpo, k7, k2tog; rep from * to last st, k1.
Row 5: K1, *skpo, yo, [k1, yo] 5 times, k2tog; rep from * to last st, k1.
Row 6: Knit.
These 6 rows form the edging.

Beaded cable cast-on

Worked from bottom edge upwards.
Starts and ends with multiple of 2 sts + 1 st.
Note: thread beads onto knitting yarn before casting on, 1 bead for every alt st, less 2, to give a selvedge st at each end.
Place a slip knot on the needle.
Cast on 1 st.
*Slide 1 bead up to sit behind the st, insert right-hand needle knitwise into st and draw loop through, drawing bead through with it. Sip loop onto left-hand needle and ensure bead is sitting at base of st.
Cast on 1 st.
Rep from * until 1 less than required number of sts are on left-hand needle.
Cast on 1 st.
This forms the edging.
Cont as required. Usually row 1 will be a RS row to show the beads to best effect.

Catherine wheels braid

Cherry basket

Worked lengthways over 19 sts.

Special abbreviation:

Work 5tog (work 5 sts together): Skpo, k3tog, pass the st resulting from skpo over the st resulting from k3tog.

Row 1 and every alt row (WS): Sl 1, k2, p to last 3 sts, k3.

Row 2: Sl 1, k7, sl 3, yf, pass same slipped sts back to left-hand needle, yb, knit 3 slipped sts, k8.

Row 4: Sl 1, k5, k3tog, yo, inc2, yo, k3tog tbl, k6.

Row 6: Sl 1, k3, k3tog, yo, k2tog, yo, inc2, yo, skpo, yo, k3tog tbl, k4.

Row 8: Sl 1, k2, [k2tog, yo] 3 times, k1 tbl, [yo, skpo] 3 times, k3.

Row 10: Sl 1, k3, [yo, k2tog] twice, yo, sk2po, [yo, skpo] twice, yo, k4.

Row 12: Sl 1, k2, [skpo, yo] 3 times, k1 tbl, [yo, k2tog] 3 times, k3.

Row 14: Sl 1, k3, inc, yo, skpo, yo, work 5tog, yo, k2tog, yo, inc, k4.

Row 16: Sl 1, k5, inc, yo, work 5tog, yo, inc, k6.

Rep these 16 rows.

Worked from bottom edge upwards.

Starts and ends with multiple of 11 sts + 2 sts.

Note: cast on using the thumb method.

Special abbreviation:

MB (make bobble): (K1, p1, k1, p1, k1) in next st, turn, p5, turn, 1 at a time, lift 2nd, 3rd, 4th and 5th sts over 1st st. (K next st tbl).

Work 3 rows in garter st.

Row 4 and every alt row: Purl.

Row 5 (RS): *K5, k2tog, yo, k4; rep from *, ending k2.

Row 7: *K4, k2tog, yo, k1, yo, ssk, k2; rep from *, ending k2.

Row 9: *K3, [k2tog, yo] twice, k1, yo, ssk, k1; rep from *, ending k2.

Row 11: *K2, [k2tog, yo] twice, k1, [yo, ssk] twice; rep from *, ending k2.

Row 13: *K3, k2tog, yo, k1, MB, k1, yo, ssk, k1; rep from *, ending k2.

Row 15: *K4, MB, k3, MB, k2; rep from *, ending k2.

Row 17: *K6, MB, k4; rep from *, ending k2.

Row 19: Knit.

Row 20: Purl.

Work 4 rows in garter st.

These 24 rows form the edging.

Cast off or cont as required.

Wheatsheaf cable rib

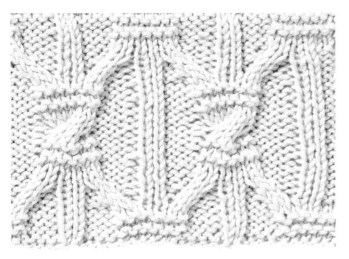

Leaf braid

Worked from bottom edge upwards.

Starts and ends with multiple of 16 sts + 8 sts.

Note: cast on using the thumb method.

Rows 1, 3 and 5 (RS): P1, k6, *p4, k2, p4, k6; rep from *, ending p1.

Rows 2 and 4: K11, p2, *k14, p2; rep from *, ending k11.

Row 6: K1, p6, *k4, p2, k4, p6; rep from *, ending k1.

Row 7: P3, k2, *T4F, p2, k2, p2, T4B, k2; rep from *, ending p3.

Row 8: K3, p2, *k2, p2; rep from *, ending k3.

Row 9: P3, k2, *p2, T4F, k2, T4B, p2, k2; rep from *, ending p3.

Row 10: K3, p2, *k4, p6, k4, p2; rep from *, ending k3.

Rows 11, 13 and 15: P3, k2, *p4, k6, p4, k2; rep from *, ending p3.

Rows 12 and 14: K3, p2, *k14, p2; rep from *, ending k3.

Rows 16 and 18: As row 10.

Row 17: P3, k2, *p4, C6B, p4, k2; rep from *, ending p3.

Rows 19, 21 and 23: As row 11.

Rows 20 and 22: As row 12.

Row 24: As row 10.

Row 25: P3, k2, *p2, T4B, k2, T4F, p2, k2; rep from *, ending p3.

Row 26: As row 8.

Row 27: P3, k2, *T4B, p2, k2, p2, T4F, k2; rep from *, ending p3.

Row 28: As row 6.

Row 29: As row 1.

Row 30: As row 2.

These 30 rows form the edging.

Cast off or cont as required.

Worked lengthways over 17 sts.

Row 1 (RS): Sl 1, k3, [k2tog, yo] twice, k1, [yo, skpo] twice, k4.

Row 2: Sl 1, k5, p5, k6.

Row 3: Sl 1, k2, k2tog, yo, k2tog, k1, [yo, k1] twice, skpo, yo, skpo, k3.

Row 4: Sl 1, k4, p7, k5.

Row 5: Sl 1, k1, k2tog, yo, k2tog, k2, yo, k1, yo, k2, skpo, yo, skpo, k2.

Row 6: Sl 1, k3, p9, k4.

Row 7: Sl 1, k2tog, yo, k2tog, k3, yo, k1, yo, k3, skpo, yo, skpo, k1.

Row 8: Sl 1, k2, p11, k3.

Row 9: Sl 1, k2, yo, skpo, k7, k2tog, yo, k3.

Row 10: Sl 1, k3, p9, k4.

Row 11: Sl 1, k3, yo, skpo, k5, k2tog, yo, k4.

Row 12: Sl 1, k4, p7, k5.

Row 13: Sl 1, k4, yo, skpo, k3, k2tog, yo, k5.

Row 14: Sl 1, k5, p5, k6.

Row 15: Sl 1, k5, yo, skpo, k1, k2tog, yo, k6.

Row 16: Sl 1, k6, p3, k7.

Row 17: Sl 1, k6, yo, sk2po, yo, k7.

Row 18: Sl 1, k7, p1, k8.

Rep these 18 rows.

Openwork picot

Worked lengthways over 3 sts.

Cast on 3 sts.

*Cast off 2 sts. (1 st)

Slip this st onto left-hand needle.

Cast on 2 sts. (3 sts)

Rep from * for required length.

Cast off 2 sts. (1 st)

Without turning, work along straight edge of picot: **yo, put tip of left-hand needle under bar across top of picot and knit into this bar; rep from ** to end.

Work 2 rows in garter st.

This cast on and 2 rows form the edging.

Cast off or cont as required.

Little bobble rib

Worked from bottom edge upwards.

Starts and ends with multiple of 8 sts + 3 sts.

Special abbreviation:

MB (make bobble): (P1, k1, p1, k1) in next st, then, 1 at a time, lift 2nd, 3rd and 4th sts over 1st st.

Note: cast on using the thumb method.

Row 1 (RS): K3, *p2, MB, p2, k3; rep from * to end.

Row 2: P3, *k5, p3; rep from * to end.

Row 3: K3, *p5, k3; rep from * to end.

Row 4: As row 2.

Rep these 4 rows once more then rep row 1 once more.

These 9 rows form the edging.

Cast off or cont as required.

Diamond edge

Worked lengthways over 12 sts.

Row 1 and every alt row (RS): K1, yo, p2tog, k to end.

Row 2: K2, yo, k3, yo, skpo, k2, yo, p2tog, k1. (13 sts)

Row 4: K2, yo, k5, yo, skpo, k1, yo, p2tog, k1. (14 sts)

Row 6: K2, yo, k3, yo, skpo, k2, yo, skpo, yo, p2tog, k1. (15 sts)

Row 8: K1, k2tog, yo, skpo, k3, k2tog, yo, k2, yo, p2tog, k1. (14 sts)

Row 10: K1, k2tog, yo, skpo, k1, k2tog, yo, k3, yo, p2tog, k1. (13 sts)

Row 12: K1, k2tog, yo, sk2po, yo, k4, yo, p2tog, k1. (12 sts)

Rep these 12 rows.

Twisted fringe

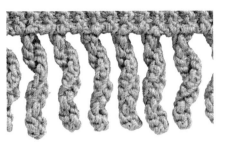

Worked lengthways over 3 sts.
Work 3 rows in garter st.
Row 4 (WS): Cast on 10 sts, inc in each
of these 10 sts, casting off one st as each
st is made, k2. (3 sts)
Rep these 4 rows, ending with row 2.

Beaded garter edge

Worked lengthways over 4 sts.
Note: Thread beads onto knitting yarn
before casting on, 1 bead for each row 3.
Row 1 (RS): Sl 1, k3.
Row 2: As row 1.
Row 3: Slide a bead up to needle, wyif
insert right-hand needle tbl in first 2 sts,
yo, k2tog tbl, k2.
Row 4: Sl 1, k3.
Rep these 4 rows.

Beaded cord

Worked lengthways over 5 sts on double-
pointed needles.
Note: Thread beads onto knitting yarn
before casting on, 1 bead for every row 3.
Rows 1–2: Knit, do not turn, slide sts to
other end of needle.
Row 3: K2, PB, k2, do not turn, slide sts
to other end of needle.
Rep these 3 rows.

Bird's eye edging

Worked lengthways over 7 sts.
Row 1 (RS): K1, k2tog, yo2, k2tog, yo2,
k2. (9 sts)
Row 2: K3, [p1, k2] twice.
Row 3: K1, k2tog, yo2, k2tog, k4.
Row 4: Cast off 2 sts, k3, p1, k2. (7 sts)
Rep these 4 rows.

Picot point cast-off

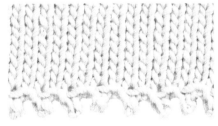

Worked from upper edge downwards.
Multiple of 3 sts + 2 sts.
Note: cast on using the cable method.
Cast off 2 sts, *slip rem st on right-hand
needle onto left-hand needle, cast on 2
sts, cast off 4 sts; rep from * to end and
fasten off rem st.

Ribbed rib

Worked lengthways over 17 sts.
Rows 1, 3 and 5 (RS): K5, [p2, k4] twice.
Row 2 and foll 2 alt rows: [P4, k2]
twice, p5.
Row 7: K1, [p4, k2] twice, p4.
Row 8: [K4, p2] twice, k4, p1.
Rows 9–10 rows: As rows 1–2.
Rep these 10 rows, ending with row 4.

Beaded loop rib

Unravelled fringe with eyelets

Cabled fringe

Worked from bottom edge upwards.
Starts and ends with multiple of 2 sts
+ 1 st.

Note: thread beads onto knitting yarn
before casting on, 5 beads for each loop.

Row 1 (RS): [K1, p1] to last st, k1.

Row 2 and foll alt row: [P1, k1] to last
st, p1.

Row 3: K1, p1, *k1, yf, slide 5 beads up
to right-hand needle, p1 tbl, k1, p1; rep
from * to last st, k1.

Row 5: *K1, yf, slide 5 beads to the base
of the right-hand needle, p1 tbl, k1, p1;
rep from * to last st, k1.

Row 6: As row 2.

These 6 rows form the edging.

Cast off or cont as required.

Worked lengthways over any number
of sts.

Row 1 (RS): K5, k2tog, yo, k to end.

Row 2: Purl.

Rep rows 1–2 as required, ending with
row 2.

Next row: K5, cast off rem sts.

Slip 5 sts off needle and unravel across
knitted fabric to create fringe.

Worked lengthways over 14 sts.

Note: two colours of yarn, A and B, are
used, but the edging can be worked in
one colour if preferred.

Using cable method, cast on 9 sts with A
and 5 sts with B.

Rows 1 and 5 (RS): K5 B, k9 A.

Row 2 and every alt row: P9 A, p5 B.

Row 3: K5 B, with A, C6F, k3.

Row 7: K5 B, with A, k3, C6B.

Row 8: As row 2.

Rep rows 1–8 as required, ending with
a row 2.

Next row: K4 B, cast off rem sts.

Slip 4 sts off needle and unravel across
knitted fabric to create fringe. Loops can
be cut to make strands.

Fancy leaf edging

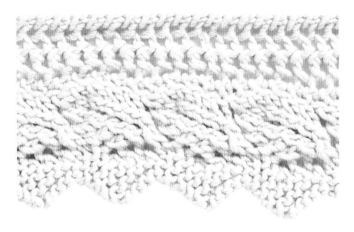

Lacy arrow edging

Worked lengthways over 17 sts.

Row 1 (RS): K3, yo, p2tog, yo, p2tog, yo, k1 tbl, k2tog, p1, yb, skpo, k1 tbl, yo, k3.

Row 2: K3, p3, k1, p3, k2, yo, p2tog, yo, p2tog, k1.

Rep rows 1–2 once more.

Row 5: K3, yo, p2tog, yo, p2tog, yo, k1 tbl, yo, k2tog, p1, yb, skpo, yo, k4. (18 sts)

Row 6: K4, p2, k1, p4, k2, yo, p2tog, yo, p2tog, k1.

Row 7: K3, yo, p2tog, yo, p2tog, yo, k1 tbl, k1, k1 tbl, yo, sk2po, yo, k5. (19 sts)

Row 8: K5, p7, k2, yo, p2tog, yo, p2tog, k1.

Row 9: K3, yo, p2tog, yo, p2tog, yo, k1 tbl, k3, k1 tbl, yo, k7. (21 sts)

Row 10: Cast off 4 sts knitwise, k2, p7, k2, yo, p2tog, yo, p2tog, k1. (17 sts)

Rep these 10 rows.

Worked lengthways over 21 sts.

Row 1 (RS): K3, yo, k2tog, p2, yo, skpo, k3, k2tog, yo, p2, k1, yo, k2tog, k2.

Row 2 and every alt row: K3, yo, k2tog tbl, k2, p7, k3, yo, k2tog tbl, k2.

Row 3: K3, yo, k2tog, p2, k1, yo, skpo, k1, k2tog, yo, k1, p2, k1, yo, k2tog, k2.

Row 5: K3, yo, k2tog, p2, k2, yo, sk2po, yo, k2, p2, k1, yo, k2tog, k2.

Row 6: As row 2.

Rep these 6 rows.

Double picots and eyelets

Worked from bottom edge upwards.
Worked over any odd number of sts.

Note: Use cable cast-on throughout.
Cast on 6 sts, cast off 4 sts, slip st on right-hand needle onto left-hand needle, cast on 4 sts, cast off 4 sts, slip st on right-hand needle onto left-hand needle, *cast on 5 sts, cast off 4 sts, slip st on right-hand needle onto left-hand needle, cast on 4 sts, cast off 4 sts, slip st on right-hand needle onto left-hand needle; rep from * until a single picot less than the required number of sts has been made.

Row 1 (RS): *K1, yo; rep from * to last st, k1.

This cast-on and row form the edging.
Cast off or cont as required.

Garter bunting

Worked lengthways over 8 sts.
Row 1 (RS): Sl 1, k7.
Row 2: Ssk, k6. (7 sts)
Row 3: Sl 1, k6.
Row 4: Ssk, k5. (6 sts)
Row 5: Sl 1, k5.
Row 6: Ssk, k4. (5 sts)
Row 7: Sl 1, k4.
Row 8: Ssk, k3. (4 sts)
Row 9: Sl 1, k3.
Row 10: Cast on 4 sts, k all 8 sts.
Rep these 10 rows, ending with row 9.

Puff ball cluster edging

Worked lengthways over 13 sts.
Row 1 (WS): K2, k2tog, yo2, k2tog, k7.
Row 2: K9, p1, k3.
Work 2 rows in garter st.
Row 5: K2, k2tog, yo2, k2tog, k2, [yo2, k1] 3 times, yo2, k2. (21 sts)
Row 6: K3, [p1, k2] 3 times, p1, k4, p1, k3.
Work 2 rows in garter st.
Row 9: K2, k2tog, yo2, k2tog, k15.
Row 10: K12 wrapping yarn twice round needle for each st, yo2, k5, p1, k3. (23 sts)
Row 11: K10, (p1, k1) in next st, slip next 12 sts to right-hand needle dropping extra loops, return sts to left-hand needle then k12tog. (13 sts)
Row 12: Knit.
Rep these 12 rows.

Square filet edging

Worked lengthways over 15 sts.
Foundation row: Knit.
Row 1 (RS): K1, k2tog, yo2, k2tog, k1,
yo2, k7, yo2, k2. (19 sts)
Row 2: K3, p1, k8, p1, k3, p1, k2.
Row 3: K1, k2tog, yo2, k2tog, k1, [yo2,
k2tog] twice, k3, k2tog, yo2, k4. (22 sts)
Row 4: K5, p1, k6, p1, k2, p1, k3, p1, k2.
Row 5: K1, k2tog, yo2, k2tog, k1, yo2,
[k2tog, k1, k2tog, yo2] twice, k6. (24 sts)
Row 6: K7, [p1, k4] twice, p1, k3, p1, k2.
Row 7: K1, k2tog, yo2, k2tog, k1, yo2,
k2tog, k3, k2tog, yo2, k3tog, yo2, k8.
(26 sts)
Row 8: K9, p1, k2, p1, k6, p1, k3, p1, k2.
Row 9: K1, k2tog, yo2, k2tog, k21.
Row 10: Cast off 10 sts, k8, k2tog, k2,
p1, k2. (15 sts)
Rep rows 1–10.

Flower bud trim

Worked lengthways over 7 sts.
Row 1 (RS): K1 tbl, [p2, k1 tbl] twice.
Row 2: P1, [k2, p1 tbl] twice.
Row 3: K1 tbl, p2, (k1, p1, k1, p1, k1) in
next st, p2, k1 tbl. (11 sts)
Row 4: P1, k2, p5, k2, p1 tbl.
Row 5: K1 tbl, p2, k5, p2, k1 tbl.
Row 6: As row 4.
Row 7: K1 tbl, p2, skpo, k1, k2tog, p2,
k1 tbl. (9 sts)
Row 8: P1, k2, p3, k2, p1 tbl.
Row 9: K1 tbl, p2, sk2po, p2, k1 tbl.
(7 sts)
Row 10: As row 2.
Rep these 10 rows, ending with a row 1.

Picot point chain

Worked lengthways over 5 sts.
Note: cast on using the cable method.
*Cast off 4 sts, slip st on right-hand needle
onto left-hand needle, cast on 4 sts; rep
from * until chain is required length.

Garter scallops

Worked lengthways over 7 sts.

Foundation row: Knit.

Row 1: K4, inc, k2. (8 sts)

Row 2: K1, inc, k6. (9 sts)

Row 3: K6, inc, k2. (10 sts)

Row 4: K1, inc, k8. (11 sts)

Row 5: K8, inc, k2. (12 sts)

Row 6: K1, inc, k10. (13 sts)

Row 7: K10, inc, k2. (14 sts)

Row 8: K1, inc, k12. (15 sts)

Row 9: K12, k2tog, k1. (14 sts)

Row 10: K1, k2tog tbl, k11. (13 sts)

Row 11: K10, k2tog, k1. (12 sts)

Row 12: K1, k2tog tbl, k9. (11 sts)

Row 13: K8, k2tog, k1. (10 sts)

Row 14: K1, k2tog tbl, k7. (9 sts)

Row 15: K6, k2tog, k1. (8 sts)

Row 16: K1, k2tog tbl, k5. (7 sts)

Rep rows 1–16.

Simple ruffle

Worked from bottom edge upwards.

Starts with twice the number of sts needed.

Note: cast on using the thumb method. If an odd number of sts are required, delete 1 st from the final count, cast on double that number of sts + 1 st and on the decrease row, end k1.

Row 1: Knit.

Row 2: Purl.

Rep rows 1–2 as required, ending with row 2.

Next row: [K2tog] to end.

These rows form the edging.

Cast off or cont as required.

Star flower appliqué

Put a slip knot on the needle.

Row 1 (RS): (K1, k1 tbl, k1) in st. (3 sts)

Row 2 and every alt row: Purl.

Row 3: K1, [M1, k1] twice. (5 sts)

Row 5: K1, M1, k3, M1, k1. (7 sts)

Row 7: K1, M1, k5, M1, k1. (9 sts)

Row 9: K1, M1, k7, M1, k1. (11 sts)

Row 11: K1 tbl, k2tog, k5, ssk, k1. (9 sts)

Row 13: K1 tbl, k2tog, k3, ssk, k1. (7 sts)

Row 15: K1 tbl, k2tog, k1, ssk, k1. (5 sts)

Row 17: K1 tbl, sk2po, k1. (3 sts)

Row 19: Sk2po. (1 st)

Fasten off.

Make 4 more petals.

Press.

With slip knots in the centre and taking 1 st from each edge into seam, join the five petals from row 1 to row 10.

Crown edging

Worked from upper edge downwards. Multiple of 5 sts.

Note: if working this as a separate edge to be sewn on, cast on using the cable method.

Row 1 (WS): Knit.

Row 2: Cast off 2 sts, * slip st on right-hand needle onto left-hand needle, [cast on 2 sts, cast off 2 sts, slip st onto left-hand needle] 3 times, cast on 2 sts, cast off 6 sts; rep from * to end and fasten off rem st.

These 2 rows form the edging.

Tassel rib

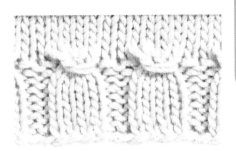

Worked from bottom edge upwards. Starts and ends with multiple of 6 sts + 1 st.

Note: cast on using the thumb method.

Row 1 (RS): *K4, p2; rep from *, ending k1.

Row 2: P1, *k2, p4; rep from * to end. Rep rows 1–2, 3 more times.

Row 9: *Place right-hand needle between 4th and 5th st from tip of left-hand needle and draw through a loop, k this loop tog with next st, p2, k3; rep from *, ending k1.

These 9 rows form the edging.

Cast off or cont as required.

Tip

Appliqué shapes, such as the star flower shown here, the loop flower on page 242, the heart on page 250 and the leaf and daisy on page 254, can be sewn on as embellishments to a knitted piece. They can also be used individually, for example, as brooches.

index

A

abbreviations 20, 26–7
accordion pleat 240
acrobats 231
all-over eyelets 165
alternate bobble stripe 40
alternated cable 95
alternated smooth stitch and tier 29
alternating triangles 58
alternating twists 83
anchor 63
angel wings lace panel 134
antique edging 262
appliqué shapes 242, 250, 254, 269, 283
arch, small 185
arched cables 86
arched windows 150
arches lace 257
Argyll check 218
Argyll diamond motif 223
arrow braid 238
arrowhead: little arrowhead 139
   small arrowhead 188
arrowhead tweed border 198
arrowhead zigzag 209
astrakhan bobbles 148
aubrieta 211

B

baby cable and garter ridges 80
back stroke 184
bannock trellis pattern 200
basket rib 58
basket stitch, small 51
basket weave 58
   large basket weave 68
basket weave rib 71
battlements (3-count) 189
battlements (4-count) I 190
battlements (4-count) II 190
battlements (5-count) 197
bead stitch 146
beaded cable cast-on 273
beaded cast-off 264
beaded cord 277
beaded frill 263
beaded fringe 271
beaded garter edge 277

beaded loop rib 278
beaded rib 42
beaded thumb cast-on 234
bear paw panel 150
bell cable 112
bell edging I 257
bell edging II 262
bell lace 172
belladonna 232
berry ladder 76
Berwick 205
biba trellis 62
big lace check 249
big twisted candle 82
birds, little 38
bird's eye edging 277
bluebell insertion 136
bluebell ribs 142
bobbins 18
bobble rib 71
bobble rib, little 276
bobble rib edging 264
bobble stitch 30
bobble stitch, mini 58
bobble tree panel 158
bobble with cable 115
bobbles and waves 122
bold cable 94
bowknot 31
box and dot 195
box pleats 235
box stitch 35
bramble stitch 58
breakers 190
brick stitch 74
broken crests 196
broken fence 187
broken rib 60
broken rib diagonal 68
broken rows I 187
broken rows II 187
broken zigzags 196
bud stitch 54
bulky cable 110
butterfly edging 237
butterfly lace 143
buttoned tags 245

C

cabbages 204
cable and dot 101
cable and eyelet rib 269

cable and lace check 144
cable fabric 105
   little cable fabric 121
cable needles 8, 110
cable rib 254
cable rope 270
cable stitch 124
cable with bobbles 89
cable with braid 104
cable with grooves, small 80
cable with horn detail 100
cable with segments 122
cable with stripes 93
cable with swirl 116
cabled fringe 278
cabled moss stitch 99
cactus ladder 49
cairn 227
campion 233
campion and pannier border 228
candelabra panel 140
Canterbury bells 151
captive diamond border 203
cartridge stitch 29
cascading leaves 176
casing and drawstring 251
cast-off fringe 236
casting off 13
casting on 10
castle edging 255
castle window 212
castle window I 213
castle window II 213
caterpillar stitch 66
Catherine wheels 159
Catherine wheels braid 274
cell stitch 139
Celtic rose 203
centipede stitch 66
centred cables 87
chain link I 205
chain link II 215
chain stitch rib 73
chalice cup panel 174
charts, reading 20
check stitch 48
checkerboard 42
checkerboard lace 169
checkered cable 110
checkered dot border 195
cherry basket 274
chevron 70

chevron and feather 142
chevron rib 66
   little chevron rib 66
chevron stripes 38
chunky braid 121
chunky cable 96
circle cable: large circle cable 108
   small circle cable 130
climbing cable 95
climbing leaf pattern 170
close checks 79
clover pattern 146
cockleshells 144
cockleshells trim 272
cogwheel eyelets 172
colours: changing 18
   joining in 16–17
compass check pattern 54
cosmea 211
country lane cable 98
country lanes 215
creeping vines 173
criss-cross cable with twists 123
cross motif pattern 36
crossed battlements 198, 199
crossed cables 131
crossed grooves 84
crosses 50
crossing paths 113
crossroad squares 77
crossroads 216
crossroads cable 90
crown edging 283
crowns of glory 151
crowns I 139
crowns II 149

D

daisy appliqué 254
daisy braid 255
dancing ballerinas 231
dancing bears 189
dancing cable 114
dancing diamonds 226
dash 182
decreasing 15
defined diamonds 93
dewdrop pattern 138
diagonal bobble stitch 57

diagonal checks 62
diagonal garter ribs 41
diagonal knot stitch 79
diagonal lattice 194
diagonal openwork 147
diagonal rib and scallop 248
diagonal rib I 62
diagonal rib II 67
diagonal ridge I 31
diagonal ridge II 32
diagonal ridges 169
diagonal ripple 126
diagonal tramline cable 128
diagonals 45
diamond and block 46
diamond and bobble panel
    179
diamond and cross 207
diamond and cross
    windowpane I 207
diamond and cross
    windowpane II 212
diamond and eyelet pattern
    161
diamond and lozenge banded
    border 224
diamond and lozenge tweed
    border 224
diamond and snowflake paths
    221
diamond box border 206
diamond diagonal 171
diamond edge 276
diamond filigree 204
diamond flower border I 220
diamond flower border II 221
diamond footpath 201
diamond lace I 155
diamond lace II 181
diamond link and dot 203
diamond links 214
diamond net mask 63
diamond panels 69
diamond pattern 73
diamond tweed pattern 203
diamond zigzag bands 219
diamonds, little and large 163
diamonds in the snow 217
dianthus and pannier border
    228
disappearing cable 109
divided boxes 61
divided cable I 107
divided cable II 109
divided circles 88
divided triangles 46
dot and dash 183
dot and long dash 183

dot stitch 34
dots (double), little 182
dots (single), little 182
dotted chevron 72
dotted ladder stitch 53
double basket weave 43
double diamond edging 246
double diamonds 116
double eyelet rib 79
double fleck stitch 48
double knot edge 270
double lace rib 178
double moss stitch 35
double moss stitch triangles
    52
double parallelogram stitch 44
double picots and eyelets 280
double pintuck 251
double rice stitch 42
double-row diamond 201
double signal check 44
double spiral cable 125
double woven stitch 42
dramatic curves 82

E
ears of corn 173
edgings 23, 234–83
eight-stitch cable 88
elongated chevron 78
embossed diamonds 33
embossed leaf pattern 136
embossed lozenge stitch 76
embossed rib 61
embossed rosebud panel 175
ends, eliminating 19
enlarged basket stitch 69
equipment 8–9
extended openwork stitches
    132
eyelet boxes 167
eyelet cable 127
eyelet diamonds 162
eyelet fan panel 141
eyelet lace 165
eyelet lattice insertion 178
eyelet mock cable ribbing 43
eyelet panes 145
eyelet quadrants 133
eyelet rib 250
    large eyelet rib 43
eyelet rib variation 132
eyelet ribs 177
eyelet rows 140
eyelet twigs 179
eyelet twigs and bobbles 180
eyelet twist panel 137

eyelet V-stitch 155
eyelets 139

F
faggoted panel 148
Fair Isle 16, 198, 212
falling leaves 136
fan edging 259
fan lace panel 157
fancy diamond 75
fancy leaf edging 279
fancy openwork 171
farrow rib 34
feather and fan 178
feather lace 156
feather openwork 133
fern and bobble edging 252
fern diamonds 145
fern lace 139
fern lace edging 240
filigree cables pattern lace 137
filled oval cable 112
fir cone and twig lace 256
fish scale lace panel 175
fishtail lace 153
fishtail lace panel 154
fishtails 159
five and one 192
flag pattern 49
fleck stitch 43
flight 199
floating snake pattern 85
flora 209
floret 233
florette pattern 171
flotsam 189
flower and chalice 207
flower bud trim 281
flower buds 176
flowers, little 143
foaming waves 139
folded cable 103
forked cable 124
foundation rows 20, 23
fountain pattern, little 143
fountains panel 167
four-section cable 94
four-stitch ribs 43
framed cross cable 91
framed heart motif 232
free cable 101
fuchsia stitch 92
fur stitch 30

G
garden path cable 98

garter and slip stitch 70
garter bunting 280
garter scallops 282
garter slip stitch 55
garter stitch 28
garter stitch checks 48
garter stitch eyelet chevron
    138
garter stitch lace, simple 142
garter stitch lacy diamonds 152
garter stitch points 253
garter stitch ridges 71
garter stitch steps 61
garter stitch triangles 45
garter stitch twisted rib 59
gate and ladder pattern 178
gathered stitch 29
geometric twisted candles 84
grand eyelets 142
granite rib 71
gull wings 196

H
H-border 192
half brioche stitch (purl version)
    59
harbour flag 57
harbour walls motif 219
harvest furrows 193
heart appliqué 250
hearts braid 258
heather peerie 190
Hellenic wave 226
heraldic border 193
herbaceous border 229
herringbone I 29
herringbone II 51
hexagon stitch 39
high tide 188
holly leaf appliqué 269
honeycomb pattern 96
horizontal dash stitch 67
horizontal herringbone 48
horizontal rib 242
horn cable 89
horseshoe print 181
hunter's rib 246

I
increasing 14, 22, 165
inserted cable 114
interlocking cable 113
internal diamonds 122
interrupted rib 55
intertwined texture stitch 70
inverted hearts 172

K
K1, p1 rib 28
K2, p2 rib 28
King Charles brocade 45
King Charles lace 149
Kirkwall 218
Kirkwall border 188
knit stitch 11
knitwise 13
knot pattern 53
knotted boxes I 153
knotted boxes II 154
knotted cable 81
knotted openwork 142
knotted rib 59

L
laburnum edging 266
labyrinth 33
lace, little 268
lace and bobble 239
lace and cable pattern 158
lace and cables 127
lace and moss stitch 135
lace bells 266
lace bunting 256
lace cable 245
lace cable pattern 104
lace chain panel 161
lace check 152
lace diamond border 146
lace diamonds 267
lace knitting 22
lace panel, little 165
lace picot 252
lace rib panel 158
lace ruffle 249
lace stripes 260
lacy arrow edging 279
lacy chain 181
lacy checks 163
lacy diagonals 170
lacy diamonds 177
lacy lattice stitch 147
lacy openwork 178
lacy stars 138
ladder braid 237
ladder stitch 51
ladder tile 72
lads and lasses I 230
lads and lasses II 230
lattice lace, large 180
lattice pattern I 111
lattice pattern II 120
lattice stitch 56
lattice window I 202
lattice window II 208

layered leaves braid 272
layered picots 270
layered rib 235
layered ruffle 271
layered tags 267
leaf and fringe 243
leaf appliqué 254
leaf braid 275
leaf edging 234
leaf panel 151
leafy lace 144
leafy trellis 132
leafy trim 243
line and dot 214
linen stitch 28
linked ribs 60
linking ovals 103
lizard lattice 35
long dash 183
long loop fur 261
loop flower appliqué 242
loop pattern 29
loop trim 259
loose V stitch 117
loose woven cables 127
lozenge lace panel 157

M
maypole lace 263
maze pattern 44
medallion moss cable 94
medallion rib 48
medium circle cable 106
Melissa 217
Michaelmas 229
mimosa shoot 134
Minerva 193
mistakes 137
mock cable left 79
mock cable on moss stitch 54
mock cable rib 74
mock cable wide rib 86
mood boards 68
mosaic path 212
moss and faggot 238
moss diamonds 65
moss diamonds edging 253
moss lace diamonds 152
moss panels 63
moss rib 60
moss slip stitch 59
moss stitch 35
moss stitch cable, small 97
moss stitch cord 236
moss stitch diagonal 39
moss stitch diamonds 47

moss stitch double parallelograms 49
moss stitch hearts 115
moss stitch panes 40
moss stitch parallelograms 37
moss stitch squares 38
moss stitch triangles 37
moss stitch zigzag 78

N
needles 8, 110
noughts and crosses trim 251

O
oblique rib 35
ocean wave 78
open and closed cable I 91
open and closed cable II 99
open bobble pattern 111
open cable 106
open chain ribbing 39
open check stitch 43
open honeycomb 86
open twisted rib 67
open V-stitch 114
openwork mullions 34
openwork picot 276
openwork points 261
ornamental cable 126
ornamental stitches 31
ornamental tulip pattern 162
outline triangle 191
overlapping cable 108
oyster shells lace 258

P
padded cable 123
papyrus lace 134
parasol lace 265
parasol stitch 147
parterre 216
pattern repeats 20, 102
peacock plume 150
pearl, little 81
perforated rib 242
phlox 201
picot braid 236
picot point cast-off 277
picot point chain 281
pillar cable 89
pillar openwork 148
pillar stitch 67
pine cone pattern 156
piqué rib 71
plain diamonds 33

pleat patterns 34
pleats 32
ploughed furrows 193
points and bobbles 247
post and hook 186
pretty maids 198, 199
propellor cable 104
puff ball cluster edging 280
puff stitch check 176
puffed rib 55
purl stitch 12
purl triangles 47
purled ladder stitch 60
purlwise 13
purse stitch 133
pyramid lace panel 174
pyramid triangles 65
pyramids I 36
pyramids II 74

Q
quatrefoil 223
quatrefoil panel 160

R
raindrops 157
raised circle cable 102
raised curve cable 108
ray of honey 86
repeated circles 129
repeated ovals 129
reverse stocking stitch 28
reverse stocking stitch chevrons 50
rhombus 81
rhombus delight 85
rhombus lace 166
rib checks 46
ribbed extended stitches 32
ribbed rib 277
ribbed tags 248
ric-rac 273
ridge and furrow 61
ridge and hole pattern 149
ridged eyelet border 142
ridged eyelet edge 236
ridged eyelet stitch 133
ridged lace 148
ridged lace pattern 156
ridged rib 55
rippled diamonds 119
ripples border 209
rocky shore 198
Roman cable 97
rose and thistle 201
rose crest 222

rose garden 131
rose stitch 60
ruched edging 264

S
sand wind 81
scallop edgings 273
scallop lace edging 241
scallop shell lace 265
scalloped eyelet edging 247
scalloped ruffle 244
Scottish thistles I 225
Scottish thistles II 225
seed stitch checks 40
seeded back stroke 195
seeded vertical stripe 186
shadow triangles 168
shell insertion, little 178
shell pattern, little 148
Shetland eyelet panel 169
Shetland fern panel 167
shield and cross 227
shingle stitch 57
shoots and seeds 191
short dash 182
short loop fur 265
simple cable 128
simple ruffle 282
single eyelet rib 79
single fence 187
single lace rib 133
six-stitch spiral cable 95
slanted bamboo 76
slanting diagonals 130
slanting diamonds 56
slanting eyelet rib 135
slanting openwork stitch 133
slanting stripes 117
slip stitch rib 71
slipped double chain 96
slipped rib 59
slipped three-stitch cable 87
sloping cable 88
sloping diamonds 82
smocking stitch pattern 92
smoked rib 246
snail shell lace 239
snakes and ladders 164
snow shoe pattern 174
snowflakes I 160
snowflakes II 161
spaced checks 75
spaced knots 52
speckled fence 188
speckled trellis 206
speckled zigzag 209
spiral and eyelet panel 140

spiral rib 72
spiral rib edging 263
square filet edging 281
square rib 79
squares 77
stacked cable 98
staggered fern lace panel 175
star braid 260
star flower appliqué 283
star lace 269
steps 56
stitch diagrams 24–5
stocking stitch 28
stocking stitch checks 55
stocking stitch ridge 66
stocking stitch triangles 35
stormy sea 197
stripe pillars 68
striped slip stitch edging 260
sugar scallops 268
supple rib 34
swatches 53, 62, 68, 105
sweeping cable 105
swinging triangles 164
symbols 20, 24–5

T
tall blocks 186
tassel fringe 247
tassel rib 283
tension swatches 8
texture stitch 29
textured cable 90
textured tiles 69
textured triangle stack 47
thick and thin rib 241
threaded squares 185
three-stitch twisted rib 59
three-wave 184
tight braid cable 103
tile stitch 61
tiny bobble braid 250
tools 8–9
top hat pattern 41
topiary stitch 64
touching paths 113
travelling vine 168
tree of life 194
trefoil bunting 236
trellis lace 160
trellis pattern 166
trellis stitch 53
trellis with blocks 208
triangle and dot 191
triangle and square I 185
triangle and square II 186
triangle ribs 77

triangle stacks 189
triangle wave border 192
triangle wave I 185
triangle wave II 191
triangle wave III 192
triangle zigzag 199
triangles and strokes 195
trims 234–83
triple wave 60
trophy cable I 111
trophy cable II 112
tulip cable 97
tulip wave 197
tweed pattern 73
tweed stitch 67
twelve-stitch braid 110
20-stitch twisted candle 81
twin leaf lace panel 170
twinkling diamonds 196
twist cable and ladder lace 179
twist edge 236
twisted and crossed cable 128
twisted cable rib 50
twisted candles 83
twisted check 52
twisted eyelet cable 100
twisted fringe 277
twisted moss 61
twisted openwork pattern 153
twisted stocking stitch 58
twists with knotted pattern 80
two-colour fringe 268
two-stitch ribs 42
two-wave 184

U
uneven rib 55
unravelled fringe 262
unravelled fringe with eyelets 278
unusual pattern check 65

V
Vandyke lace panel I 154
Vandyke lace panel II 155
vertical bar lines 34
vertical basketweave lattice 210
vertical stripes 214
vertical strokes II 214
vertical zigzag moss stitch 41
vine and twist 125
vine cable 107

waffle stitch 67
wall-walk 207
wandering zigzag 204
waterfall pattern 180
wave, small 184
wave and diamond border 202
wave crest I 197
wave crest II 200
wavy border 237
wavy cable, small 126
wheatsheaf cable rib 275
whelk pattern 30
whirligig 220
wide cable panel 123
willow edging 244
winter rose medallion 222
woven cable 118
   large woven cable 100
woven cable stitch 81
woven horizontal herringbone 37
woven rib 48
woven stitch I 42
woven stitch II 66

Y
yarn 9, 124
yarnover 165

Z
zigzag cable 118
zigzag eyelet columns 148
zigzag eyelet panel 159
zigzag eyelets 162
zigzag fence 204
zigzag lace 177
zigzag moss edging 255
zigzag panel 141
zigzag, small 183
zigzag stitch 75
zigzag tweed 210

Acknowledgements

Thanks to Kate Haxell, Susie Johns and Erika Knight for selecting and compiling the stitches.
Thanks to Nicola Hodgson for putting together this volume.
Knitters: Rosalind Campbell, Carole Downie, Sarah Hazell, Melina Kalatzi, Cathy MacDonald, Jenny McHardy, Annette Travers
Photography: Geoff Dann, Holly Jolliffe, Michael Wicks
Chart illustrator: Lotte Oldfield
Technical editor: Luise Roberts

This latest volume in Collins & Brown's bestselling Ultimate series reveals all the techniques of the masters in an easy-to-understand format.

PAVILION

Whatever the craft, we have the book for you — just head straight to Pavilion's crafty headquarters.

Pavilioncraft.co.uk is the one-stop destination for all our fabulous craft books. Sign up for our regular newsletters and follow us on social media to receive updates on new books, competitions and interviews with our bestselling authors.

We look forward to meeting you!

www.pavilioncraft.co.uk

the ultimates

The Ultimates are a growing series of comprehensive reference guides, with everything you could possibly want to know about a wide variety of craft subjects. Each title contains clear, concise text and step-by-step illustrations, making these books the perfect companion for both beginners and experts.

All titles retail at £25 and are available direct from our website: www.pavilioncraft.co.uk

978-1-84340-411-8

978-1-84340-450-7

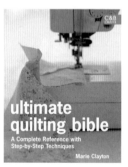

978-1-84340-502-3

978-1-90939-797-2

978-1-909--39-718-7

978-1-84340-563-4

978-1-84340-574-0

978-1-84340-672-3

978-1-90844-901-6

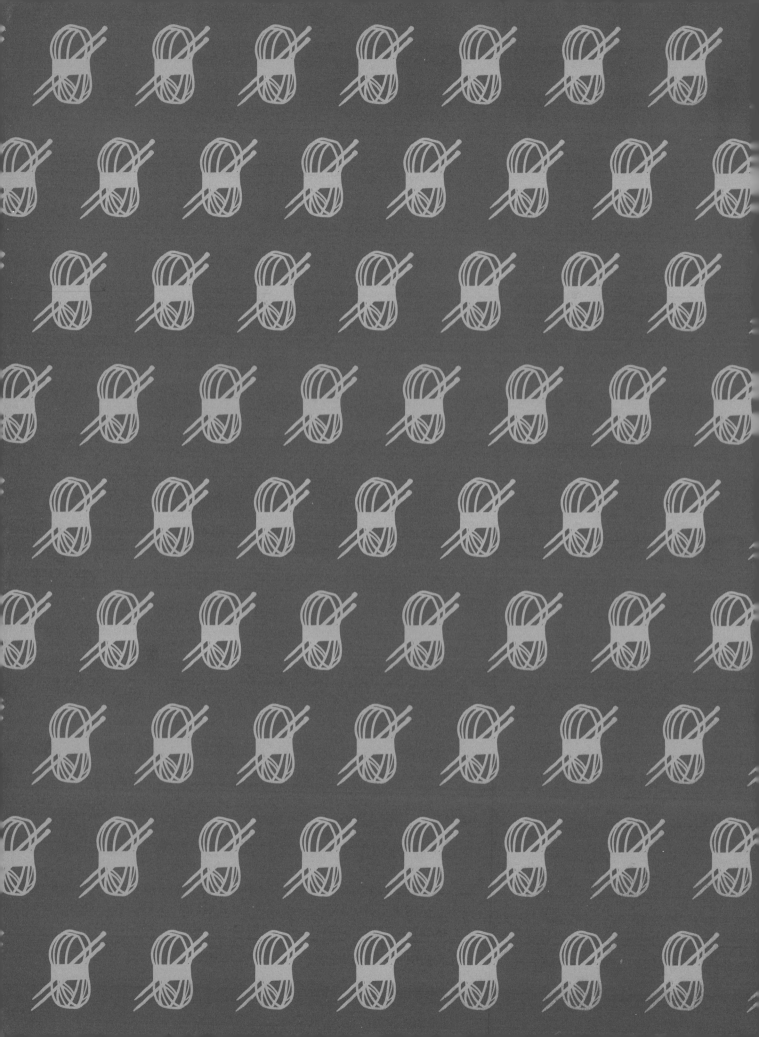